T0303608

Women Making
WAR

Women Making
WAR

FEMALE CONFEDERATE PRISONERS
AND UNION MILITARY JUSTICE

THOMAS F. CURRAN

Southern Illinois University Press
Carbondale

Southern Illinois University Press
www.siupress.com

Copyright © 2020 by the Board of Trustees,
Southern Illinois University
All rights reserved
Printed in the United States of America

23 22 21 20   4 3 2 1

Publication of this book has been underwritten by the Elmer H.
Johnson and Carol Holmes Johnson criminology fund.

Cover illustration: Cover illustration: detail of "United States
Volunteers Attacked by Mob, Corner of Fifth and Walnut Streets, St.
Louis, Missouri," *Harper's Weekly*, June 1, 1861, p. 349. LIBRARY OF
CONGRESS PRINTS AND PHOTOGRAPHS DIVISION.

Library of Congress Cataloging-in-Publication Data
Names: Curran, Thomas F., author.
Title: Women making war : female Confederate prisoners and Union
    military justice / Thomas F. Curran.
Description: Carbondale : Southern Illinois University Press, [2020] |
    Includes bibliographical references and index.
Identifiers: LCCN 2020001452 (print) | LCCN 2020001453 (ebook) |
    ISBN 9780809338030 (paperback) | ISBN 9780809338047 (ebook)
Subjects: LCSH: Women prisoners of war—United States—History—
    19th century. | United States—History—Civil War, 1861–1865—
    Participation, Female. | United States—History—Civil War, 1861–
    1865—Prisoners and prisons. | United States—History—Civil War,
    1861–1865—Women. | Women—Confederate States of America—
    History. | Women—Confederate States of America—Social
    conditions. | Women—Missouri—St. Louis—History—19th century.
    | Military courts—United States—History—19th century.
Classification: LCC E628 .C865 2020 (print) | LCC E628 (ebook) | DDC
    973.7082—dc23
LC record available at https://lccn.loc.gov/2020001452
LC ebook record available at https://lccn.loc.gov/2020001453

Printed on recycled paper ♻

To Debby and Megan

CONTENTS

Gallery of illustrations beginning on page 137

ACKNOWLEDGMENTS

T he road to completing this book has been very long, with many twists, bumps, detours, distractions, traffic jams, and stops for repair work. Along the way, many people helped me put together the pieces of this story. At the National Archives DeAnne Blanton assisted me early and often on a number of issues. Also facilitating my research were Kimberly Harper, Missouri State Historical Society; Patricia Luebbert, Missouri State Archives; Lauren Sallwasser, Jaime Bourassa, and Amanda Claunch, Missouri Historical Society; Jim Stimpert, Holly Callahan, and Jeannette Pierce at the Milton S. Eisenhower Library, Johns Hopkins University; John Rhodehamel, Huntington Library; Kathleen Casey and Richard Amelung, Saint Louis University Law Library; Liz Plummer and Shelby Beatty, the Ohio History Connection; Geoffrey Stark, Special Collections, University of Arkansas; Sr. Theodore Bollati, ASCJ, and Kathleen Koboldt, Cor Jesu Academy Library; Michael (Sonny) Trimble and Natalie M. Drew, U.S. Army Corps of Engineers; and staff members of the Law Library and Photoduplication Services of the Library of Congress.

Many provided specific information or materials concerning particular women or issues. DeAnne Blanton and Lauren Cook assisted in documenting Mary Ann Pitman, while Richard A. Nichols helped organize my materials on her. Judy Yaeger Jones, LaVonne Barac, and Merritt R. Blakeslee aided me in my research on Clara Judd. Ann Christian provided information on the Fox and Huckshorn women. Scott Williams and Jack Davis clarified Caroline Billingsley's story. Mercedes Graf shed light on the elusive Barbara Ann Donovan or Duravan, or whatever her name was. Ollie Sappington offered information about his ancestor Drucilla Sappington, while Betsy Deiterman provided me with a photograph of Drucilla's final resting place.

Sylvia Frank Rodrigue of the Southern Illinois University Press showed continued interest in and support for the project from its early stages. I was pleased to bring it to her and SIU Press once it was completed. Jennifer Egan at the press also has provided valuable assistance. Wayne Larsen and Linda Jorgensen Buhman diligently guided the manuscript through the production process, and Lisa Marty meticulously copyedited the work, adding polish to the finished product.

At the project's early stages, Rosemary Hopkins helped me to shape exactly what I intended, while the Rev. Garth Hallett, SJ, Saint Louis University, proved to be a valuable sounding board and delightful lunch partner. Matthew J. Mancini, Saint Louis University, shared his insight on Francis Lieber and the writing of Lieber's Code. Benjamin G. Cloyd, Hinds Community College in Raymond, Mississippi, confirmed my assessment of the place of prisons in Civil War memory. Anne Stirnemann, Missouri Regional Poison Control Center, informed me on the effects of drinking chloroform. Susan Youhn discussed the stories of childbirth in prison camps that circulated during the war. Randy Watkins at the Jefferson Barracks National Cemetery explained the meaning of the stones marking the interred in the Civil War section and the difference between Union stones and Confederate stones. Dan Gedden of St. Patrick's Cemetery (formerly Greenwood Cemetery) confirmed that the site has no record of Mrs. Reynolds resting there. And Jim Gioia of Cor Jesu Academy translated *Deo Vindice* for me before I learned that it was commonly known as the national motto of the Confederacy.

At several conferences I benefited from the comments of panelists and audiences as I presented portions of my research. Special thanks go to Frank Nickel, Southeast Missouri State University; Randall Allred, Brigham Young University, Hawaii; Daniel Sutherland, University of Arkansas; and William G. Piston, Missouri State University. Many insights and questions I could not answer that later I pursued came from these conferences, as well as the numerous talks I gave on the subject as a member of the Speakers Bureau of the Missouri Humanities Council. I am particularly grateful to the late Barbara Jane Walrand Gill of the Speakers Bureau for the support she gave me over the years. John F. Marszalek, Mississippi State University, was kind enough to read and comment on my chapter on Henry Halleck and Lieber's Code, while DeAnne Blanton once again helped by reviewing my chapter on Mary Ann Pitman. And the anonymous readers for the Southern Illinois University Press provided thoughtful recommendations that have made this book a much stronger contribution. Finally, Jane Laurentius generously volunteered to read the entire manuscript, catching many embarrassing mistakes and unclear statements. My apologies to anyone I have overlooked.

I thank my colleagues and the administrators at Cor Jesu Academy, past and present, for their support and friendship, particularly Donna Johnson,

Brian Hohlt, Mark Tueth, Jennifer Ahrens, Audrey Ploesser, and Kevin Knickman. I also appreciate the interest my students have taken in this project over the years. I thank all my friends whom I subjected to long monologues on these women and why their story is important, especially Teresa Harvey, who gave the project its working title, "Bad Girls." (With all due respect to Inner Circle.) I thank my sister, Sue, and brother Gary, who are always there with a kind word or a laugh when I need it, and nephew Jake and niece Jeanne, who would make their father proud. Finally, I thank and give my never-ending love to my daughter, Megan, and my wife, Debby, who have put up with all my research and writing. Megan, who—as I write this—is starting college, has never known me *not* working on this project. And Debby tolerated sharing me with these women, whose numbers only grew as time went on, for most of our marriage. To Debby and Megan I dedicate this book.

Women Making War

Introduction

U pon his release from the Alton, Illinois, Military Prison in early
June 1863, Sergeant Edward Herndon Scott of the Confederate Sixth
Missouri Infantry wrote an extensive letter to his father in Kentucky.
In this missive, Scott recounted in brief his first year and a half of service in
defense of "the holiest cause that men can aspire next to Christianity and his
church, the cause of civil liberty." After relating in greater detail his capture at
Grand Gulf, Mississippi, at the hands of Ulysses S. Grant's advancing forces
during the Vicksburg campaign, Scott graphically pictured the conditions
he and his fellow captives met at the Alton prison: overcrowding, rampant
disease, vermin of every kind, overzealous guards who heaped insults and
worse on the prisoners. But these were just some of the "countless and name-
less indignities and outrages" that Scott saw "committed all over our State and
our land" under the auspices of the Federal government. Scott had to pause
his litany and calm down before registering the final villainy he witnessed.
With all the contempt he could muster, Scott pronounced, "They have five
ladies, and a child . . . at Alton also as prisoners. Isn't that Chivalrous?"[1]

Captain Griffin Frost, who spent two extended periods incarcerated at
Alton and the Federal military prisons in nearby St. Louis, would have agreed.
In his postwar memoir based on diaries he secretly kept, Frost condemned
the "Yanks" for "making war on women." How, in the "progressive age" of
the nineteenth century, could women be kept as "political prisoners"?[2]

The presence of the women that Scott and Frost witnessed in the St. Louis-
area military prisons was not an anomaly. At least four hundred and forty
women are known to have been arrested in St. Louis or to have been sent
there after their arrest elsewhere. A large majority of them spent time either
in the Alton facility or in one of the several military prisons that appeared
in the city of St. Louis during the war. Elsewhere, other Southern partisan

women also faced incarceration at the hands of the Federal army, charged with a variety of infractions. While some women came into custody as victims of what Abraham Lincoln under different circumstances referred to as a "mere friction and abrasion . . . of the war,"[3] many of these women boldly and openly took credit for the actions for which they were held accountable, all in the name of the Confederate cause.

Edward Herndon Scott and Griffin Frost were not alone in their criticism. Southern newspapers and Confederate military and political leaders regularly condemned the arrest of women they depicted as innocent and defenseless; they blamed it on the Federal government's and army's frustration caused by military loss combined with the evil-hearted nature of the Yankees.[4] Scott, Frost, and other Confederates failed, or perhaps refused, to realize that the rebel women imprisoned during the war often had been combating for that same cause that they and other Southern men had been defending.

The women arrested and, in many cases, imprisoned in the St. Louis area represent a fraction of the number of female Southern partisans who found ways large and small to advance the Confederate military cause. More significant than their numbers is what the records of these women, though fragmentary, reveal about the activities that led to their arrests, the reactions women partisans evoked from Federal authorities who confronted them, and the impact that women's partisan activities had on Federal military policy and military prisons. As the book's title suggests, the war the disloyal women waged on the United States army and the war with which the army responded form the subject of this study. The records of the Union provost marshals, the military prisons involved, newspaper reports, military correspondence, and first-hand accounts from participants in the war all document the numerous ways that some Southern women actively and with deadly earnest contributed to the war effort and the many new roles they willingly performed.

Indeed, these activities ranged from overt displays of support for the Southern Confederacy to offering aid and comfort to those fighting against Federal authority to more direct activities such as spying, smuggling, sabotage, and even service in the Confederate army itself. As residents of the region within which the war was predominantly fought, Southern women often showed their loyalty to the Confederate cause in ways that put these women in harm's way, and in some cases brought them into conflict with, and often the custody of, Federal military authorities. This was particularly true for women in Missouri. Some of the women arrested and imprisoned during the conflict were truly victims of war, arrested for no other reason than their relation to a Confederate soldier whom they had not seen for months or even years or for simply being in the wrong place at the wrong time. For the majority, however, arrest and imprisonment were consequences of conscious decisions they made to do what they could to advance the Southern cause and assist those in armed rebellion against the United States government.

In the century after the Civil War, the literature on women and the war was dominated by two types: accounts of women performing functions within their traditional roles as nurturers and caregivers, such as working as nurses and serving with agencies designed to bring relief to soldiers; and tales of a few well-known women such as Rose O'Neal Greenhow and Belle Boyd, who transcended traditional roles to serve as spies. Indeed, for a century after the war women received scant attention in the vast and growing Civil War literature.[5]

In 1966, Mary Elizabeth Massey produced *Bonnet Brigades*, a ground-breaking study of women and the war that broadened our understanding of the numerous roles women performed.[6] Now half a century old, Massey's *Bonnet Brigades* and her other historiographical contributions were recently commemorated in a special issue of *Civil War History* with a collection of short reflective essays by historians who have written on women and the war.[7] If anything can be taken away from this collection, it is that as innovative as Massey's study was when it appeared, *Bonnet Brigades* still had serious omissions, biases, and inaccuracies. Fortunately, in the decades since *Bonnet Brigades* appeared, numerous studies have expanded our knowledge of women's multifaceted activities and experiences during the Civil War era.[8]

Many of the authors of these works followed Massey's lead in delving into diaries and letters left behind by women, providing rich source material for expanding our understanding of women's wartime experiences. Still, such an approach is not without its limitations. These documents contain a wealth of information, but these types of sources were most often left behind by middle- and upper-class white women who had the time and ability to produce such records. Furthermore, Southern white women who wrote diaries and letters probably belonged to the slave-owning class, and represent a small segment of Southern society. The social status of these Southern white women helps to explain why historians have observed that many desired to do more to aid directly the Confederate cause, as their husbands and sons did, but they reluctantly, if not resentfully, suppressed these longings, constrained by notions of domesticity and separate spheres and the reality that women had no legitimate or legal political voice. In short, societal norms made direct participation in the war unacceptable.[9]

Other studies have found that Southern white women did act politically during the war, but not always in ways designed to aid the Confederate war effort. In *Confederate Reckoning*, Stephanie McCurry investigates yeomen and poor Southern women who rose up in protest during the war to force the Confederate national government and their respective state governments to respond to their plight. Portraying themselves as "soldiers' wives" deserving of special treatment and protection from the government because their husbands left them to go off and fight for the Confederacy, McCurry affirms, these women protested the Confederate "government's manpower policies, soldiers' wages, government prices for women's work, relief, Federal taxes, impressment, and monetary policy, to name the main ones," in their efforts to provide for themselves and their families. These women's discontent and frustration eventually led to the infamous bread riots of 1863, during which these lower-class women organized to obtain flour and other food items from merchants, many of whom had been charging exorbitant prices and had contracts with the Confederate government.[10]

Historian Paula Baker's definition of "politics" as "any action, formal or informal, taken to affect the course or behavior of government or the community"[11] certainly describes the actions of the soldiers' wives. Yet during this time of civil war, when the self-proclaimed Confederate States of America waged a rebellion against the United States government to establish an independent sovereign nation, the soldiers' wives in their actions did not seek a regime change. McCurry accurately characterizes the actions of these women as "a politics of subsistence." They acted politically for personal, familial, indeed domestic purposes—literally bread and butter issues—and not to advance a political agenda.[12]

Although not her main focus, McCurry acknowledges that some Confederate women did act in political and partisan ways against the Federal government, especially in border regions and areas under occupation.[13] However, a few scholars have written in more depth on rebel partisan women and their efforts to advance the Confederate cause as spies, smugglers, even soldiers, and other military contestants.[14] Some Confederate women, indeed, took part in the war effort, knowledgeable that their actions could and often did have consequences. Contrary to what one author suggests, they were not merely "playing at war."[15] Union officers and soldiers who encountered rebel partisan women would have begged to differ with that characterization. At the outset of the war, McCurry explains, men believed that "women were not parties to the war, that they played no role in the politics that had brought it on and would take no part in waging it." In short, women "were innocent parties, entitled to protection, even perhaps from enemy men."[16] It did not take long for the Federal military to adapt their views to the reality posed by rebel women. Federal authorities took women's activities seriously, considering them treasonous, and responded with measures they deemed the women's actions justly deserved.

McCurry notes that the soldiers' wives who challenged Confederate policies in their politics of subsistence rarely identified themselves as "citizens,"
in keeping with notions of women's proper role.[17] Federal officials who dealt
with Confederate partisan women, however, did identify them as such; they
not only considered but routinely referred to these rebellious women as citizens of their native states, and citizens of the United States. The United States
army created a policy that endowed female citizens with the same obligations
that male citizens had during time of war and rebellion.[18] In some instances,
officers adjudicating the cases of accused women determined that the women
had "forfeited their rights of citizenship by their continued acts of disloyalty
toward the U.S Government."[19] Attributing the arrest and treatment of these
women simply to men's attempts to restrain them from stepping out of their
proper gender sphere is to underestimate the seriousness with which Federal
officials responded to the women as well as to misinterpret the strength of
the women's political convictions, as disloyal and treasonous as they were.[20]

The women's own admissions attest to their awareness of the political nature of their actions. "When within the Confederate lines," Annie B. Martin
asserted, "[I] would do all I could to aid the Southern Confederacy. Because
I believe them right, the people of the South." Emma English admitted that
she was a "Rebel from principle" and "despised the Government of the U.S.
worse than anything." Hattie Snodgrass, arrested because she "hurrahed"
Jefferson Davis, among other things, probably would have taken exception
to English's self-characterization as a "Rebel." When questioned about her
brother-in-law in the "Rebel army," Snodgrass insisted that he served in the
"Confederate" and not the "Rebel Army," affirming the legitimacy of the
Confederate States. Margaret Johnston more directly praised "the course
Jefferson Davis had taken" in her testimony, and defiantly predicted success
for the "Southern Confederacy." Twenty-two-year-old Mary Simpson referred
to herself as a "secessionist," as did many other women in custody. Also like
many other partisan women, admitted "Southern sympathizer" Harriet Snead
refused to take an oath of allegiance to the United States government because
of her political convictions.[21]

In their defense, some women echoed the arguments used by the "Peace"
wing of the Democratic Party, often referred to as the Copperheads.[22] Specifically, they connected their Confederate sympathies with their opposition
to emancipation. Accused of harboring and feeding bushwhackers, Sarah
Moss revealed that she wished "to see the Government of the U.S. restored
as it once was," with slavery intact. Eliza Spencer, also accused of aiding
bushwhackers, averred, "I sympathize with the South and want them to gain
their Independence but I would prefer the Government as it was." Elizabeth

Campbell, who had assaulted a Unionist neighbor, was more forthright in her opinion. She told the detective who questioned her that "she was Union, *provided*, they would keep the Nigger out of the question."[23] While military authorities and Unionist observers occasionally criticized women in gendered terms, the evidence shows that their arrests and treatment came in response to their disloyal activities, not any transgression of gender norms. In other words, if authorities arrested a woman for using "improper language," and many like Elizabeth Campbell faced that charge, they deemed the language improper because it was disloyal, not because it had been uttered by a female. Men also experienced arrest for using improper language. As for spying, smuggling, and other wrongdoings, the disloyalty should be self-evident.

That is not to say that the issue of the appropriateness of arresting women did not arise. It did, but the discussion was usually one-sided. It was not uncommon for incarcerated women and their friends and family members to play the gender card, so to speak. And in some cases, gender did mitigate the nature of the treatment and punishment that women received. By the second year of the war, however, Union army personnel had no doubt that Confederate women's rebellious activities deserved punishment.

The story of women arrested and imprisoned during the Civil War has received scant attention in the vast body of literature produced in the century and a half since the conflict's end, and when it has, the significance of the subject has been minimized or underestimated. In his Pulitzer Prize-winning study of civil liberties during the Civil War, Mark Neely Jr. notes that at least 13,535 civilians came into Federal custody during the conflict, the vast majority from the border states or occupied parts of the Confederacy. Further, he holds that the number of arrested women he encountered in his research numbered only in the "dozens." This study documents four hundred and forty women—more than thirty-six dozen—who came into custody in the Department of the Missouri alone. In *The Hard Hand of War*, Mark Grimsley does not broach the subject of the arrests of women. The same is true for Dennis K. Boman's *Lincoln and Citizens' Rights in Civil War Missouri*.[24] On the other hand, Thomas Lowry describes one hundred and twenty women found guilty of various crimes by military tribunals during the war in his *Confederate Heroines*. Nevertheless, Lowry's encyclopedic approach, broken down by state and then by case, limits the ability to draw broader conclusions about women's activities and their interaction with the military justice system.[25] John Fabian Witt's award-winning study of the laws of war during the Civil War mentions in passing the arrest of only two women, including St. Louisan Zaidee J. Bagwell, charged with writing letters of encouragement to a friend in the South. Likewise, William A. Blair's *With Malice toward*

Some, focusing on treason during the war, acknowledges that women were held accountable for their actions, but provides few details or examples. The same is true for Jonathan W. White's unpublished dissertation "'To Aid their Rebel Friends': Politics of Treason in the Civil War North."[26] To be sure, analyzing Confederate women's partisan activities was not the intention of these scholars, but the limited attention given to women reflects how little we know about those activities and their consequences.

Likewise, the histories of military prisons and prisoners of war have told us little about Confederate partisan women's experience in Federal custody and the activities that got them there. William B. Hesseltine's groundbreaking 1930 study *Civil War Prisons* ignores women prisoners altogether. Appearing nearly seven decades later, Lonnie R. Speer's *Portals to Hell* devotes only two separate paragraphs to women prisoners. Other recent studies overlook female prisoners completely.[27] In "Stress, Suffering, and Sacrifice: Women POWs in the Civil War," Mercedes Herrera-Graf covers a small number of women who faced imprisonment, focusing on the psychological toll it may have taken on them.[28] More recently, Elizabeth Belanger utilizes geographic information systems to investigate St. Louis women accused of disloyalty, especially by other women, "through the lens of neighborhood development." Her essay, however, does not delve too deeply into the stories of these women.[29]

Similarly, as valuable as they are, most studies of wartime Missouri and the border area have given limited attention to the arrest of women, barely scratching the surface. Michael Fellman's investigation of the guerrilla war in Missouri devotes a chapter to women and covers a broad spectrum of issues. He discusses the arrests of a number of women in or near Missouri in connection with the guerrilla conflict but with two exceptions avoids the discussion of imprisonment. Daniel Sutherland's sweeping study of the significance of guerrilla warfare across the South details even less. Louis Gerteis's history of wartime St. Louis also gives brief attention to the subject, and Christopher Phillips's book on the border states offers a small number of examples of arrested partisan women.[30] While these studies have contributed much to our understanding of the specific topics and issues they address, their coverage of partisan women is narrow.

A few scholars have been more diligent in giving attention to partisan women. For instance, in his recent study of guerrilla warfare in Missouri, Joseph M. Beilein Jr. devotes considerable attention to the role women played in what he calls the "household war," where the men in the brush relied heavily on their womenfolk to sustain them with shelter, food, and other supplies. For their effort, many of these women found themselves arrested and banished or imprisoned. Michael Stith's *Extreme Civil War* also maintains that "women were *active* players in the guerrilla war," but their activities centered around strategies of survival, not advancing a cause.[31] Several contributions to a collection of essays edited by LeeAnn Whites and Alecia P. Long advance our knowledge of Confederate partisan women and their interaction with Federal authorities. In particular, Kristin L. Streater explores the "She-Rebels" of Kentucky, the aid they gave to the Confederate cause, and the response it evoked from Union officials. In "(Mis)Remembering General Order No. 28," Long challenges the notion that many of the women of New Orleans bowed to Union major general Benjamin Butler's infamous "Women's Order" but rather openly protested or defied it. Whites revisits the arrest and banishment of a group of wealthy and influential St. Louis women in the spring of 1863 (which this study revisits in chapters 4 and 12).[32]

More recently, Stephanie McCurry offers an analysis of the traditional laws of war in relation to women, which treated women as innocent noncombatants to be protected, and the challenge to that belief posed by Confederate women's partisan activities. The Union army's experience with enemy women contributed to the inclusion of women as combatants to be dealt with harshly when warranted in General Orders No. 100, also known as Lieber's Code, adopted in 1863. The code, McCurry demonstrates, "fundamentally rewrote the distinction" between civilian and combatant, "breaking down the wall between soldiers and noncombatants including the assumption of women's innocence." Lieber's Code made the arrest and punishment of rebellious women a matter of formal policy.[33]

Despite these contributions there is still much to be learned about Confederate women's participation during the war and the impact their activities had. This study will expand that knowledge, reinforcing the fact that rebellious women were held accountable for their disloyal actions—actions that intentionally bore significant political meaning—just as men were. It also shows the broad variety of military infractions disloyal women perpetrated. Furthermore, the narrative reveals that Federal military authorities usually prosecuted disloyal women in the same way they did men. By 1863 the arrest of rebel women had become routine and the policies employed and practices used to deal with them more regularized. While Union officials often proved quick to arrest suspected offenders, both male and female, and while the wheels of military justice usually moved slowly, efforts to investigate accusations usually were surprisingly thorough for the purpose of ferreting out the truth.

The women examined here came from all points across the socioeconomic spectrum. Some had significant wealth while others represented the lowly working class. Most appear to be native born, but some were immigrants.

St. Louis residents made up a large portion of the women who came before the provost marshal general, but he also dealt with numerous women from rural Missouri, as well as other states, North and South. Even a handful of African American women passed through the military justice system, although almost always as witnesses to other's offenses.

Before proceeding, two issues need to be addressed here due to the lack of evidence that appears in the record. Both of these issues regularly arose as questions when I presented papers or lectures on my research in academic and nonacademic settings. The first issue concerns postwar political activism. The records indicate that the partisan women's activities during the war did not serve as a springboard for political activism, at least related to women's rights, once the war ended. However, some of these women did participate in the politically charged movement to promote the myth of the Lost Cause in the late nineteenth and early twentieth centuries.[34] The second issue relates to the subject of sexual assault and rape. While compelling research has appeared in recent years challenging the notion that the rape of women, at least white women, by Union soldiers was extremely rare during the war,[35] this investigation revealed no evidence of sexual assault or rape committed against arrested disloyal women. That is not to say that it did not occur. Violated women may have kept silent out of fear of retribution or embarrassment or a combination of a variety of factors. Nevertheless, the records investigated here reveal no instances of these types of attacks on women, despite claims made by Confederate leaders to the contrary during the war.

An 1880 publication issued by the Department of War concerning opinions of the judge advocate general reported in a footnote that during the war "nearly one hundred and fifty cases of *women*" had been "tried by military commission," according to the general orders issued during the war.[36] What this finding neglects is that not all cases of accused civilians, male and female, had been adjudicated by formal military commissions. Therefore, the general orders issued in the various military commands and by the War Department tell only part of the story. This study relies heavily on two collections of documents from Record Group 109 of the National Archives: the three hundred microfilm rolls of the Union Provost Marshals' File of Papers Relating to Individual Civilians [M345] and the ninety-four rolls of the Union Provost Marshals' File of Papers Relating to Two or More Civilians [M416]. These records, while often also not telling the whole story of the subjects involved, provided a wealth of data that made this research possible. In addition, the investigation utilized portions of the Select Records of the War Department Relating to Confederate Prisoners of War, 1861–1865 [M598] from Record Group 109.

Contemporary newspapers also proved invaluable. In particular, the *Missouri Democrat*, the Republican-leaning, pro-Union St. Louis-based paper, regularly reported on the comings and goings at the Office of the Provost Marshal as well as the local prisons, and often provided details no other source had. The *Democrat* proved to be a consistent supporter of military policy, including the arrest and confinement of women.

Of course, most studies of anything military-related during the Civil War rely on the *War of the Rebellion: A Compilation of the Official Records of the Union and Confederate Armies*, and this one is no exception. The *O.R.*, as historians have come to know it, proved indispensable as a source, especially in providing background information and tracking down obscure individuals. Collections at various archives and libraries in Missouri and elsewhere proved useful, as well. Finally, this study is indebted to the works of numerous scholars, most of whom are cited in this book.

With that said, piecing together this narrative did not come without difficulties. Incomplete records, misfiled documents, misspelled names, bad penmanship, and more all contributed to headaches in understanding the stories told here. Of the records of the provost marshal, Mark Neely accurately observes: "The jumble of papers is unsystematic to the point of chaos." Added to that are the various layers of participants functioning as provost marshals of different types, what William Blair identifies as "provost marshal confusion,"[37] and the habitual changes in personnel in these and other military positions in the Department of the Missouri. Indeed, at times completing this study seemed like trying to make sense of a puzzle of an M. C. Escher print with missing pieces.

Despite the shortcomings of the records, the documentation left behind concerning Confederate women who ran afoul of the Union military justice system in Missouri is fairly extensive, more so than for other places. Furthermore, Missouri's history and location provided a set of circumstances that reflected the broader sectional divide in the nation. In many respects mid-nineteenth-century Missouri represented a border state, where North met South and East met West, where slavery met freedom. The state found itself at the center of many of the key events in the sectional disagreements of the half century prior to the war: the debate over the spread of slavery west of the Mississippi River and the compromise reached in 1820 that created Missouri as a slave state; the 1837 murder of abolitionist newspaper editor Elijah Lovejoy by a proslavery mob in nearby Alton, Illinois, after his exile from St. Louis; the early stages of the Dred Scott freedom case, ultimately decided against Scott and against the notion that Congress could limit the spread of slavery; the violence of "Bleeding Kansas," which spilled over the border into Missouri after the passage of the Kansas-Nebraska Act. While slaves made up less than 10 percent of the state's population in 1860, the shared practice of human bondage and the fact that a majority of residents were of Southern birth or a generation or two removed from a slave state tied Missouri's interests to those of the Southern states.[38]

On the eve of the Civil War, St. Louis's population stood segmented and factionalized. More than half of the city's 1860 population was of foreign birth, with Germany contributing the largest share, more than 50,000, while Ireland ran a distant second with almost 30,000 souls. The city attracted Northerners as well: 21,000 inhabitants in 1860 were of free-state birth compared to 7,400 slave-state natives, excluding the city's 56,782 native Missourians. St. Louis's white population dwarfed the 5,359 inhabitants with African roots, more than 80 percent of whom were slaves. Many of the native-born whites traced their heritage back to Southern or French origins, and the older wealthy families of these groups dominated St. Louis's social elite. During the two decades prior to the Civil War, the old slave-owning elite found their political standing eroding, as recently arrived entrepreneurs from the northeastern states and from Germany came to dominate the expanding economy of the city.[39]

While Missouri rested on the periphery of the main conflict during the war and witnessed only a few significant battles, none of which matched in magnitude the major confrontations between Union and Confederate forces that occurred east of the Mississippi River, the state suffered countless small engagements, skirmishes, and guerrilla-style clashes, a product of the type of partisan warfare that engulfed the Gateway to the West. Nevertheless, St. Louis became a place of great significance in the war's Western Theater. As the center of the Department of the Missouri and strategically located near the confluence of the Mississippi and Missouri Rivers, St. Louis served as the supply distribution hub and a training center for newly raised regiments from Missouri and neighboring loyal states.[40] The importance of St. Louis ensured that disloyalty in the city and the rest of the state would be dealt with severely.

The Southern partisan women who serve as the focus for this study represent only those who were caught by the Union military. Certainly many others gave similar support for the Confederacy and never faced arrest. Unfortunately, their stories may be lost forever. Furthermore, disloyal women could be found in custody elsewhere during the war. As incomplete as the records are for the Confederate women dealt with in the St. Louis region, they are even sparser for those handled in other locations. Some of those women left a trace in the published record. For instance, besides Rose O'Neal Greenhow and Belle Boyd, Washington's Old Capitol Prison held many female prisoners.

Other rebel women felt the sting of military justice in the District of Columbia and nearby Maryland and northern Virginia.[41] Women could be found in custody in the contested Shenandoah Valley and western Virginia, later West Virginia.[42] Women judged guilty in the East were often sent for confinement to the Worcester County House of Corrections, also referred to as Fitchburg Prison, in Massachusetts.[43] In the Western Theater, Memphis's notorious Irving Block Prison housed rebel women in custody, although these women often were shipped to the Alton Prison for confinement once found guilty or until their trial.[44] In occupied New Orleans, the military prison occasionally entertained females per order of controversial Union major general Benjamin Butler and other commanding officers. At least four of those women ended up being sent to the prison camp at Ship Island in Mississippi.[45] Women could be found among the political prisoners at Camp Douglas Prison in Chicago and Camp Chase Prison in Columbus, Ohio,[46] and by the end of the war, Louisville had enough demand for space for rebel women in custody that it created a separate military prison for them. It is most remembered not for those it incarcerated but rather for its one-time surgeon of the prison's hospital, Dr. Mary Walker. Coincidently, Walker herself had spent time in a Confederate military prison, having been captured in Virginia and sent to Castle Thunder Prison in Richmond until exchanged four months later.[47] The Confederates, too, placed women in custody and put them in their prisons, even the notorious Andersonville.[48] In addition, many other rebel women not considered here faced arrest and confinement in various Union-controlled towns and garrisons in Missouri; because they were never sent to St. Louis, they fall out of the scope of this study.

The book is arranged chronologically, allowing the narrative to examine the escalation of partisan women's wartime activities and to analyze the evolution of the Union military response to the women's disloyalty. The first chapter considers the Federal government's early response to Confederate sympathizers in St. Louis and the early arrests of men and women. It shows that Union officials remained reluctant to arrest women until their conduct could no longer be tolerated. As women's disloyal activities escalated, officials proved ill-prepared to deal with female prisoners who merited confinement. By the time Union general Henry Halleck took command of the Department of the Missouri, Confederate-sympathizing women had already proved troublesome. Recognizing that the danger posed by disloyal women equaled that of men, Halleck guided the establishment of a military policy for treating civilians, both loyal and otherwise, during time of war and rebellion that made no distinction for gender. Halleck's role in the writing of General Orders No. 100, also known as Lieber's Code, is addressed in chapter 2. The next chapter explores the growing seriousness of women's partisan activities in Missouri and the parallel response to their actions by Federal authorities, now equipped with clearer guidelines for punishing treasonous civilians through Lieber's Code. Eighteen sixty-three witnessed the first of a series of banishments to the South of women—many of them wealthy and well-connected—from St. Louis and elsewhere in the state for their part in the illicit Confederate mail network as well as for spying for the rebels and smuggling contraband beyond the lines. The year also saw a growing intolerance among Union soldiers and officers for disloyalty in whatever form, accompanied by an increased number of women arrested and held in custody for unacceptable behavior.

The Alton Military Prison, a former state penitentiary on the Illinois side of the Mississippi River just north of St. Louis, came under the jurisdiction of the Department of the Missouri. Although it housed primarily Confederate prisoners of war, in early 1863 Alton welcomed the first of many female prisoners, the subject of chapter 4. Before the end of the war, several dozen Confederate women would spend time incarcerated in Alton, having been sentenced to significant periods of time under lock and key for serious wartime infractions. While many came from states along the Mississippi River south of Missouri, a significant number were from the western part of the state and had been arrested for their involvement in the guerrilla warfare that plagued that region, the focus of chapter 5. The arrival of women from out-state Missouri grew in anticipation of and as a result of Confederate general Sterling Price's ultimately unsuccessful raid into the state. This chapter also considers the scrutiny given suspected treasonous organizations operating secretively in the state and elsewhere in the nation and the women connected with the investigation begun in 1864. One particular woman who served as a witness in the investigation merits further attention, indeed her own chapter. Captured in the spring of 1864, Mary Ann Pitman came into custody with an astounding tale of having served in the Confederate military disguised as a man before becoming a smuggler for Nathan Bedford Forrest as a woman. She also claimed to have extensive knowledge of the secret pro-Confederate conspiracy, leading her to become a key witness. Having proven her sincerity in her recent rejection of the Confederacy and her reaffirmed loyalty to the United States, Pitman became a spy for the provost marshal general in St. Louis, a task she carried out through the rest of the war.

Chapter 7 explores some of the more unique cases of arrested Confederate women and troublesome and distinctive issues that Federal officials faced as a result of the incarceration of female prisoners. The issue of adequate space for female prisoners, as well as life within the female prisons themselves, is addressed in chapter 8. The next chapter focuses on the waning months of the war and the ongoing issues rebellious women posed as they continued to come into custody while Union officials began anticipating an end to the conflict. Finally, chapter 10 assesses the story of the Confederate women investigated in this book and its place, or lack thereof, in the larger scope of Civil War memory. In particular, it argues that in the postwar years the narrative of these women became refashioned to comport with the Lost Cause myth that celebrated the valor of Southern men who went off to protect home and family, especially defenseless women.

While the story presented here uses St. Louis as its nexus for examining Confederate partisan women, it nevertheless broadly enriches our understanding of these and other actively disloyal women, their agency in trying to advance the Southern cause, and the responses they evoked in Union military authorities.

CHAPTER 1

"The Line Is Being Drawn Every Day"

T he fissures that tore apart the nation in the spring of 1861 had been apparent in St. Louis long before the South Carolina militia under the banner of the Confederate States of America attacked Fort Sumter in Charleston Harbor. For the duration of the war, St. Louis remained bitterly divided, despite being under control of Federal forces, while outside of the city, Missouri became a contested land, consumed by irregular warfare conducted by both Confederate and Unionist partisans. Under such conditions, it became difficult, if not impossible, for Missouri's citizens, both male and female, to remain neutral in this struggle. One month into the conflict, a St. Louis woman of secessionist sentiments observed, "The line is being drawn every day."[1] She, and other Southern-sympathizing women, knew on which side of that line she stood. Many women like her in Missouri and elsewhere proved willing to act on their convictions, no matter what the consequences. During the early weeks and months of the war, Missouri's Confederate women primarily remained observers of the conflict. As the war intensified, however, some felt compelled to contribute. For most of these rebellious women, their actions amounted to showing open support for the Confederate cause in different ways. For others, their convictions induced them to more serious methods such as encouraging recruitment in the Southern army, raising funds for the Confederates, helping prisoners escape, spying and smuggling, and more. In response, Union military authorities proved reluctant to act at first. As these disloyal activities became more common, authorities found themselves in the unenviable position of determining how to deal with rebel women, something for which the Union army and Federal government were ill-prepared.

After the attack on Fort Sumter, President Abraham Lincoln called for volunteers from the loyal states to put down what had become an armed rebellion. In response four more slave states joined the initial seven that had proclaimed themselves out of the Union. Missouri threatened to join them. Newly elected governor Claiborne Jackson supported secession, as would a majority of the state legislature. Nevertheless, the special convention that met in the late winter of 1861 to decide Missouri's fate concluded by a large majority that no "adequate cause" existed to justify Missouri's break from the Union. The convention then moved to adjourn until December unless a special committee of seven delegates deemed it necessary to meet earlier. The like-mindedness of the secession convention nowhere near resembled the conflicting sentiments of St. Louis's diverse population. Tensions heightened between Unionists and secessionists as a cloud of uncertainty and apprehension fueled by rumors of impending violence descended upon the city. After refusing to heed Lincoln's call for volunteers, Governor Jackson met with St. Louis-area militia commander General Daniel M. Frost and ordered him to call out the state militia—the Missouri State Guard—for a training muster. Frost planned to encamp the militia on the heights overlooking the Federal arsenal south of the city and from there to launch an attack. To bolster the militia's strength, Jackson sent a request to the newly created Confederate government for artillery pieces, which arrived in the city disguised as crates of marble on May 8. By then, Frost's initial plans had been foiled by U.S. captain Nathaniel Lyon, who commanded the arsenal and temporarily controlled all Federal troops in Missouri.[2]

This course of events forced Frost to locate his muster at Lindell Grove, a wooded area on the western edge of the city. The troops quickly dubbed the location Camp Jackson, in honor of the governor. The level of support for secession varied among Camp Jackson's men. Reminiscing four decades after the events of 1861, native St. Louisan Philip Stephenson captured the spectrum of sentiments in the camp: "A good deal of feeling, indeed, was in the camp, sympathy for the south of varying degrees, from downright state-secessionism thro' state neutrality, to mere sympathetic feeling and indignation at the high handed aggressions of the north." There were also nativists who allied themselves with the secessionists simply because the city's German population gave overwhelming support to the Federal government. Still, a strong secessionist sentiment appeared evident, as Confederate flags flew from tent poles and militiamen named some Camp Jackson streets after Confederate president Jefferson Davis and the hero of Fort Sumter, General Pierre G. T. Beauregard.[3]

By early May 1861 Frost had amassed between seven hundred and nine hundred men at Camp Jackson.[4] Alerted to the arrival of the crates carrying the cannons, which recently had been confiscated by the Confederates from the arsenal at Baton Rouge, Louisiana, Captain Lyon allowed them to be delivered to Camp Jackson. According to one account, the following day, Lyon, disguised as the mother-in-law of pro-Union Missouri congressman Frank Blair—complete with "dress, shawl, and bonnet"[5] and riding in the carriage of Blair's brother-in-law Franklin Dick—surreptitiously inspected the camp for the move he planned to make on it the next day, May 10. Troops began preparing early the next morning, and by midafternoon, six thousand Federal soldiers, mostly drawn from the recent militia volunteers, encircled Camp Jackson. Daniel Frost protested Lyon's actions, arguing accurately that the muster was both legal and within the letter of the state constitution, but he could do little else to halt the inevitable. What Frost did not explain was the presence of the goods stolen from the Baton Rouge arsenal at the muster. Without a shot fired, the Missouri State Guard at Camp Jackson surrendered.

Lyon took into custody some fifty officers and six hundred and thirty-nine men.[6] The prisoners were marched to Olive Street, which bordered the northern side of Lindell Grove and headed eastward into the heart of the city. A delay in moving the prisoners downtown allowed the crowd of spectators to grow rapidly. Soon secessionists among the throng began heckling the militia, aiming their most insulting invectives at the Germans. Clods of dirt and rocks flew down on the militia, and then shots rang out. Firsthand accounts on the origins of the first shots of the incident vary, but within seconds the Federal militia began firing into a crowd. When the skirmish ended, at least twenty-seven civilians lay dead or dying, including two females, one only fourteen years old, and several teenage boys. At least one Federal militia member also died, but conflicting reports suggest that there may have been more. Numerous others received wounds in the fray as well.[7]

The Camp Jackson affair threw the city into a state of panic. New rumors spread like wildfire. Fears that German militia were planning to massacre secessionists gripped Southern sympathizers, while the German-American community residing on the city's south side prepared for an attack by secessionists in retribution for the dead of May 10. According to one witness, there were "[a]rms in every man's hands, vengeance lighting the faces in the crowd, the threats to murder or drive out all participants on the horrible outrages." Several small and violent scuffles erupted involving Union militia and civilians, one in which six were killed. Meanwhile, other Southern sympathizers fled the city for safety, some never to return. The panic dwindled in a few days, but anxiety in St. Louis continued to remain high as Missouri's future remained in question.[8]

In a last-ditch effort to avoid open warfare in the state, moderate Missouri Unionists arranged a conference between Lyon, now formally in command of troops in Missouri, and Claiborne Jackson on June 11. The meeting in the governor's suite at Planter's House, St. Louis's premier hotel, included Lyon and Frank Blair on one side and Jackson, the governor's secretary Thomas Snead, and former Missouri governor Sterling Price on the other. The exchange, heated at times, continued for four hours, but Lyon refused to relent to Jackson's demand that the Federally controlled Home Guard be disbanded because to do so would serve as a recognition of the limits of Federal authority. In the end, Lyon stormed from the room with the words "This means war," ordering Jackson and his compatriots to leave the city. Jackson hastened back to Jefferson City, where he and Snead then quickly prepared a proclamation from the governor accusing Lyon and the Federal government of trampling on the rights and liberties of Missouri residents, a claim calculated to arouse the anger of Missouri's independent, freedom-loving Westerners. The proclamation further called for the enlistment of fifty thousand militia volunteers "for the protection of the lives, liberty, and property of the citizens of the state."[9] Any hope of salvaging peace in Missouri was lost.

Unionists tentatively held on to St. Louis. One secessionist woman described the city ten days after Camp Jackson: "The town is filled & surrounded by troops. . . . Regulars occupy Russell & Bennett's Houses on 4th St. & there are Dutch regiments out by the fair grounds, at the Water Works all around & in the arsenal, on the Gravois Road, at the Rail road depots, & every where. . . . My blood boils in my veins when I think about the position of Missouri—held in the Union at the point of Dutchmen's bayonets."[10] While the rest of the state was still up for grabs, certainly the Unionist bayonets were a reality in the streets of St. Louis. Elevated to the rank of brigadier general, Nathaniel Lyon refused to allow the Confederates to go unchallenged after the ill-fated Planter's House meeting. First, he occupied Jefferson City, abandoned by Jackson and other state officials, including a majority of the state legislature. For the rest of the war, the legally elected–turned secessionist government remained in exile. Next, Lyon's forces managed to drive the much larger but unorganized Missouri State Guard to the southwestern part of the state and then to occupy Springfield. Despite his success, Lyon's position remained precarious. His supply lines extended two hundred miles back to St. Louis, and rebel forces numbered about eight thousand men, with some five thousand more on their way from Arkansas. On August 10, the two armies clashed outside of Springfield along Wilson's Creek and the Confederates came out victorious. One of the Union dead was Nathaniel Lyon.[11]

Under these circumstances Major General John C. Frémont took command of the newly designated Western Department, which included the entire region between the Mississippi River and the Rocky Mountains. Mexican War hero, noted Western explorer, and the first presidential candidate of the Republican Party, Frémont inherited a "threatening situation" in which "all operations had to be initiated in the midst of upturned and revolutionary conditions and a rebellious people, where all laws were set in defiance." At Frémont's disposal were twenty-three thousand troops, of which the three-month enlistments of some eight thousand were about to expire. The general's earliest attentions in Missouri focused on defending the region from the Missouri State Guard concentrated south of Springfield and from an anticipated Confederate attack at Cairo, Illinois, an important river city south of St. Louis. The situation for the Union in St. Louis, and the state as a whole, was growing graver.[12]

The capture of Camp Jackson temporarily quieted secessionist sentiment in St. Louis, but within weeks, secessionists brazenly displayed their sympathies by flying Confederate flags from windows and sending up cheers for Jefferson Davis. Emboldening the city's secessionist element was the growing pro-Confederate Missouri State Guard, led by Mexican War hero and former state governor Sterling Price. Even in the city, recruiters openly enlisted men to join Price. Secessionists and Unionists alike remained ever aware that the river city represented the key to controlling the rest of state. Shortly after arriving, Frémont decided to confront "the untoward and obstructing conduct of the people of Missouri" against Federal authority. In a terse announcement, Frémont declared martial law in St. Louis city and county on August 14, 1861. He then appointed Major Justus McKinstry as St. Louis's first provost marshal. Martial law followed throughout the state on August 30, the proclamation reading: "All persons engaged in treasonable correspondence, in giving or procuring aid to the enemies of the United States, in fomenting tumults, in disturbing the public tranquility by creating and circulating false reports or incendiary documents, are in their own interests warned that they are exposing themselves to sudden and severe punishment." Thus began a steady stream of civilians entering Federal custody in the region, arrested for activities or utterances considered disloyal and treasonous.[13]

Provost Marshal McKinstry showed little hesitancy in exercising the powers of martial law. According to one observer, when asked "What does martial law do?," McKinstry replied, "Martial law does as it d——d pleases." To house the first of these civilians arrested under martial law, the provost marshal utilized an abandoned structure on Fifth and Myrtle Streets used before the war as housing for slaves awaiting sale. The former owner, Bernard Lynch of proslavery and secessionist sentiments, had fled to the South at the war's outset.[14]

A contemporary account of the building, later to be called the Myrtle Street Prison, described it as "well adopted to the purposes of a prison, the back yard enclosed by high brick walls, affording a comfortable degree of freedom to the inmates, and the two large rooms of the upper story of the building being tolerable sleeping quarters for a large number of prisoners." The structure was one of two "slave pens" operated by Lynch before the war. According to one source, Lynch used this location to confine slave children that he had for sale; his other site, a much smaller building just a few blocks away, held adult slaves. By September 3, 1861, the newly converted military prison housed twenty-seven prisoners, including civilians and some Federal soldiers arrested for ordinary military offenses. Before long, civilians arrested by the military also could be found in the Gratiot Street Military Prison, a location much larger than the Myrtle Street Prison that primarily housed Confederate prisoners of war. Formerly the McDowell Medical College, it had been confiscated by Federal authorities after its prosecessionist owner Joseph Nash McDowell absconded to the South.[15]

It is unlikely that Southern-sympathizing women remained silent at this time. In fact, Unionist pastor of the Second Baptist Church of St. Louis Galusha Anderson recounted in his wartime memoir numerous instances of women lashing out against Federal authority, Unionist acquaintances, and the German militia during the early month of the war. He even related one story in which a secessionist woman unsuccessfully plotted to take the life of Frank Blair. Nevertheless, at the war's outset, Union and Confederate authorities considered women as nonparticipants in the war, who were to be protected and treated with respect and proper decorum, in keeping with the traditional laws and customs of war.[16]

In St. Louis, it appears that the activities of Confederate women at first evoked little concern in Provost Marshal McKinstry and his successor John McNeil. Perhaps, at first, the provost marshal could discount the actions of women as insignificant. However, by the fall of the war's first year, Confederate women's partisan activities would not go unchallenged. In St. Louis, the subversive activities of Ann Bush and a Mrs. Burke could not be overlooked. The two women, according to a newspaper account, had been "using their influence to make rebels of young men of their acquaintance." On October 20, 1861, Bush and Burke became the first women arrested in St. Louis for disloyal activities.[17]

Mrs. Burke first came to John McNeil's attention in early September 1861, and on the ninth of the month, the provost marshal ordered her arrest. According to evidence presented to the provost marshal from steamship captain James Doyle, Mrs. Burke had been corresponding with her husband, a captain in the Confederate army, and sending him information. Doyle noted, Burke "visited the different camps for the avowed purpose of collecting information to send" to her husband. Thus, Mrs. Burke became the first rebel woman sought out for arrest in St. Louis. When soldiers arrived at her home, they found Burke "sick of the fever" and unable to leave her residence. Burke remained free until October 20 when she was taken into custody. The connection between Burke and Ann Bush is not made clear in the records of the provost marshal. It may be just coincidence that they were arrested on the same day. Burke was released on that day, as no evidence was found in her possession showing her guilt; the same would not be true for Ann Bush, who was known by several aliases, including Mary Ann Bush, Mary Bushey, Mrs. Blackburn, and Mrs. Flynn.[18]

Particularly during the early stages of the war, women on both sides of the battle lines proved themselves effective recruiters for the armies, encouraging the men in their lives, especially suitors, to prove their manhood by enlisting. Bush took a somewhat opposite approach. Prior to Bush's arrest, McNeil received a letter from C. Brown of Albany, New York, dated October 12, 1861, concerning Bush. Brown described the woman as "a creature of the worst reputation." According to her accuser, Bush had been sending prosecession newspaper clippings, copies of which he included, to men in Albany, where Bush had previously resided, in order to dissuade them from enlisting in the Union army. Further, according to the letter, "She has the use of a great deal of money, and by misrepresenting things she has great influence over men that have associated with her." Brown concluded that "she ought to be under arrest." Evidently McNeil agreed.[19]

Immediately after Bush's arrest, McNeil received two petitions regarding her case. The first, signed by nine people seeking her release, characterized the prisoner as "an honest . . . woman who supports her family by sewing." The second, a much more cryptic plea bearing the names of two petitioners, stated simply that "I have lived next door to [Bush] for a year and know what she is." Bush gained her release after spending one night in confinement at Benton Barracks, a military training facility north of the city. She also had to sign a pledge promising "to refrain from writing to any person or persons with a view of persuading them in any manner against the Government of the United States, and that I will not speak disloyally of said government. . . . If I break [the pledge] I render myself liable to banishment from the state." Evidently the pledge did not convince Brigadier General Samuel R. Curtis, in command of Benton Barracks at the time. He noted in her file: "Look out for this woman. She needs watching. Our spy man may interject himself in her affair."[20]

Ann Bush disappeared from the records after her release, but in mid-February 1864 Mrs. Burke's premises were ordered searched for "property belonging to the U.S. Government." The search turned up only "one blanket not worth takin [*sic*]."[21] Nevertheless, Burke and Bush had the dubious honor of breaking the gender barrier on civilian arrests in St. Louis. They would not be the last women to come into the custody of the Office of the Provost Marshal.

On November 19, 1861, Major General Henry W. Halleck arrived in St. Louis to replace John Frémont and take command of the newly designated Department of the Missouri. Halleck also took charge of supervising operations penetrating into the western Confederacy and inherited responsibility for meeting the activities of Confederate sympathizers who challenged Federal authority from within the lines. Halleck learned through experience that women partisans could be just as much a threat as their male counterparts. Shortly after taking command, Halleck confronted manifestations of disloyalty in St. Louis. Symbols of Confederate sympathy had reappeared throughout the city, and within one hundred yards of city hall recruiting for the state guard resumed. Halleck put a stop to these activities. In particular, St. Louis's disloyal women had been showing their solidarity in opposition to the Federal government by wearing bright red rosettes. The general handled the situation by purchasing scores of similar rosettes and having them distributed among the city's prostitutes, who gladly put them on. Once the local newspapers publicized Halleck's generosity to the ladies of the evening, the flowers quickly disappeared from the breasts of Confederate sympathizers, who did not want to be equated with the streetwalkers.[22] In this instance, Halleck chose an informal route to counter female Confederates' show of support for the enemy, but the general appeared ready to take a strong stance against Confederate women's more serious partisan activities.

Halleck was more suited to administrative work than battlefield command. A native of New York, he graduated third in West Point's class of 1839. He earned the nickname "Old Brains" through his study of military science and other academic pursuits; he also briefly taught French at the military academy. During the Mexican War, Halleck spent his time far from the battle lines in California, where he proved himself an able administrator. He helped to establish a provisional government in that conquered region and then participated in the organization of the constitutional convention that would help pave the way for California statehood. Leaving the army in 1854, the former captain entered the field of law and did not return to active duty until August 1861. The impression Halleck had made on General-in-Chief Winfield Scott many years back secured him a commission as major general.[23]

In Missouri under Halleck, Federal soldiers from the highest levels to the common private in the field began to respond to the violations committed by women in a manner consistent with the women's actions and the new roles they adopted, roles that placed them in the ranks of enemy partisans. Halleck made this clear in his General Orders No. 13, issued two days after Abraham Lincoln confirmed that a state of martial law already existed in Missouri. The order of December 4, 1861, gave permission to officers in the field to "arrest and place in confinement all persons in arms against the lawful authorities of the United States, or who give aid, assistance, and encouragement to the enemy." Such persons would be tried by a military commission or tribunal similar in most ways to a court-martial, and those found guilty would be punished accordingly. Throughout the document, Halleck employed gender neutral language to refer to those subject to arrest and punishment except when discussing men acting as guerrillas in the field. In section 6 of the order the major general became more specific on the range of individuals who could be held answerable. After prescribing death by firing squad for those arrested for spying, he added that "in this respect the laws of war make no distinction of sex; all are liable to the same penalty." These people, he articulated early in the document, "have forfeited their civil rights as citizens by making war against the government and upon their own heads must fall the consequences."[24]

Through General Orders No. 13, Halleck made it clear that women were not beyond the reach of Federal authority and would be held responsible for their actions. Other commanders under Halleck concurred with this conclusion. For instance, writing from Jefferson City five months later, Brigadier General James Totten issued orders calling for the arrest of "all persons making disloyal speeches against the Government of the United States and the authorities thereof." Such language constituted "treasonable conduct," and as such would be met with the charge of "encouraging rebellion against the Government of the United States." Totten was explicit in including women among those "citizens" who could be held accountable for their defiance of the government: "Neither sex nor age among those who have reached the years of discretion and legal responsibility will be overlooked. All must be taught to obey and respect the laws of the land or submit to punishment for their disloyalty whether it consists of word, act or deed."[25]

Both Halleck and Totten agreed that women were citizens with certain responsibilities. Gender would not serve as a shield to protect them from punishment. They differed in that what Halleck implied, Totten made explicit: Actions of disloyalty constituted treason—a political crime and the only crime defined by the Constitution. Still, Totten stopped short of charging the women with treason. Halleck also had reason for refraining from using the term treason in his order. Prior to his arrival in Missouri, military commissions had attempted to try partisans on the charge of treason with

little success. Experience had proven that it was near to impossible for a
military court to convict a person of treason as defined by the Constitution
under the wartime conditions of Missouri. For one thing, two witnesses to
the same overt act of treason were required for a conviction; on top of that,
treason was a matter for civilian and not military courts.[26]

Halleck, a prewar author of a book on international law, clarified the matter in his first general order of 1862, issued on New Year's Day. The order set
procedures for military trials of civilian offenders who violated the "laws of
war." It also established the format for the tribunals that would judge the
cases. According to General Orders No. 1: "Treason as a distinct offense is
defined by the Constitution and must be tried by courts duly constituted by
law; but certain acts of a treasonable character such as conveying information
to the enemy, acting as spies, &c., are military offenses triable by military
tribunals and punishable by military authority."[27] Halleck no doubt saw treason in the actions of Southern partisans, but as the law stood, he could not
accuse them directly of being traitors. Nevertheless, those that challenged
the authority of the United States government, whether male or female, had
to face the consequences.

In Missouri, actions of Southern partisan women were defined within the
public sphere as political, and as such, women would be held accountable for
their political misdeeds. Here the orders of Halleck and Totten harmonized
with Benjamin Butler's General Orders No. 28, issued in New Orleans in May
1862. Butler's notorious "Women's Order" threatened the city's women with
treatment as common prostitutes for abusing Federal soldiers and officers. As
historian Drew Gilpin Faust has noted, "General Orders No. 28 held women
accountable for their actions in the public sphere; Butler would not permit
them to stand outside political responsibility or retribution. In taking such
a position, Butler acknowledged women as politically powerful."[28]

Neither would Halleck or Totten allow women to stand beyond political
responsibility and retribution, but they differed from Butler in the intention
of their orders. Mark Grimsley has observed that Butler's strategy with this
and other commands he issued while at New Orleans was "to make a few
dramatic examples that would give citizens of the occupied city pause before
trifling with Federal authority." In the case of Orders No. 28, Butler's plan appears to have proved effective.[29] Halleck and Totten, on the other hand, faced
a much different situation. Butler's order affected a city firmly in the hands
of the Union army. Halleck and Totten dealt with a vast territory heavily
contested by Unionists and Confederate sympathizers. The action of handing out flowers similar to those worn by secessionist women to prostitutes,

as Halleck had done early in his tenure, might work against that particular show of Confederate support, but Halleck and his subordinates confronted an ongoing problem that would not go away with similar symbolic countermoves or the issuance of any type of order from Federal authorities. Experience had already proven women capable of rebellious and treasonous sentiments; even before Halleck took command in Missouri, Ann Bush and Mrs. Burke had come before the provost marshal in St. Louis. Many more would follow, not only from St. Louis but also from elsewhere in Missouri and throughout the growing area of Confederate territory coming under Union occupation.

Henry Halleck expressed his willingness to punish rebellious women within his command. He reasserted it in his Special Orders No. 80, issued on January 26, 1862, regarding "women . . . in the habit of approaching the vicinity of the military prison, waving hostile flags, for the purpose of insulting the troops, and carrying on communication with the prisoners of war." Halleck ordered the commanding officer of the prison guard to "arrest, and place in confinement, all women so offending." He also ordered the confiscation of all carriages, along with their harnesses and horses, bearing the enemy's flag and the arrest of "any person wearing or displaying a hostile flag in this city." The pro-Union *Missouri Democrat* applauded the measure. Such women "seem to suppose they could do such things without impunity, under the protection of womanhood," an editorial asserted. "The time has come when disloyal persons (whatever their attire) must pay decent respect to that military authority which rebellion has rendered necessary in this city."[30]

Still, Halleck's first few months in charge in St. Louis witnessed the arrest of only three women, two of them for acts unrelated to the Confederate cause. A Mrs. Walton, arrested with her husband for defrauding the government on a cord wood contract, spent a few nights behind bars before her release.[31] Bridget Connors, taken in for "keeping a disorderly dram shop," gained release after five nights in custody "upon taking an oath not to sell any more liquor in the city to soldiers without special permit from" the provost marshal's office.[32] Only Mary E. Cole did anything disloyal: uttering "treasonable language." Indeed, a list sent to Washington on March 3, 1862, comprised of the names of "all persons received and held in confinement at Saint Louis and Alton other than prisoners of war since March, 1861" contained the names of no women, even those known to have been arrested during this time period.[33]

By early April 1862, Halleck had grown weary of the activities of Southern-sympathizing women, however. In declining a request that the wife of a chaplain in Sterling Price's army be allowed to pass through the lines to visit her husband, Halleck complained:

> Nearly all the secessionists of this State who have entered the rebel service have left their wives and daughters to the care of the Federal troops. There is scarcely a single instance where this confidence has been abused by us. But what return have these ladies made for this protection? In many cases they have acted as spies and informers for the enemy and have been most loud-mouthed in their abuse of our cause and most insulting in their conduct toward those who support it. Under any other government they would for such conduct be expelled from the country or confined within the walls of a prison.[34]

Despite the paucity of arrests of rebel women, Halleck seemed quite aware of their activities. Certainly military matters under his command preoccupied the major general: Ulysses S. Grant's successful attacks on Forts Henry and Donelson; the taking of Island No. 10; the victory snatched from defeat at Shiloh; and then the laborious crawl toward the Confederate enclave at Corinth, Mississippi—Halleck's only campaign as commander in the field—only to find the town abandoned.[35] Nevertheless, within a few weeks of making his complaint, the arrest of a string of pro-Confederate women commenced, albeit for relatively minor infractions compared to what was to come. For instance, two women draped a rebel flag out of an apartment window, several publicly sang secessionist songs, while others uttered "improper [i.e. disloyal] language." A Mrs. Bruneen destroyed a small United States flag in front of neighbors, and Margaret Ferguson's second visit to the Myrtle Street Prison to wave at prisoners in the windows secured for her a few hours in custody. Fanny Barron and Margaret Kelson came before the provost marshal for "inducing one Ja. Tho. Jilton to join a rebel band of bushwhackers." And the family of a Miss Bull found themselves under house arrest, with guards at all exits, because someone allegedly waved a Confederate flag out of one of the house's windows at prisoners arriving from the Shiloh battlefield. The family remained confined for two weeks before the guards were removed.[36]

In another instance, an arresting officer turned a woman who expressed disloyalty over to the local police. The highly intoxicated woman made a public spectacle as she led two cows through the streets of St. Louis while "hurrahing for Jeff. Davis." After an interview with the commandant of the Gratiot Street Prison, guards accompanied the woman to the "city calaboose" to be held on civil charges, thus removing from St. Louis's most recent provost marshal George E. Leighton the responsibility of handling her case.[37]

Major Leighton usually dealt with arrested women by requiring them to take a loyalty oath, in and of itself an act that acknowledged women's political significance, and then releasing them. When that failed, the women faced banishment from the city, county, or state, a punishment commonly meted out by civil authorities when dealing with recalcitrant criminal offenders. For instance, in one of the most serious cases within this early group of prisoners, Mrs. Fanny Coons was ordered banished from the state for failing to hand over to the provost marshal money raised by a benefit held in early July 1862 for which she was the treasurer. Held ostensibly for the aid of the poor, the event attracted almost exclusively secessionists of the city. According to one newspaper account, the "numerous and distasteful" decorations for the festivities were devoid of "any patriotic and national symbols." Leighton feared that the proceeds would be funneled to the Confederates, and he demanded that he be the one to make sure that the funds were distributed to the needy, regardless of Unionist or Confederate sympathies. After an extensive investigation, during which Coons proved uncooperative, Leighton determined that the benefit was "illegal and treasonable in its character." Leighton's order banishing Coons threatened her with imprisonment should she return to the state before the end of the war.[38]

Fanny Coon's Confederate activities probably went beyond raising money for her cause. According to an acquaintance, Coons had been allowed to visit rebel prisoners in St. Louis's military prisons and hospitals. She used this privilege to affect "the escape of a number of soldiers, under the guise of feminine garments," justifying her actions with the adage "all is fair in war." Perhaps one of those that Mrs. Coons intended to free was Captain Hampton L. Boon, captured at the Battle of Blackwater on December 19, 1861. Boon previously had escaped but was recaptured in southwest Missouri just a few miles from Sterling Price's lines. He nearly made good on his desire for freedom on April 22, 1862, simply by walking out of the front doors of the Myrtle Street Prison, clad in "a mottled straw bonnet, brown veil, black silk dress, hoop skirt, and new hoops, dark grey cloak, plaid scarf and embroidered slippers . . . with his hair daintily parted in the middle." Boon almost vanished into the city, but moments after the "presentable though somewhat tall lady" exited the prison, the assistant jailor realized that no women had entered the facility that day. Rearrested a block away, Boon claimed that he had carried the women's garments on his person into the prison at the time of his arrest, an assertion the jailors quickly discounted. Instead, they suspected that the apparel had been smuggled in by a female visitor, although none was mentioned by name in the account. The incident prompted prison officials to place severe limitations on future visits from women. They also questioned Fanny Coons in the matter, but found no solid evidence to hold against her.[39]

Because these women were arrested by his order, Provost Marshal Leighton had discretion over the way the women were treated. Clearly he exhibited a reluctance to confine the women in prison. The cases of most of them were dispensed with on the same day as the arrest, and those women not let go within a few hours spent only a night or two behind bars. Furthermore, Leighton did not pursue action against every woman that came to his attention. When Mary Powderly complained that a Mrs. Lyons abused her because of her family's Unionist leanings, regularly calling Powderly names like "Black Union nigger" and throwing "the offal of chickens" at her, Leighton failed to make an arrest.[40] Meanwhile, elsewhere women like Rose Greenhow, Ellie Poole, and Medora Onderdonk were confined for weeks and even months. Unlike these women, however, none of the St. Louis detainees was accused of spying or another comparable infraction. The most serious charges appeared to be those leveled against the banished Fannie Coons. That soon changed.

A speedy release would not be the case for Isadore Morrison, who on July 25, 1862, became the St. Louis region military prisons' first female inmate ordered confined indefinitely.[41] Arrested on July 12, 1862, in Cairo, Illinois, for spying and then sent to St. Louis to be confined, Morrison's fate rested in the hands of the Federal officer that ordered her imprisonment, Brigadier General William K. Strong, and not with St. Louis's provost marshal. Leighton could not order her release under any circumstances. Morrison had been found on the streets of Cairo in the middle of the night "under very suspicious circumstances." Several papers in her possession confirmed that she was up to no good. They included a list containing an enumeration of troops in the area. She also had a letter written by someone supposedly from St. Louis that she admitted she was to use "to help her in deceiving the officers and getting to Corinth [Mississippi]." She refused to divulge the name of the author of the letter because she said she could not "give an Explanation without *Criminating herself* [sic]."

Morrison claimed to be a native of Virginia and a prewar resident of Memphis, Tennessee. At one point she asserted that her name actually was Larina Cunningham. She freely admitted to having been engaged in spying for eight months but would not give any specifics because if she did so, "she was afraid she would be Shot." Morrison's admissions raise a number of questions. She was so candid about being a spy, but consistently refused to discuss any of her activities. Perhaps she naively thought that without her own admission of specifics, Federal authorities would release her in a few days, as she told the detective who interviewed her.

In her interview Morrison spoke often of Eugenia Phillips, the outspoken secessionist who had run afoul of Federal power in two well-publicized instances. The wife of a prewar congressman from Alabama, Phillips remained in Washington when the war commenced. In response to her unyielding expressions of support for the Confederate cause, the secret service first placed Phillips and her two daughters and sister, all secessionists, under house arrest before moving them to Rose O'Neal Greenhow's home, which had been converted into a prison for rebel women. No proof could be found that she corresponded with the rebels as accused, and so after several weeks, Federal officials decided to release the Phillips women, provided that they pass through Confederate lines, not to return. Phillips went to New Orleans, where in May 1862 she once again came under Federal rule and the jurisdiction of Benjamin Butler. It took little time for Phillips to get Butler's dander up; on June 20, Butler ordered Phillips's arrest for "traitorous proclivities and acts" and had her imprisoned at Ship Island on the Mississippi.[42] Perhaps Isadore Morrison simply tried to achieve the same attention and notoriety that Phillips had received. On the other hand, she may have hoped that her captors would dismiss her as a young woman only seeking attention but posing no harm.

Whatever the case, while Morrison admitted no specifics that could be used against her, the document she carried revealing troop strength around Cairo certainly was "criminating." Unless she truly was naive, or incredibly stupid, Morrison had to know that her captors would not release her to go "where she pleased." Instead, she may have been using this act to put the officers at ease, hoping to engineer a chance to escape. Morrison's story became more complex once she arrived in St. Louis. On the fourth day of her confinement at the Gratiot Street Prison, Morrison requested an interview with the prison's commandant, a Lieutenant Bishop. In his office, in dramatic fashion, Morrison pulled out a vial of chloroform and attempted suicide with it. Bishop intervened, stopping Morrison from ingesting most of the liquid.[43]

Perhaps Morrison saw herself as a nineteenth-century Antigone, the title character of the play by Sophocles. Antigone kills herself to expose the corruptness of and bring shame to the ruler of Thebes, a land locked in its own civil war. Or perhaps Morrison did not have martyrdom in mind; perhaps she sought to create an opportunity. Morrison had to have known that her jailor would try to stop her from drinking the chloroform. The vial had been small enough for her to bring undetected into the prison, and she did not ingest its entire contents. She may not have ingested any at all. If she did swallow any, she may have known that it would pass from her body in a few short hours. It was logical for Morrison to assume that she would be hospitalized once the suicide was foiled, either because of concerns for her physical or emotional state, or both.[44] The record is silent on whether Lieutenant Bishop sent Morrison to the hospital at that time, but three weeks later, according to the *Missouri Republican*, Missouri Provost Marshal General Bernard G. Farrar ordered that Morrison be sent to the nearby hospital for women run by the Sisters of Charity "on account of sickness." The conclusion of the story of Morrison's imprisonment is tersely, yet revealingly, summed up on the paper jacket of her case file: "Has been paroled to Sister's Hospital. Escaped from there." Isadore Morrison disappeared from confinement and from the records, but it is quite presumable that her partisan activities did not end there.[45]

Morrison's case exposes a woman's willingness to take extreme measures to further the Confederate cause. After the experience with Morrison, officials in St. Louis evinced less hesitancy in imprisoning women arrested on their orders. Between late July and the end of December 1862, at least twenty-four women faced arrest in St. Louis and several spent at least one night, some women many more, in confinement by order of the Office of the Provost Marshal. The general accusation of disloyalty, including the charge of expressing support for the Confederacy, proved to be common charges aimed at women during this period. At the same time, the women displayed a rather militant posture toward the Federal government and those who supported it. A Mary Wolfe, arrested in September 1862, regularly taunted her Unionist neighbors. She also allegedly asked her young son if he had enough "secesh" in him to hit their Unionist neighbor's son on the head with a "little hatchet, the little damn black republican." Lucinda Clark, reportedly a "very quarrelsome woman" who continually abused Unionist neighbors, sang this version of the song "Dixie": "I wish I were in the land of cotton and see old Lincoln dead and rotten." Her wish that "the Union folks ought to be shot for arresting secessionists" did not deter the provost marshal from having her arrested.[46]

According to numerous depositions against her, Catherine Farrell's "reputation for loyalty is bad." Described as a "strong secessionist . . . violent and abusive," Farrell supposedly "kept a rendezvous for disloyal persons since the breaking of this Rebellion." She referred to the German American militia who took part in the Camp Jackson affair as "Damn Dutch Butchers" and called one Unionist woman she met in the street a "Black republican Bitch," while threatening to "cut her heart out." She also abused a particular neighbor and his family because he had taken a position with a government office: at one point Farrell threw a tumbler at the man's mother as she walked past Farrell's open window. At the time that these depositions were taken, Farrell had already been arrested once and ordered banished from the Department of the Missouri, but due to a change in personnel in the provost marshal's office, the order slipped through the cracks. She was given five days to leave the state, "under penalty of being removed by force."[47]

In July 1862, Provost Marshall Leighton ordered that the house of Edward William Johnston be searched for weapons and ammunition. No doubt suspicion fell on Johnston because he was the brother of Confederate General Joseph E. Johnston. While soldiers went about their task, Edward's wife, Margaret, who, according to the officer in command, was "treated with all courtesy and leniency," launched into a scorching tirade that would lead to her arrest for using abusive language against the government. According to the charges brought against her, she said

> that she was a true daughter of the south, that if she had ten lives to loose, she would cheerfully loose them for the success of the Southern Confederacy; that she gloried in the course Jefferson Davis had taken and was still pursuing, that he was all which was great and chivalrous, and quite a contrast the mean, blackguard, negro stealing, contemptible abolition President Abraham Lincoln . . . that he gloried in her brave brother in Law, Gen. Johnson who had made the Union Soldiers feel his heavy hand more than once, and she hoped and prayed he would do so again.

Although not taken into custody immediately, Margaret was arrested by Leighton's order in mid-August. Not surprised and clearly unfazed by this turn of events, she once again asserted her Southern devotion and "repeatedly used insulting language against the men and hurrahed for Jeff. Davis."[48]

Mary Wolfe, Lucinda Clark, Catherine Farrell, and Margaret Johnston fought their own war against the Federal government and those who sought to uphold it. Never denying the charges against them, these women defiantly expressed their Confederate allegiance and their hostility toward Federal authority, despite the consequences. As the number of women prisoners expanded, the charges against them grew more complicated and the methods of sentencing them more severe. Paralleling this growth was the dedication the women evinced in carrying out their work. The case of Drucilla Sappington reveals both these processes. Sappington was the daughter of St. Louis-area judge Olly Williams, who according to one source was a cousin to two presidents, Zachary Taylor and James Buchanan. After her first husband died in the 1850s, Drucilla married William David Sappington, and settled on his farm about ten miles west of the city in St. Louis County. By 1860, William David owned land valued at $10,000, plus $2,560 in personal property. According to the 1860 slave census, he also owned one twenty-six-year-old male slave.[49]

William David joined the Confederate army, serving in the Fourth Missouri Cavalry, while his wife remained at home fighting the war from behind the lines. Mrs. Sappington first came to the attention of Federal authorities in August 1862 when they received a report that "a camp of secessionists was recently upon her premises with her knowledge and consent." A visit by a patrol of some seventy soldiers turned up nothing. Nevertheless, Sappington, characterized as "the wife of a bitter secessionist now in the rebel army," complained that the men had killed all her ducks, turkeys, and chickens and had stolen clothes, jewelry, and money, and almost made off with a bed. Ten days later, intelligence divulged by a man who had joined a band of guerrillas but had second thoughts and turned himself in confirmed that Mrs. Sappington's house and property were being used by the rebels not only with her consent but her cooperation.[50]

A second visit to the Sappington property proved more fruitful. In early September, a Confederate officer and his staff were found quartered at the Sappington house and arrested. The officer proved to be none other than Hampton L. Boon, who having failed in his escape from the Myrtle Street Prison while disguised as a woman finally succeeded using other methods. Sappington was not immediately taken into custody, but she would not go unpunished. For "having given information to the traitors of the movement of the U.S. forces and having harbored and aided men in arms against the United States government," Missouri Provost Marshal General Bernard G. Farrar ordered on September 3 that Sappington swear an oath of parole and pay a bond of $2,000. Farrar further demanded that Sappington leave the state of Missouri and relocate to Massachusetts. (It is unclear why he specified Massachusetts.) From there she was to lodge by mail monthly reports to Farrar concerning her good conduct.[51]

When Sappington learned that she was about to be served with Farrar's order, she fled the county, headed for southwestern Missouri, and presumably Confederate lines. A few days later one hundred miles from the city, authorities found and arrested her and a female traveling companion, Elisabeth Sigler, who had also gained a reputation for disloyalty. The women were returned to St. Louis and on September 15 were placed in a residence adjacent to the Gratiot Street Prison, where the owner of the former medical college once lived. Sappington did not let prison walls stop her from aiding the Confederate cause. In custody she and Sigler shared a room adjacent to the cell occupied by Absalom Grimes, a noted Confederate mail carrier who recently had been captured in St. Louis and sentenced to be shot. The two women helped Grimes to escape confinement to resume his clandestine pursuits. Not surprisingly, Grimes already knew Sappington and recently had been at her home.[52]

Sappington left the prison about a month after her arrival, her father having posted a one thousand dollar bond on her behalf. It is doubtful that Sappington ever traveled to Massachusetts, but evidently the threat of further imprisonment or losing her father's money did not shake her commitment to the Confederacy. Soon Sappington was once more arrested, probably for involvement in smuggling. This time she would be detained briefly in a temporary prison before being banished to the South beyond Federal lines. At some point she returned to Missouri, perhaps because there she could act upon her political convictions better than she could within the Confederacy. As late as March 1864, Lieutenant General Edmund Kirby Smith, commanding the Confederate Trans-Mississippi Department, received secret communications from Sappington, written from St. Louis, concerning military affairs in Missouri, Indiana, and Illinois. Smith passed the message along to Sterling Price, now a regularly commissioned Confederate general preparing to launch a campaign to liberate his home state.[53]

Drucilla Sappington was not the only disloyal woman to have been arrested more than once. After her first arrest, she spent about one month in custody before her release, as did her friend Elisabeth Sigler. For the women arrested in St. Louis during the first two years of the war, Sappington, Sigler, and Isadore Morrison proved to be the exception, not the rule. Morrison remained in custody for a little over a month from the time of her arrest in Cairo until her escape. For the rest of the women known to have been arrested in 1861 and 1862 in and around St. Louis, about forty in all, most of whom faced some charge related to disloyalty, their time behind bars ranged from a few hours to a few days. An oath of allegiance and promise of future good conduct usually sufficed to gain release for most, although some had to pay a bond to back up their promise. During this same time, the punishments men received for similar offenses seem a bit harsher. For example, Edward D. Trainor earned a twenty-day imprisonment sentence, after which he had to swear an oath of allegiance and pay a three thousand dollar bond for his disloyalty. William Embree, convicted of "using language disloyal to the government and tending to encourage Bushwhacking" spent about ten days in prison before being paroled. That Federal authorities in St. Louis had regular facilities to confine men while they had no permanent location for women prisoners yet may explain the difference. During this same time, at least eight women were banished from the city or state, as well, but so were men. The *Missouri Democrat* made a great deal about the banishment of four women who had habitually and violently harassed Unionist neighbors and otherwise acted disloyally, but mentioned only as an afterthought that also banished with them was one of their husbands, who had acted with equal nastiness.[54]

For the most part, the records suggest a thoroughness in investigating suspected women. Detectives working under the provost marshal questioned witnesses and suspects and took depositions, often before making an arrest.

George Leighton had great confidence in his detectives, as they had been "invaluable" in the St. Louis area and elsewhere in the state "in discovering facts which it has been impossible to obtain by the ordinary means." Most, if not all, cases appear to have been resolved by the provost marshal himself, rather than the military commissions that had been designated to hear civilian cases. The cases were also handled expeditiously. Leighton rendered judgment commensurate with the actions of the women. In cases of expressing disloyal sentiments, the most common charge during this period, a stern warning to cease such displays usually sufficed. Bridget Kelly, for instance, had been arrested in August 1862 for singing "secession songs." The provost marshal's office let her go, "as she is sufficiently warned . . . without being kept a night in prison." Thus, numerous women like Kelly spent just a few hours in custody. Suspicion alone did not prove guilt. For example, accusations that a Mrs. Keating was guilty of "disloyalty and annoying Union people" were "satisfactorily disproven" by the evidence collected in her case. Likewise, the charges of materially aiding in the recruitment of Confederate soldiers faced by Mary M. Barclay were dropped within about twenty-four hours once they were proven unfounded. Admitted secessionist sympathizer Catherine Duffey, detained for having used "improper language" to an army surgeon while visiting a St. Louis hospital, gained released after apologizing to the doctor. Her language was "improper," no doubt rude and unladylike, but not disloyal.[55]

The evidence suggests that the first few women arrested in the St. Louis area early in the war were held in rooms at Benton Barracks, northwest of downtown. Women imprisoned in 1862, however, were sent to the Gratiot Street Prison, including the empty residence adjacent to it. Because of the short duration of most women's imprisonment during this time, Federal authorities probably felt no pressing demand to designate extensive space for women prisoners. Or vice versa, the lack of accommodations might very well have explained the brief confinements. Whatever the case, the *Missouri Democrat* reported in September 1862 that the Gratiot Street Prison "furnishes very slender accommodations for secession in crinoline." Contrary to the paper's assertion that a section of prison would soon be "reserved for ladies,"[56] the sparse room allotted for women continued well into 1863.

By the end of 1862, women coming before the St. Louis provost marshal had become a matter of course. One might question whether the shift in responsibility for handling civilian arrest cases from the State Department to the War Department in February 1862 accounted for the spate of female arrests that began in mid-spring. A close look at the records, however, reveals otherwise; civilian arrests eased in the months after the shift to allow

Secretary of War Edwin Stanton time to review the record amassed by Secretary of State William Seward.[57]

It is surprising, considering the divided loyalties of the area, that the arrest in force of disloyal women in St. Louis and its surroundings did not take place sooner. When in mid-February 1862 Seward requested from all Federal military prisons a list of the names of all civilians confined for any period of time in the prisons in St. Louis and Alton since March 4, 1861, George Leighton included no women in his reply. In contrast, in response to the same request, Washington, D.C.'s provost marshal general Andrew Porter reported that fourteen women had been "arrested by [Porter's] command or sent to [him] for safe-keeping" at the Old Capitol Prison. The earliest arrests took place in August 1861, and all but one of the women on the list came into custody before the war entered its second calendar year. The officer who compiled the list further noted that it was incomplete due to missing records, so there may have been more women arrested.[58]

A subsequent list of prisoners confined in Old Capitol on March 17, 1862, revealed the names of three women found on the previous enumeration who were still in confinement, including the notorious Rose O'Neal Greenhow. After her arrest, Greenhow remained confined in her own house, along with several other women arrested for disloyal activities. In mid-January 1862, authorities transferred Greenhow and the other women to Old Capitol.[59]

In her study of women's partisan activities during the Civil War, Elizabeth Leonard suggests that a combination of Victorian chivalry and a lack of appropriate prison space hindered Federal authorities in the East from imprisoning women early in the war. The same was probably true in St. Louis. Certainly finding adequate space factored in the dearth of arrests of women during the first year of the war. Federal authorities in the area struggled to find sufficient facilities to handle Confederate prisoners of war, whose numbers were added to by the male civilians arrested for disloyal activities. Nevertheless, department commander Henry Halleck and those under him remained aware of the nature of Confederate women's covert activities in the region. By late spring 1862, it could no longer go unchecked. The policies Halleck established in Missouri essentially remained in place when the general left for Washington to become general-in-chief of the entire Union army. The arrest and imprisonment of disloyal women continued under the command of his successor John Schofield.[60]

As Mark Grimsley has shown, by late 1862 the Lincoln administration and the Union army began backing off from the conciliatory approach they had taken in conducting military operations. The war for the Union was hardening, highlighted by Lincoln's announcement that liberating slaves would now be a military objective of the war.[61] After a cautious and limited approach to women's disloyalty in St. Louis during the conflict's first two years, the hardening of war included more arrests of Confederate women, longer periods of imprisonment for them, and a series of very public banishments to the South of prominent Missouri women involved in a multitude of covert activities against the Union cause. Nationally, the hardening of the war would also include the adoption of a comprehensive policy for dealing with civilians living in war zones and areas under Union army occupation, one that would recognize both men and women as potential threats to Federal authority. With his experience dealing with disloyal women in Missouri fresh in his memory, Henry Halleck played a key role in the shaping of that military policy.

CHAPTER 2

"No Difference on Account of the Difference of Sexes . . . concerning the War-Traitor"

B y late 1862, Confederate-sympathizing women in St. Louis and the outlying region had made it abundantly clear that they were not going to remain passive observers of the war. Indeed, many rebellious women decided to take their stand against the Federal government, and they did so in a variety of ways that carried them beyond the traditional domestic sphere that nineteenth-century women were supposed to occupy. Through their actions, Confederate women attempted to further the political cause of secession and to contribute to the war being waged to secure Southern independence. Federal army officials, not only in St. Louis but also in Washington, certainly grew concerned about the actions of these women, though not necessarily because they transcended the boundaries of womanhood. Confederate women were proving to be a significant threat to the Union cause in ways both large and small, just as their male counterparts were. Major General Henry Halleck's experience in Missouri exposed him to a civilian population rife with secessionist sympathizers, bent on resisting the authority of the Federal government. It also showed him that Confederate-sympathizing women willingly participated in furthering the cause they supported, and Halleck had no tolerance for such rebellious activities. Whether or not the military courts could try defendants for treason, Halleck saw these rebels behind the lines as traitors. Halleck, therefore, responded accordingly, authorizing women's arrests, their imprisonments, and in some cases their banishments from the state. Halleck's elevation to general-in-chief of the army and his removal to Washington placed him in a position where he could help to set policy for the entire army concerning the appropriate treatment of rebellious civilians. The lessons he learned in Missouri would ensure that any such policy he endorsed would not overlook the wrongdoing of Confederate women.

The policy went into effect on April 24, 1863, when the Department of War issued General Orders No. 100, "Instructions for the Government of Armies of the United States in the Field." Also known as Lieber's Code, the document represented the first such code ever adopted by the nation's military, or by any other nation for that matter.[1] Written primarily by international law expert Francis Lieber and endorsed by Halleck, Lieber's Code delineated the rights and responsibilities of governments at war, soldiers in the field, and civilians in occupied territories. In practical terms, the code set guidelines for the Federal army concerning how troops were to conduct themselves and what the army expected of civilians they encountered as they marched into enemy territory. In many respects, it simply formalized practices already evolved through wartime experience. It also made women accountable for their actions—actions deemed treasonous—as a matter of policy throughout the Union army. In addition, Lieber's Code introduced the concept of the war traitor into the military lexicon. The term, an invention of Henry Halleck, carried no added punitive weight. Nevertheless, its use allowed Halleck and other military personnel the satisfaction of leveling the charge of treason, or at least a version of it, at civilians accused of aiding the Confederacy, including women.

The idea for the code itself originated with Lieber. As early as August 1861, he began to consider writing what he envisioned as "a little book on the Law and Usages of War, affecting the combatants." Over the next several months, Lieber delivered a series of lectures at Columbia College in New York on that general topic. Halleck, a respected specialist in the study of international law himself, became interested in what Lieber had to say. Still commanding in St. Louis and grappling with the legalities of fighting a civil war, Halleck requested a summary of the lectures from Lieber. Before Lieber could respond, he learned that one of his two sons serving in the Union army had been wounded at the Battle of Fort Donelson, and so he dashed off to Tennessee to find the injured lad. This trip to the West gave Lieber the opportunity to meet and develop a friendship with Halleck. It also set in motion the circumstances that led to the creation of Lieber's Code.[2]

A few months after their initial meeting, Halleck wrote to Lieber requesting his opinion on "the matter of guerrilla war" and men captured in the act of war while wearing "the garb of peaceful citizens." Lieber's response came in the form of an extended essay entitled "Guerrilla Parties Considered with Reference to the Laws and Usages of War." With this done and Halleck now in Washington as general-in-chief, Lieber once again proposed clarifying "the Laws and Usages of war" in November 1862, but rather than in the form of a "little book," he suggested that it be done as "a set of rules and definitions providing for the most urgent cases" and issued directly by President Lincoln. Lieber pressed the issue, and before long Halleck appointed a committee, made up of four generals and chaired by Lieber, to carry out this task.[3]

The end product became Lieber's Code, ready for issuance as the Department of War's "General Orders No. 100" in April 1863.[4] The code contained ten sections and 157 individual articles. Broadly written to apply to all armed conflict and to allow flexibility, the document became the general policy for soldiers in the field. Much of the code dealt with enemy combatants. It addressed matters related to prisoners and exchanges, flags of truce, treatment of wounded partisans and guerrillas, and more. According to the definitions of the types of armed conflicts set forth by Lieber, the present hostility represented a rebellion: "a war between the legitimate government of a country and portions or provinces of the same who seek to throw off their allegiance to it and set up a government of their own." Under these terms, Confederate soldiers could be treated as belligerents under the law of war, but the "legitimate government" (as opposed to the military) still had the right to try "leaders of the rebellion or chief rebels for high treason."

The civilians of the Confederate states were also still subject to Federal law. In this context, the code described three categories of civilians in areas of occupation: those who remained loyal to the government, those who sympathized with but did not positively aid the rebellion, and those who "without taking up arms, give positive aid and comfort to the rebellious enemy without being bodily forced thereto." While the first group merited the full protection of the army, the latter two could be deprived of property for the benefit of the military or subjected to retaliatory acts in response to the depredations of Confederate soldiers and guerrillas. The code's ambiguous treatment of what constituted "military necessity" and "retaliation" allowed officers in the field to follow a harsh policy toward civilians under occupation, or in contested areas like Missouri.[5]

Ambiguous or not, General Orders No. 100 made the punishment of Confederate partisan women a matter of policy. It specifically stated that women violating its policies would be held accountable in the same way as men: "The laws of war, like the criminal law regarding other offenses, make no difference on account of the difference of sexes, concerning the spy, the war-traitor, or the war-rebel."[6] In effect, the policy served as a set of guidelines for provost marshals and other Federal officers with whom rebellious women ran afoul. With the approval of the government, Union authorities could treat these enemy women using the same punishments leveled against their male counterparts.

Holding women accountable for their actions appears in Lieber's original draft of the code, which he had printed for circulation among the committee members in February 1863. After that the draft underwent many changes and additions. In a letter to Halleck sent a month after the issuance of General Orders No. 100, Lieber acknowledged that "the Generals of the Board" assigned to draft the code "have added some very important additions." Yet it was Halleck, who was not part of the committee assigned to write the code, that Lieber claimed merited special acknowledgment for his contributions: "I regret that your name is not visibly connected with this code," Lieber wrote. "Some opportunity will occur . . . when I shall yet chisel your name on this marble tablet of the code." Lieber had asked Halleck for his comments and suggestions on the February draft when he sent a copy to the general, and in following letters sent numerous revisions and additions to Halleck for his consideration. Indeed, Halleck biographer John Marszalek called the general "the patron of General Orders No. 100."[7]

Evidence confirms that one of Halleck's more unique contributions to the code was the inclusion of the concept of the war traitor. Article 90 of the code defines the "war-traitor" as one who was a "traitor under the law of war," presumably rather than a traitor as specified by the Constitution. It further states that a war traitor "is a person in a place or district under martial law who, unauthorized by the military commander, gives information of any kind to the enemy, or holds intercourse with him." Subsequent articles give further examples of what constitutes a war traitor.[8] Significantly, by holding the accused war traitor accountable only for having contact with the enemy, military authorities did not have to prove what information was revealed and what consequences it had.

The term "war-traitor" does not appear in Lieber's February draft, but the term traitor does. For instance, article 65 of Lieber's February draft reads: "If a person belonging to the territory of the enemy, occupied by a hostile army, gives information to the enemy, unauthorized to do so by the occupying or conquering authority, such person is either a spy or a traitor, and in either case is punished with death." More specific to the ongoing rebellion, article 67 reads, "If a citizen of the United States obtains information in a legitimate manner, and betrays it to the enemy, be he a military or civil officer, or a private citizen, he is a traitor, and is condemned to death."[9] Such cases, according to the code, would be heard by a military court or commission. The description of the offense found in article 67 arguably fits the definition of treason found in article 3, section 3 of the U.S. Constitution: "Treason against the United States shall consist only in levying war against them, or in adhering to their enemies, giving them aid and comfort." Henry Halleck knew, however, that the military could not rule on cases of treason. Treason was a civilian offense defined by the Constitution. As commander of the Department of the Missouri, Halleck made this clear in his first general order of 1862, which set procedures for military trials of civilian offenders.[10] Thus, the term "traitor" in the final draft of Lieber's Code would have to be replaced with "war-traitor," one who was not protected by the constitutional definition of what constituted treason and could be tried by a military court or commission.

Evidence points directly to Henry Halleck as the originator of the concept of the war traitor, or war treason, but he first used the term "military traitor" to refer to one who committed "military treason." Halleck certainly believed that the actions of Confederate partisans such as the ones he encountered in Missouri while commanding there were treasonous. Once in Washington, Halleck gave his wholehearted approval to a proposal from Major General William Rosecrans in Tennessee calling for "more rigid treatment of all disloyal persons within the lines." At the time, Rosecrans confronted a number of troublesome cases concerning civilians, including that of accused smuggler and spy Clara Judd, whom the general sent to the Alton Military Prison in Illinois while he decided what to do with her. In his March 5, 1863, response to Rosecrans's proposal, Halleck affirmed his view that in his opinion disloyalty constituted treason, something he had only previously intimated. He also now held that military courts had authority in such cases. He did this by distinguishing a difference between the political offense of treason and this notion of "military treason." According to his definition of the term, "military treason" was "a military offence punishable by the common law of war." Military courts, and not civilian ones, had jurisdiction over the cases, and so the burden of proof was much less rigorous. "The party" who committed military treason "not only forfeits all claims to protection, but subjects himself *or herself* to be punished either as a spy or a military traitor, according to the character of the particular offense." Through this feat of mental gymnastics, Halleck redefined treason to meet military needs and his own desire to try rebellious civilians as traitors.[11]

Halleck reiterated the concept of the military traitor in a March 17, 1863, letter to Major General Edwin V. Sumner, who recently had been appointed to take command of the Department of the Missouri: "All of Missouri is now in the military occupation of the United States. The inhabitants are, therefore, bound by the law of war (without any regard to their civil allegiance to the Government of the United States as the sovereign power) to render obedience to the occupying military authority. If they take up arms in insurrection, or render aid and assistance to the enemy, they become military insurgents or military traitors, and therefore forfeit their lives and property."[12] The same day that Halleck wrote to Stanton, Lieber wrote to Halleck requesting two copies of the March 5 letter that Halleck had sent to Rosecrans.[13] Lieber borrowed heavily from the letter in writing an added section of the code on civil wars and rebellions.[14] For instance, on March 22, he sent the general a draft of a new article for the code concerning the particularly thorny issue of whether or not a spy or a "military traitor," once returned to the protection of his own army, could be punished for those past offenses if he were later captured.[15]

The evidence in the draft copies of the code supports Halleck as the inventor of the terms "military traitor" and "military treason." Neither can be found in usage in this context prior to the March 5, 1863, letter from Halleck to Rosecrans. Further supporting Halleck as the term's inventor is an 1865 essay on the illegality of the use of military commissions to try civilians during the war written by U.S. senator and former U.S. attorney general Reverdy Johnson. He explained: "During the pendency of this rebellion, (never before,) it has been alleged that there exists with us the offence of military treason, punishable by the laws of war. It is so stated in the instructions of General Halleck to the then commanding officer in Tennessee, of the 5th of March, 1863." Johnson, a former Whig turned Democrat who defended accused Lincoln conspirator Mary Surratt, used as his source an 1863 edition of Henry Wheaton's *Elements of International Law,* edited by William B. Lawrence, although that source simply reprints Halleck's letter to Rosecrans in its entirety without any substantial comments. Johnson continued: "The term *military treason* is not to be found in any English work or military order, or before this rebellion, in any American authority."[16]

Missourian Edward Bates, Lincoln's attorney general from 1861 to 1864, agreed. "*Military treason!*" he confided in his diary in late June 1865. "I confess my ignorance. I never heard of it till I read just now, a sketch of Reverdy Johnson's argument (in Mrs. Surat[t]'s case) before the *Military* Commission. . . . *Halleck's treason,* seems to me a new invention. It certainly is not Treason *against the U.S.,* which (says the constitution—Art. 3 § 3) shall consist *only* in levying war against them, *or* adhering to their enemies giving them aid and comfort." He punctuated his comments with one last scoff: "*Halleck's treason!!*"[17]

The term had actually been used prior to Halleck's employment of it, but not imbued with the meaning Halleck gave it. Scottish politician and historical writer Archibald Alison, for instance, published an essay first appearing in 1831 titled "Military Treason and Civic Soldiers." His subject, however, concerned members of the military who committed treason, not what Halleck had in mind.[18]

Halleck's concept made its way into Lieber's Code, but at some point, the military traitor became the war traitor, perhaps because a civilian by nature is not part of the military, even though he or she might be taking part in a war. Lieber claimed to be the first person to use the phrase "war-traitor," and Confederate secretary of war James Seddon would also see Lieber's hand in the origins of the phrase. In a long protest against the adoption by the U.S. Army of General Orders No. 100, Seddon rejected the idea of the war traitor, claiming that it was alien to the American legal and constitutional tradition. He attributed it to the foreign origins of Lieber, a Prussian emigrant, who Seddon had inferred was familiar only with the institutions of the "imperial or military despots of the continent of Europe."[19]

Nevertheless, comments on an extant copy of Lieber's February draft of the code in what looks like Lieber's handwriting suggests that the use of war traitor instead of military traitor came at the suggestion of Halleck.[20] Whether or not the phrase "war-traitor" originated with Halleck, the idea definitely was his. Writing more than half a century ago, U.S. army major, member of the judge advocate general's corps, and Harvard law professor, Richard R. Baxter agreed. The "war treason" of Lieber's Code, he argued, evolved from the "military treason" of Henry Halleck. Furthermore, the code "specifically distinguished this species of treason from the normal domestic variety."[21] Halleck, no doubt, believed that supporting the Confederacy constituted treason. If he had not concluded so already, his experience in Missouri certainly would have convinced him. Whether it was military treason or war treason, Federal provost marshals and their commanding officers could now level the charge of treason—at least a version of it—at rebellious civilians through General Orders No. 100.

In practice, the accusation of committing war treason proved to be a symbolic gesture leveled with some other specific offense or offenses such as smuggling or spying. Symbolic or not, the charge carried with it political connotations and responsibilities that would apply to women as well as men. Holding women accountable for treasonous activities bears significance for several reasons. First, prior to the Civil War, an era when women were not considered public actors who had any legitimate political voice, no women had ever been charged with treason by the United States government. In fact, in the early days of the republic, the Supreme Court ruled that women could not be held accountable for treason because their civic identities belonged to their husbands and not to themselves. The cases in question related to the events of the American Revolution when several states found loyalist women guilty of the charge of treason, specifically for their departure from the United States under the protection of the British military.[22] Many of the women who left did so with their husbands. By the prosecuting states' laws, such action resulted in the forfeiture of any property they left behind. The two decades following the adoption of the United States Constitution witnessed several cases brought before the Federal courts concerning the forfeited property, cases brought by some of the women or by their heirs; some cases made their way to the Supreme Court. In response, the court elaborated a view that the married women who left the nation did so because of their obligations to their husbands.

In arriving at this position, the court viewed the women as *femes covert* who had no civic identity other than that of their husbands and who owed their primary civic obligations to their husbands, even when their husbands' demands conflicted with those of the state. This understanding derived from the broader doctrine of *coverture,* which initially applied to relations between parents (especially fathers) and children, and masters and servants.[23] The court ruled that the women who left with their husbands could not be held liable for treason because they had no will of their own, only the will of their husbands, which the women were obliged to obey.

The court's opinion in these cases did not necessarily result in the return of the property, but it did absolve the women from accountability for their actions. Theoretically, this opinion still stood at the outset of the Civil War, although it had never been challenged, especially under the U.S. Constitution's definition of treason. The Civil War provided a challenge to the privileges from punishment offered women through *coverture;* Federal military officials did not recognize rebellious women as *femes covert* and would hold them accountable for their actions, including ones deemed treasonous, regardless of the loyalties and activities of their husbands or fathers. Women would be judged on their own as actors in the public sphere and the penalties they suffered would reflect the nature of their transgressions. This treatment was particularly evident in Missouri, a state divided in loyalties and torn by guerrilla warfare throughout the conflict.

The military holding women accountable for treasonous activities marked a distinct departure from tradition, the second significance. Historically, the military treated enemy women as noncombatants, to be left unharmed, indeed protected, from the ravages of the very war the military waged against the women's nation. The actions of rebellious Southern women challenged that convention, forcing this reconsideration of how women who defied the military would be treated. With Lieber's Code, the laws of war applied to women, and violating those laws constituted the military's own version, Henry Halleck's version, of treason.[24]

The war treason defined in Lieber's Code did not match the rigors of the crime of treason defined in the Constitution. Nevertheless, punishment in many cases could mean death. Although a few women were sentenced to death before having their sentences commuted, no woman was executed for violations against the military during the war, and only one, Mary Surratt, was put to death in the war's aftermath.[25] Still, the threat of punishment, including execution, by the military in contested areas now carried the approval of the Federal government in Washington.

Significantly, a close examination of the records of Confederate women handled by the provost marshal in St. Louis city reveals a distinct change in pattern for the duration of imprisonment after the adoption of General Orders No. 100. With one exception, no woman imprisoned in St. Louis prior to the order's April 24, 1863, release is known to have spent more than about a month behind military prison walls. While short imprisonments were not unknown after the orders went into effect, all but one woman, who spent more than a month in custody, were arrested after the date the order was issued. Furthermore, charges such as the one leveled against Margaret Clifton, the one exception, who was arrested a day or so before the implementation of General Orders No. 100—"Treason against the Government of the United States" for having aided guerrillas—all but disappeared, replaced by the accusation of "violations of the laws of war," such as in the case of Augusta and Zaidie Bagwell, who were arrested days after the code's adoption.[26]

For the rest of the war, Lieber's Code served as a guideline in the struggle against rebellious and treasonous civilians. It provided military commanders and provost marshals with the authority of the Federal government to levy harsh punishment on both men and women caught aiding the Confederacy. The army continued to employ Lieber's Code into the twentieth century. Nevertheless, the decision of the Supreme Court in *Ex parte Milligan* in 1866 determined that the use of military courts or commissions to try U.S. civilians when civil courts were available was unconstitutional, in effect making the charge of war treason against rebellious citizens obsolete. By this point, it did not matter. The Confederacy had surrendered and the Union had been restored. The military courts and the decisions they had rendered had served their purpose and were no longer necessary.[27] The army continued to use the term "war traitor" for many years, but by implication, the accused had to be a noncitizen of the United States in territory occupied by the U.S. military.[28] Eventually, the term fell out of use, and Lieber's Code, though still influential, was supplanted with regulations more relevant to modern total war. During the Civil War, however, Lieber's Code served as a tool used to punish those who waged war against the Federal government. Furthermore, Henry Halleck's concept of the war traitor embedded within the code became a rhetorical weapon, giving Halleck and others the satisfaction of labeling rebellious civilians as the traitors he believed them to be.

Identifying the disloyal as traitors included women. "We know of no modern war," Halleck commented near the end of the war, "in which the female character has been so debased and so destitute of all the softer attributes which ought to adorn the sex."[29] Yet Halleck and other Federal authorities who confronted disloyal women concerned themselves with much more than women debasing themselves and their gender. These Confederates threatened the very fiber of the national government. Certainly, Halleck's experience in St. Louis convinced him of that, and his experience would be reflected in General Orders No. 100. Indeed, Lieber's code aided the government in bringing suitable punishment to these traitors. As the war progressed, punishment of rebellious women became more rigorous, part of what historian Mark Grimsley has called the hardening of the war.[30] Nevertheless, harsher punishment did nothing to deter disloyal women from supporting the Confederacy and acting on their convictions.

CHAPTER 3

"The Embarrassment Is to Know What to Do with Them"

I n the spring of 1863, the hardening of the war in the Department of the Missouri became evident in the treatment of rebellious women by the departmental command and the Office of the Provost Marshal General. Backed by General Orders No. 100, a more rigorous response to Confederate women's partisan activities became the rule. A new approach to dealing with disloyal women emerged in the form of banishment to the Confederate South, a punishment allowed by Lieber's Code. Federal authorities in St. Louis first used the method in response to the activities of a group of women from prominent families in and around the city, for whom they had been seeking an appropriate remedy. Soon they imposed banishment beyond the lines to women of various backgrounds who aided the rebellion. To be sure, not all women arrested were sent south. The provost marshal general's office continued to arrest and confine women for periods of time considered appropriate for their offenses. Women whose actions authorities deemed more serious, however, could face banishment for the duration of the war, with stiff penalties should they return without permission.

After Major General Samuel R. Curtis took command of the Department of the Missouri on September 24, 1862, the arrests of secessionist women begun under Halleck's regime abruptly stopped. The records suggest that between the time Curtis assumed control and the middle of March 1863 only one woman came into custody in St. Louis. The reason for the cessation of women's arrests is not clear; however, it may have been due to Curtis's own reluctance. Three months after Curtis took over, departmental provost marshal general Franklin A. Dick reported a hesitancy to punish the disloyal on Curtis's part in a letter he wrote to Abraham Lincoln apprising the president of the state of affairs in Missouri and the continued need for the imposition of martial law. The December 19, 1862, letter argued that the rebels in the city of St. Louis and the rest of the state were more active and hopeful than ever and continued to do what they could to aid those in arms against the Federal government.[1]

Dick was well aware of conditions in St. Louis and Missouri. A prewar St. Louis lawyer and brother-in-law of Francis Blair, Dick had served first as Blair's aide and then as the adjutant general of Missouri volunteers under Nathaniel Lyon before the general's death. Then he had a seat on the board of assessment in St. Louis, helping to identify and fine Confederate sympathizers. A staunch Republican who at times criticized Abraham Lincoln for being too lax in his treatment of the disloyal, Dick became provost marshal general of the Department of the Missouri in early November 1862. In the letter to the president, Dick explained there were a number of Confederate sympathizers in the state who desired to go south beyond Federal lines. He thought this a good idea, as it would remove from the state "many unchangeable enemies who will do us less injury there than here." In fact, he added, there were numerous sympathizers who should be sent south whether they requested it or not. In particular, he cited the "many female spies in good society" in St. Louis who he believed were "efficient aiders of the rebellion." Removal of such persons from the state, he assured the president, "would work a most wonderfully good effect upon Missouri, and in a short time its results would be permanent peace and tranquility to the State." Dick also noted that he had not initiated such a plan because General Curtis feared that it would not be acceptable in Washington. The fact that Dick went over Curtis's head all the way to the president to propose the plan is also telling of the general's reluctance to punish women. Whatever Curtis's reasons were, his days in Missouri were numbered. After several clashes between the general and civilian authorities in the state, President Lincoln moved to replace Curtis, first with Edwin V. Sumner, who died before he could take command, and then with John Schofield, whom Curtis initially had replaced.[2] Curtis relinquished command on May 24, but not before witnessing Franklin Dick carry out his plan to remove the troublesome rebel women.

On March 5, 1863, Dick informed the Union army commissary general of prisoners William Hoffman that he now had sufficient evidence to arrest and convict "a large number of women . . . actively concerned in both secret correspondence and in carrying on the business of collecting and distributing rebel letters." He then explained his concerns: "These women are wealthy and wield great influence; they are avowed and abusive enemies of the Government; they incite the young men to join the rebellion; their letters are filled with encouragement to their husbands and sons to continue the war; they convey information to them and by every possible contrivance they forward clothing and other support to the rebels. These disloyal women, too, seek every opportunity to keep disloyalty alive amongst rebel prisoners."[3]

Dick recognized political power and influence in these women. Three months earlier Dick had termed these types of activities "acts of a treasonable character." While perpetrators could not be charged with treason *per se*, the violations themselves were triable by military tribunal, and punishable by military authority. In effect he anticipated the definition of the war traitor that would enter into military policy in April. Further, he did not think that the power and influence the women exerted, which he deemed "injurious and greatly so," could be halted by their imprisonment. He therefore recommended that the best way to stop these partisan activities was to banish the women to the Confederacy. According to Dick, his office so far had conducted a policy of leniency toward these women, believing that "leniency would reform them." But this policy, Dick insisted, had "led these people," both male and female, "to believe that it is their 'constitutional' right to speak and conspire together as they may choose." He disagreed, and would no longer condone it.[4] The "hard hand of war" would be felt by these Confederate women of Missouri.

Prominent secession-sympathizing women in St. Louis had long been suspected of smuggling, corresponding with the enemy, and other disloyal enterprises. More than a year before Provost Marshal General Dick proposed banishing known female operatives, the department commander Henry Halleck lodged his complaint against the wives and daughters of St. Louis men in Confederate service who remained behind enjoying the benefits of the protection of the Federal government while spying and committing other misdeeds against its army. Dick also noted that he had "for some time past been thinking of arresting and trying" the women in question. He did not mention Samuel Curtis's apparent reluctance to move against the women, but he did suggest another reason why nothing had been done yet: "The embarrassment is to know what to do with them" once arrested. "Many of them are wives and daughters of officers in the rebel service."[5] He then listed the names of several of the suspected women, all related to prominent Confederate officers and politicians and all fixtures in St. Louis's highest social circles.

The "embarrassment" centered on what to do with the women after their arrest. Here the commitment of Southern-sympathizing women to help the Confederates, the hardening of the war conducted by the Union army, and the influences of class and gender converged. In the past, elite secessionist women in the St. Louis area had not been shielded from the retribution of

the Federal government. Fanny Coons, banished from the state for collecting money for the Confederate cause, was the wife of a prominent St. Louis
physician and traveled among the city's highest social circles. The quarter-
of-a-million-dollar estate owned by Mary Barclay's husband did not stop
the provost marshal from investigating her on suspicion of materially aiding
the rebels. Neither did the fact that Drucilla Sappington's husband owned a
more modest but still respectable farm nor that her father was a local judge
protect her.[6] Banishing women beyond the lines represented something new.

    In the cases of women arrested by the army prior to the spring of 1863,
those in charge of military matters in St. Louis found ways other than long
imprisonments to deal with the accused. In most cases, a brief period of incarceration, often only a few hours, was followed by a release, conditional on
giving an oath of allegiance and perhaps a bond to guarantee future good behavior. In more severe cases, banishment from the state of Missouri sufficed.
By early 1863, Franklin Dick was ready to take a much harder stance against
disloyal women. He did not find the methods used in the past adequate for
dealing with the women he now wished to punish. Obviously, the dedication
with which these women went about their covert work impressed Dick and
required a response that would put the women out of business for good.
Certainly just banishing them from the state would not work. He knew that
nothing could stop the women from continuing their work from some other
location within the lines. Despite his apparent reluctance to arrest civilians,
as department commander, Curtis noted that those banished from the state
who remained within the lines do "us more harm than anything else. They
join the Copperheads, and do all the mischief possible."[7]

    A second option was to imprison the women. Lack of sufficient space for
housing women prisoners on a long-term basis may have been a factor working against this punishment. So far, the provost marshal's office in St. Louis had
not imprisoned women for any long period of time. Provost Marshal General
Dick seemed resistant to imprisoning these women in particular. He remained
conscious of the class status of the women he sought to arrest and the influence they exerted. His Victorian notions of chivalry may have hindered him
from considering Gratiot Prison as an appropriate location for women of such
standing, or he may have feared placing the women in the prison where, in
Dick's words, they sought "every opportunity to keep disloyalty alive." Finally,
Dick must have been aware that imprisoning the women permanently would
turn the women behind prison walls into a cause célèbre for the Confederate
war effort, strengthening the enemy's resolve to fight. For whatever reason,
Dick decided it best to put these women where they could do no further harm
to the Union war effort. He elected to banish them to the South.

Franklin Dick was not the first Federal officer to propose sending disloyal civilians beyond the lines and to banish wives and families of Confederates. For instance, writing from Baltimore on March 4, 1862, almost a year to the day before Dick outlined his plan to William Hoffman, Major General John A. Dix had asked Ohio Democratic congressman George Pendleton: "Should we retain within our limits the families of those who are in arms against the Government? Should they not be sent into the insurgent States to share the privations, the social disquietude and the desolation they have brought and are bringing upon themselves?" Dix concluded that such a fate "would be a much more effectual cure for secession than a residence among us where no such disturbance exists."[8]

Ulysses S. Grant also considered banishments a few months after Dix had. General-in-Chief Halleck had approved a request from Grant to put beyond the lines "a great many families of officers in the rebel service [in west Tennessee] who are very violent." Apparently Grant did not exile anyone at that time, but a few weeks later Halleck accepted another Grant request to banish civilians in west Tennessee and northern Mississippi who aided guerrillas there. Grant did send a group of civilians beyond the lines, but no evidence suggests he included any women.[9]

A month later, Brigadier General John M. Schofield, then temporarily commanding in Missouri, wrote to General-in-Chief Halleck asking for authority to banish to the South certain "men of influence and wealth" who Schofield claimed were engaged in a conspiracy to rise up against the Union army from behind the lines. Halleck consented to the request but warned Schofield to use this power sparingly, "as it is not good policy to increase the ranks of the enemy by sending South all their friends and sympathizers." It is doubtful that Schofield ever acted on this plan, but even if he had, his targets were also men, not women.[10]

Banishments beyond Federal lines of disloyal women were not unknown, however. Early in the war several high profile women had been banished from the Washington, D.C., area, for instance Rose O'Neal Greenhow and Eugenia Phillips.[11] Also, the army in the East routinely allowed women with ties to the South to pass through the lines, not to return. Yet banishing women to the South had not become a matter of regular policy for the Federal government or the Union army.

Dick's March 1863 proposal made its way through the chain of command in the War Department and received the ringing endorsement of Judge Advocate General Joseph Holt and Edwin Stanton himself. On April 29, 1863, Commissary General of Prisoners Hoffman wrote back to Dick, telling him to carry out the plan "promptly and inflexibly." By the time Dick received the approval, banishing disloyal citizens beyond the lines had, in fact, become a part of Union army policy through General Orders No. 100, which allowed military commanders to "expel . . . revolted citizens who refuse to pledge themselves anew as citizens obedient to the law and loyal to the government" during times of insurrection, civil war, and rebellion.[12] Dick also already had several of the women in question in custody.

The course that Franklin Dick took in handling the local women desig-nated for banishment had been foreshadowed by an incident that occurred a few weeks after he made his proposal to William Hoffman. On March 31, 1863, the wife of Confederate general Jeff Thompson and her friend, a Mrs. Calhoun, also married to a Confederate officer, arrived in the city with a nurse and two children after having crossed into Union lines from Helena, Arkansas. Considering the pair "improper persons within our lines" and suspicious of the circumstances that allowed these women to enter Union lines, Dick ordered the two arrested and held "in close custody in their rooms at the Everett House [Hotel]." While expedience may explain the decision to confine the two wives of enemy officers to the rooms they already inhabited, Dick sent a man arrested with the two officer's wives on the same charges to the Gratiot Street Prison. Several days later, Dick directed that the whole party be returned from whence they came.[13]

Gender may explain the exceptional treatment given Thompson and Cal-houn, although by this time the St. Louis military prisons had hosted many women. The imprisonment of women of Thompson and Calhoun's promi-nence certainly would gain widespread attention, particularly since there was no concrete evidence of wrongdoing on their part. It was better to confine them briefly in their hotel and then expel them as a preventative measure rather than imprison them with no just cause. While similarities existed between Thompson and Calhoun's treatment and that of the St. Louis women earmarked for banishment, certain differences also are apparent. First, Thomp-son and Calhoun were ostensibly visiting the city, and not residing in the area. Second, and most important, while considering the two women in St. Louis under suspicious circumstances, Federal authorities had no proof that Thompson and Calhoun had committed any disloyal acts. Such was not the case with the St. Louis women soon to be exiled. On March 20, 1863, Mar-garet McLure, who upon the death of her husband had inherited a sizeable estate including a large house on Chestnut Street, became the first of this group arrested.

Margaret A. E. McLure had been a part of the vast network of mail col-lectors and distributors, predominantly female, that Absalom Grimes had woven throughout the western border states. According to Grimes, "The lady distributors had their skirts made double in such a way that they could stow away more than a thousand letters. The hoop skirt and ruffled dresses were a most fortunate and convenient fashion at that time."[14] This clandestine mail network allowed Confederate soldiers in the field to communicate with their loved ones beyond the lines, thus aiding them in keeping their morale high. More significantly, it facilitated the flow of information to the South and the rebel army, information that could be useful in waging war against the North.

Grimes described Margaret McLure as "the most enthusiastic and lovable lady that ever lived . . . who sacrificed everything she had in the world in aiding the southern cause." On February 12, 1863, Federal detectives arrested one William S. Wright, a surgeon in the Confederate army and an accused spy, at McLure's house. They found in his possession a large amount of illegal correspondence, various medicines, and fabric for uniforms—all destined for the South. If McLure had not yet become a suspect, she certainly was now. On the afternoon of March 20, 1863, McLure left her Chestnut Street home, planning to go to the Gratiot Street Prison to deliver money designated to be spent on the Confederate prisoners of war. She did not get very far before she was stopped and placed under arrest, charged with "holding correspondence with the enemy. . . . Giving aid and comfort to the enemy," and being a "Rebel Mail Agent." Rather than confining her in the Gratiot Street Prison, Dick placed guards around McLure's house and confined her there. At some point over the next few weeks soldiers removed all of McLure's possessions from her house and replaced them with simple cots, tables, and chairs, in anticipation of the arrival of more women prisoners.[15]

Franklin Dick's decision to imprison McLure in her own house and to put the other women he planned to banish there as well may have served multiple purposes. First, Dick may have been concerned that the imprisonment of women of McLure's status in the regular facility would cause a major backlash. As it was, he received numerous letters and petitions asking that McLure be released on parole, or released altogether, or when her fate became public knowledge, that she be allowed to remain within the free states.[16] Petitions came forward for several of the other women as well.

Second, secrecy seemed to be of great concern for Dick. Keeping the women away from the military prison kept word of their arrest from spreading quickly so that others he intended to arrest and banish were not tipped off that they might be next. The local *Missouri Democrat*, always quick to publish articles exposing "rebels in crinoline," remained silent on McLure's arrest. In fact, the paper did not report of the existence of the new "female prison" until May 9. But secrets were hard to keep in Civil War St. Louis. Confederate sympathizer Ann E. Lane, daughter of St. Louis's first mayor, William Carr

Lane, reported to her sister on April 19, 1863: "They do say a great deal of ladies are to be banished." On April 30, the *Missouri Democrat* had revealed the impending banishment to the South of prominent secessionists in the St. Louis area, and on May 8 the paper noted that prison reports for the last several days had been withheld by the provost marshal's office "in consequence of the arrests of certain influential citizens" supposedly to "secure secrecy relative to these arrests."[17]

Finally, using the house as a prison allowed Dick to keep her and the other women he had arrested in one centralized place before their departure for the South. The next two women arrested were Mary Louden and Lucie Nickolson. Each spent a few days in the Gratiot Street Prison before being sent to Mrs. McLure's house as involuntary guests. The wife of Robert Louden, a partner with Absalom Grimes in the mail carrying business, Mary Louden was arrested on April 25, 1863. It is not clear from the records exactly what charges Franklin Dick leveled against her; her marriage to a known mail smuggler probably was enough to cast suspicion on her. From the Gratiot Street Prison, Mrs. Louden wrote a rather indignant letter insisting her innocence. She denied being a member of "any secret society," and further complained that she had not been "offered the privilege of signing a parole." She requested that she either be released out of hand or at least be let out on her "parole of honor." An unsigned endorsement on the letter, probably from Franklin Dick, noted, "I am aware of the fact that she was not offered a parole, which she expects being a lady (!) Paroles for such business are all 'played out' with me."[18]

Louden would soon be joined at Gratiot by Lucie Nickolson of Cooper County, Missouri. On the basis of information written in a letter confiscated from a rebel mail carrier, probably William Wright, Franklin Dick ordered schoolteacher Nickolson's arrest on April 23, 1863. The arrest was carried out in Boone County on May 3, and a few days later Nickolson arrived in St Louis. A letter to her sister "Gettie" in Kentucky, written in Lucie's hand and found in her possession at the time of her arrest, made it clear where Nickolson's loyalties rested. To her sister, Lucie admitted, "I have done all in my power to aid and comfort the 'rebels,' and have the satisfaction of Knowing I have been of considerable service, come weal or woe." Nickolson remained confident that now Confederate general Sterling Price would soon return to Missouri to liberate the state and that the Confederates ultimately would succeed, but if fortune should not shine the Southern way, she "would rather see every house in Mo burned to the ground than see it remain in the power of the Fed. Gov. or if they must have it, let them have it a ruined, wasted country, as well as a ruined subjugated people."[19]

In her interrogation, Nickolson said nothing to mitigate her case, admitting to making clothes and delivering them to Price's army, and to corresponding with the Confederates, among other things. She also claimed to be owed a commission in the rebel service promised her by Price. Finally, she reaffirmed her support for the Confederate cause: "I would like very much to see the southern confederacy established & then live under Jeff. Davis." As with Mary Louden, Nickolson petitioned General Curtis for a parole, to no avail. Instead, on May 8, 1863, she and Louden were transferred from the Gratiot Street Prison to Margaret McLure's house.[20]

At least eight more women were arrested and sentenced to banishment at this time. Most seem to have been picked up on May 8, and all went directly into McLure's Chestnut Street "prison." They included Eliza "Lily" Frost, referred to as "a most violent rebel" in a notation on the testimony she gave. The wife of Daniel M. Frost of Camp Jackson notoriety and now a general in the regular Confederate service, Eliza Frost came into custody after a letter for her written by her husband fell into Federal hands. In her testimony, she admitted to corresponding with her husband, but she denied knowing from whom she received his letters or to whom she entrusted the letters she wrote to him. Others arrested included the wives of the medical director of the Confederate Army of West Tennessee Montrose Pallen, Lieutenant Colonel John William Smizer of the 8th Missouri Infantry, and Joseph Chaytor, a captain and assistant quartermaster in the 4th Missouri Cavalry.[21]

There were also three other female Confederate mail carriers: Mrs. Charles Clark, Ada Haynes, and Harriet Snodgrass.[22] Like Lucie Nickolson, Miss Harriet "Hattie" Snodgrass taught school, and according to one deposition against her, she kept a "secesh flag in her school room." Snodgrass also was the sister of Mrs. Joseph Chaytor, whose husband, Snodgrass insisted, belonged to the "Confederate" army, not the "Rebel army" as her Federal captors called it. According to one witness, Snodgrass's house was "the resort of notorious rebel sympathizers." Another testified that "the wealthy secessionist ladies came to her house and left packages of various kinds there," presumably destined for the Confederate army.[23]

Snodgrass also gained a reputation as a friend of the Confederates in the local military prisons, as did Miss Ada Haynes. Haynes often brought goods to the prisons for the inmates, and she may have done more. In a letter smuggled out of the Gratiot Street Prison from Confederate prisoner William H. Duncan to a Dr. T. Holmes, Duncan referred to "the kind angels who are in the habit of visiting us to learn of our wants for the purpose of alleviating them." He further suggested that these women served as the conduits of the flow of clandestine communications in and out of the prisons. Perhaps Haynes was one of Duncan's "angels." Haynes's involvement with prisoners went beyond the local facilities. She also wrote to inmates at the Union prisons at Fort Warren in Boston and Point Lookout in Maryland to offer them comfort in their confinement. Because prisoners could receive mail only from relatives, she pretended that she wrote as the niece of her correspondent.[24]

Haynes's activities did not end there. She evidently used her connections to assist aspiring Confederate men to obtain positions in the rebel service. For instance, in September 1862, Haynes received a letter from one J. Isaac Jones who "understood" that she "could be of Some Service to a man wanting to go to the army under Maj. Gen. Price. . . . I would like to get a letter from some persons to him so I could get a possition [sic] after I get there." Jones wrote so matter-of-factly that his letter gives the impression that Haynes had developed a reputation for performing this kind of service. It is not clear whether Federal authorities were aware of the extent of Haynes's activities, but by spring of 1863 they at least knew that she was part of the network of contraband letter carriers in St. Louis. Thus they decided that she could no longer stay in the city. Finally, joining the group was Drucilla Sappington, once again at odds with the provost marshal general. She probably was the ringleader of the "Band Known as Mrs. Sapingtons Company," mentioned in the investigation of another St. Louisan in January 1863 and no doubt engaged in disloyal activities. Two months later, she again came under scrutiny when she paid a police officer to arrest and return to her her slave, who had been confiscated by the army and put to work building fortifications. By then Sappington had developed quite a reputation. For example, when a Mrs. C. Walton made a statement against a Mrs. Loring on the latter's Confederate sympathies, she stated that "Mrs. Loring is as disloyal to our country as Mrs. Sappington." Her arrest came shortly before the departure of the exiled women, and while no specific new charge against her can be found to cause this action, an informant had reported to the provost marshal general in late April and early May that Sappington had been associating with a known smuggler under investigation.[25]

Franklin Dick set May 13, 1863, as the date of the departure for the banished women. On the appointed day in the afternoon, the inmates of the makeshift Chestnut Street prison left the house and boarded an omnibus under the supervision of Dick's secretary, a Lieutenant Patrick, and two members of the provost guard. The vehicle then transported the women to the landing on the river where the steamer *Belle Memphis* awaited. To keep order among the large crowd of onlookers, Dick directed a company of the 23rd Missouri Infantry, U.S., to the location to form a human corridor from the omnibus to the steamer, through which the women walked upon their arrival at the river's edge. Once on the steamer, according to one account, "One of the young women ascended to the hurricane roof . . . and cheered for the 'Confederacy.' As the boat swung into the stream, this lady was joined by two others, and the trio united their sweet voices in singing 'Dixie' and the 'Bonnie Blue Flag.'" On board, the women joined a group of at least ten male prisoners, condemned to the same fate, who had been placed on the vessel during the previous afternoon. In addition, the wives and children of three of the banished men joined the group. Dick allowed the families to leave with their husbands by their own choice; the women ordered banished were not given that option. Only Charles Clark joined his wife on the southbound trip, but only because he, too, had been banished; and with one known exception, the women had to leave their children behind in the care of relatives or friends.[26]

The one exception of a child who traveled with a banished mother on the *Belle Memphis* was the son of Margaret McLure. When authorities arrested Mrs. McLure, they sent her son, "aged about 14 years," to live with an uncle in Platte County. Still, the boy had been "a party to the offense." Soon James Dwight, an assistant to Franklin Dick, wrote to his counterpart in the provost marshal's office in Platte County requesting that "the young McLure," as he was referred to, be arrested and sent back to St. Louis immediately so that he could serve as "a witness against other parties." After taking the boy's statement, Franklin Dick decided it best to send him south with his mother. Thus, the young McClure joined the party of the banished.[27]

The *Belle Memphis* left the wharf a few minutes after 5 P.M. with Major T. J. McKinney, Major General Samuel Curtis's aide-de-camp, taking responsibility for supervising the journey beyond enemy lines. He had at his disposal a company of the 1st Nebraska Infantry, assigned to guard the prisoners. The departure of the exiles drew a large crowd as expected, but it remained orderly. Aboard ship, on the other hand, was a different story. According to one account, some of the prisoners made "demonstrations of indignation" at their guards, who were quieted only by threats of close confinement for the entire trip. The steamer made stops at Cape Girardeau, Missouri, and Cairo, Illinois, before landing at Memphis on May 14. During the trip, the guards searched the prisoners' baggage and their shipboard quarters, while McKinney and a Union surgeon from Cairo "politely but faithfully" checked the rooms housing the women. Finally, a group of "Union ladies on board" were called on to search the persons of the female prisoners. They uncovered a small amount of medicines, which were confiscated. After spending the night in Memphis, McKinney and his charges then traveled by rail to LaGrange, Tennessee. From there they boarded ambulances that took them southward under cavalry escort. Traveling in this manner, it took the party about four days to pass into Confederate-occupied Mississippi, where Mc-Kinney turned the prisoners over to the general commanding at the town of Okalona, south of Tupelo in the northeast part of the state. According to an account published in the *Missouri Democrat*, the Confederates "evinced great displeasure" that this column of exiles under Federal guard had penetrated so far through their Northern defenses. These Confederates had to have felt helpless and a bit demoralized at that moment: to the south Ulysses S. Grant had just marched his army inland from the Mississippi River, occupied the state capital at Jackson, and then began laying siege on Vicksburg. Only a month earlier, a Federal cavalry raid led by Benjamin Grierson slashed past Okalona as it swept the length of the state. Now, these Confederates' lines would have proven vulnerable again had it not been for the flag of truce under which the most recent invaders traveled. The Confederates honored the flag of truce and escorted McKinney and his men back through the lines.[28]

Back in St. Louis, rumors spread of more impending banishments. In detailing the May 13 departure, the Unionist *Missouri Democrat* reported that it had learned that some three to four hundred more Confederate sympathizers had already been chosen for banishment. Two weeks later, St. Louis Confederate sympathizer Philip Gooch Ferguson confided in his diary: "It is said that a list of 800 citizens has been made for banishment."[29] Whether or not Federal authorities intended at this time to exile such a large number of secessionists is unknown, but clearly Confederate supporters like Ferguson recognized the hardening of the line that the army was now taking against them. Their fears of more banishments were not without merit because many more were to come before the end of the year. The activities of women of prominent families had first prompted Franklin Dick to propose banishment to the South as an appropriate response. While women of status and wealth would continue to stand out among subsequent groups sent beyond the lines, women of more modest circumstances involved in partisan activities were not immune from such a fate. Not three weeks passed from the first mass banishment before Union authorities rounded up and sent on its way the next party of southbound women.

Shortly after the departure of McLure and the others, the chain of command in St. Louis underwent changes in personnel. First, newly promoted Major General John M. Schofield returned to head the Department of the Missouri on May 24, 1863. Then in early June Franklin Dick resigned as provost marshal general of the department, replaced by Colonel James O. Broadhead, a former U.S. district attorney in the state. Several weeks earlier George Leighton had also resigned as provost marshal of the St. Louis district; Captain Charles C. Allen succeeded him.[30]

James Broadhead proved to be a controversial choice as provost marshal general. An established Union man, he still held rather conservative views on a number of matters. In particular, he hated abolitionists and openly criticized Lincoln's emancipation policy. Nevertheless, under Broadhead the banishments initiated under Franklin Dick continued. Before the end of 1863, six more groups of banished Confederate civilians, some women, left St. Louis for the South, departing on June 1, July 10, September 22, October 28, November 22, and November 25. As with the first shipment, the banished women included a number of wives of prominent Confederates. The June 1 party included Cornelia Polk, the wife of Trusten Polk, former Missouri governor and U.S. senator and now Confederate colonel and judge advocate general for the Department of the Trans-Mississippi. She had been accused of continually expressing support for the rebel cause and for corresponding with the enemy. General Sydney Jackman's wife Martha departed in October after being arrested at her home in Howard County. She was joined by Mrs. Colonel William H. Cundiff, both charged with giving aid and comfort to the Confederates. Cundiff admitted to passing through the lines to visit her husband and then returning. She also acknowledged "being a rebel against the U.S. government and loyal to the C.S.A." Cundiff had been given the opportunity to remain in St. Louis provided she take a loyalty oath. She refused.[31]

Absalom Grimes's Confederate clandestine mail network also lost another key operative in the June 1 banishments, Marion Wall Vail. Vail, who was Grimes's aunt, was one of the first women recruited by Grimes for his service. She was also instrumental in helping him flee St. Louis after his 1862 escape from the Gratiot Street Prison. Grimes considered Vail "one of the most energetic of all my assistants in the mail-carrying business" and praised her devotion to the Confederate cause. Numerous other women sent south had corresponded with the rebels. Most of the women thus accused admitted to keeping the correspondence, but Mary Cleveland, arrested in Troy, Missouri, fervently denied the charges. Nevertheless, the officer who investigated her case determined that she was "without a doubt guilty of all acts charged against her."[32]

In all, at least forty women took part in these mass banishments in 1863, including the initial group that left in May. That number, however, did not include the numerous women who left St. Louis for the South by choice during this time. Punishment for returning from the Confederacy without proper authorization included imprisonment and applied to those banished and those who left on their own alike.

That some of the sentenced women awaiting banishment were given their parole to prepare to depart was one difference between the first and later shipments of banished women. It appears that most of these later exiles spent some time imprisoned, and that the provost marshal general briefly paroled them from custody to allow them to gather what belongings they would bring with them. Until June 11, 1863, most of the women slated for exile, unless on parole, stayed in Margaret McLure's house, although the location proved insufficient for prisoner Eliza Murray, an accused smuggler. Arrested in late spring 1863 as part of a network of operatives smuggling quinine, morphine, and other goods to the Confederates, Murray, according to one account, proved too "intractable" to remain in the Chestnut Street women's prison and was moved to the Gratiot Street Prison. Murray was ordered banished to Canada, apparently an option for some prisoners. To prepare for her departure, she received release upon giving her oath of parole and a security of $900 in gold. She then apparently married George Skipworth, a former army sutler and one of her fellow smugglers, also out on parole. The two then disappeared. Authorities thought they had left for Canada on their own, but a few weeks later they were rearrested in Illinois.[33]

On June 11, 1863, the provost marshal guard removed the women from Mrs. McLure's house and placed them in another house on Twelfth Street, fitted as a military prison for women. The Female Military Prison, as it was now called, had been the home of Edward Dobyns and his daughter Mary. Dobyns's total wealth as of 1860 was valued at more than $150,000, so one can presume that he owned a sizeable house. The residence had been confiscated because it had been deemed abandoned by its occupants.[34] Mary Dobyns had been arrested on about May 10, 1863, according to her father's account for making "demonstrations against the Government," although exactly how he never ascertained. She apparently stayed at the Gratiot Street Prison scheduled for banishment until May 14, when Provost Marshal Leighton granted her parole and allowed her to relocate to her father's house. Edward Dobyns pled for leniency for his daughter, claiming that because of her poor health Mary would not "live three months" in the South. He proposed that she be allowed to go to Kentucky or some other Northern state instead, but to no avail. Then Dobyns learned through a third party that he could apply to take Mary to Canada. Dobyns completed an application for such a move and then delivered it to a clerk in the office of then Provost Marshal General Franklin Dick. Dobyns then saw his daughter off to Canada.

What Edward Dobyns overlooked or misunderstood was that he had to make the application for his daughter's removal to Canada to Dick in person. Leaving the written application at Dick's office did not suffice. Mary Dobyns now faced the charge of violating her parole. It did not matter that the apparent mistake had been her father's. Only her presence in Canada shielded her from arrest. Meanwhile, unaware of the new charge against his daughter, Edward Dobyns packed up all his belongings from his Twelfth Street residence, supposedly to rent it out while he took an extended trip through Illinois and Kentucky. He returned to St. Louis in March 1864 to find his daughter a fugitive, charges pending against him for "clandestinely" leaving St. Louis for "Dixie"—a claim he denied—and his house confiscated and converted into a military prison for women.[35]

Another significant difference between the first group banished and the later groups concerned children. Provost Marshal General Franklin Dick denied the first group of women the right to take with them their children, except for Margaret McLure's son, who himself had been an accessory to his mother's activities. Mothers among the later groups, however, could bring their families. Perhaps James Broadhead, who supervised the later 1863 banishments, thought it too unchivalrous to separate children from their mothers.

The later banishments also further revealed that exile was not reserved only for the elite and influential women for whom Franklin Dick first had intended it. For instance, the July 10 banishment included Elizabeth Rucker, a thirty-two-year-old dressmaker who had received permission to pass into the South to be with her husband, Thomas, a bricklayer in the employ of the Confederates in Alabama. When she returned through the lines without permission, she was caught in Memphis and sent back to St. Louis. According to two anonymously written letters received by the provost marshal's office, Rucker had returned as a rebel spy. Whether or not a spy, Rucker was sent back to the Confederacy. Rucker traveled aboard the same steamer that carried the Clifford sisters, Joe and Ellen, southward. The two St. Joseph millinery workers had performed one too many pro-Confederate demonstration to warrant their continued presence in Missouri. Six weeks before Rucker and the Cliffords departed, the Federals sent south Lucretia E. Rose and her stepdaughters Susan and Selma Lemon because they had been "engaged in harboring, feeding, secreting, and encouraging bushwhackers." Likewise, Lucretia's husband David, a modest Pike County farmer, was charged and sentenced. David's transgressions had nothing to do with the fate of the women, however. They were held accountable for their own complicity in helping guerrillas.[36]

While the departure of the women sent south in the seven mass banishments received considerable attention in the local newspapers, further newspaper accounts, the provost marshal general's files and other records show that many more women received banishment orders in 1863 than those scheduled for passage in the seven shipments. At least fourteen others faced exile, and there very well may have been many more. Some of the women ordered south never made the trip, however. For example, a military commission found sixteen-year-old Hannah Jane Martin of Andrew County guilty of disloyal conduct, specifically spitting on a United States flag in front of others at a Baptist Church, "thereby showing a contempt and hatred for the United States government, which that flag represents." The commission at first ordered Martin to be transported beyond the lines, but upon reconsideration recommended that because of "the youth of the prisoner and her inexperience," the sentence be remitted and she be allowed to remain in Missouri provided that she post a one thousand dollar bond. General Schofield agreed, noting that "the conduct of the prisoner indicates a want of good sense and good manners, and the circumstances justify a mitigation of her punishment." He approved the commission's recommendation. Likewise, three young women related to a Confederate officer received permission to remain in the city on the intercession of family friends at the last minute. Their youth probably served to affect this decision.[37]

Augusta Bagwell and her daughter Zaidie also received reprieves from their May 22 banishment sentences because of the elder Bagwell's poor health. Zaidie was allowed to remain to tend to her ailing mother. Both faced charges related to corresponding with and giving encouragement to the Confederates. To ensure that they did not continue their rebellious ways, Schofield ordered that both pay hefty bonds for their good behavior, $10,000 for Augusta and $5,000 for her daughter. For the rest of the war the two women reported regularly to the provost marshal general's office by way of the mail from their Macon County home.[38] Finally, through the intercession of influential friends, Hannah Ward, the sister of former St. Louis mayor John M. Wimer, went to Canada rather than experience southern exile. That would not be the last Federal officials would hear of Hannah Ward.[39]

Like Eliza Skipworth (nee Murray), Hannah Ward could not elude the long arm of the military justice system, but three other banished women, Amanda and Mattie Maddox and Mary Hall, apparently did. Having been given their parole to report to the steamer *Swanery* on the appointed day of departure, the three were never heard from again. Where they went and whether they continued their active support of the Confederate cause are unknown.[40]

A thorough accounting of the 1863 banishments is impossible because of the incomplete nature of the records. Newspaper accounts provide the most comprehensive recounting of the individual departures of the seven large shipments of banished civilians, but as the process became more common, coverage diminished. For instance, the first group sent south merited nearly a full column of detailed description in the *Missouri Democrat*. A week later, a briefer article outlined the trip beyond the lines. Then followed a lengthy firsthand account of the journey made by one of the officers, probably expedition leader Major McKinney, that filled more than a column. Coverage for the subsequent departures gradually waned; when the November 25 shipment of exiles left St. Louis, the *Missouri Democrat* allowed just over an inch of column space for coverage, and after almost a week had passed.[41] By the end of the year, banishments had become commonplace, a routine part of Federal military policy.

Throughout the rest of the war, banishments remained a regular part of the punishment meted out to rebellious women who passed through the military justice system in St. Louis. Of course, for Federal authorities, banishment had no guarantee of permanence. Some exiled women gained permission from the secretary of war to return to Missouri, usually to tend to the health of a loved one in the city or nearby. For instance, in early 1864 Eliza Frost, the wife of General Daniel Frost, received permission to return to St. Louis to care for her mother, provided that she take the oath of allegiance to the Federal government. Authorities allowed Cornelia Polk to return with her daughter to be closer to her ailing husband, now a prisoner at the Sandusky Military Prison in Ohio. Likewise, Mary Louden reentered the city with permission because of her imprisoned husband, Robert Louden, who was under a death sentence for carrying Confederate mail, smuggling, spying, and boat burning. Louden's execution was eventually called off, and later when being transferred to the Alton Prison from St. Louis he escaped. Mrs. Louden, then in Philadelphia with Robert's family and her children, would be held hostage temporarily by Federal authorities in the City of Brotherly Love in case her husband showed up there. Marion Wall Vail, mail operative in Absalom Grimes's network, gained consent to return as a "consequence of the intercession of influential Union men of St. Louis" just three months after her banishment.[42]

Not all women who returned bothered to obtain the proper authorization, and several suffered the consequences. Annie B. Martin, the sister of Theresa Blannerhassett, learned this the hard way. Authorities arrested Blannerhassett late in the summer of 1863 and sentenced her to banishment to the South. Although the records are unclear on the charges against Blannerhassett, she was related to Ada Haynes and may have been involved in mail carrying. Upon her sister's sentencing, widow Annie Martin elected to travel downriver with Blannerhassett; thus, Martin imposed exile on herself. Martin was no stranger to the provost marshal's office. On April 1, 1863, she had given a statement proudly admitting that she had a brother serving as a lieutenant in the Confederate army and that she would rather have him in that role than "as Maj. Gen'l in the Union." She also told after some hesitancy that she had received letters from her brother and had written to him "Hundreds of times," but she would give no information on how the letters were exchanged. She added that she expected her brother to return soon to Missouri "with old [Sterling] Price." When pressed on just when Price planned his invasion, Martin replied, "We look for him during the summer, am not at liberty to tell the *exact date.*" Evidently the provost marshal decided not to arrest Martin for corresponding with the enemy or for her blatant secessionist sympathies. Nevertheless, on November 22, 1863, Martin and her sister left for the South.[43]

In September 1864, Annie Martin returned to St. Louis without permission and was arrested. At first the *Missouri Democrat* reported that Martin faced spying charges, but in the end, authorities held her accountable only for violating the order that she not return without the authorization of the secretary of war and sentenced her to remain confined for the duration of the war. Martin's sister Theresa Blannerhassett evidently avoided any further trouble with the Union army, but their relative Ada Haynes did not. Having been sent south with Margaret McLure, Eliza Frost, and the others, Haynes returned to St. Louis the following March without proper authorization after passing through the lines and receiving a pass under suspicious circumstances from the provost marshal in Cairo, Illinois. Having been detected and arrested again, Haynes asked to take the oath of allegiance and to stay in the city, promising to remain a loyal citizen. Nevertheless, then-provost marshal general J. P. Sanderson reported that

> If her statement could safely be believed and relied upon, her case, though she is here in violation of a positive order, and in defiance of it, would perhaps be entitled to consideration and she recommended to a generous clemency. But her whole demeanor since her arrival, in every way, directly and emphatically contradicts the sincerity and truthfulness of her statement. Notwithstanding the protestations in that statement, she has continued, by her action in every respect, without disguise or any attempt at disguise, to be rebel in all her manifestations, feelings, sympathies, declarations and actions, and I am thoroughly satisfied that she is not a safe person to be allowed her liberty in the community.

Sanderson recommended that Haynes be banished again, but this time to New York or one of the New England states. General William Rosecrans, now commanding the Department of the Missouri, concurred and on July 20, 1864, Ada Haynes was exiled again, "not to reside west or south of the State of New York during the present rebellion."[44]

Not all the women banished from Missouri left by way of St. Louis. In July 1863, Brigadier General Thomas Ewing, commanding the Military District of the Border on the volatile western edge of the state, issued General Orders No. 10, which permitted officers in the field to force the wives and families of known guerrillas and women heading families who willfully aided guerrillas to leave the district and the state. If the families failed to comply promptly, the officers were to send the women and their children under guard to Kansas City to be banished south. This order predated by a week Ewing's notorious General Orders No. 11, which ordered the complete depopulation of nearly four counties in his district.[45]

Ewing's August 25, 1863, General Orders No 11 was indiscriminate, immediately impacting Confederate sympathizers and Unionists alike. Those who could prove their loyalty were allowed to return to their homes. Those who could not, or refused to, had to leave the state, whether or not they had been engaged in helping guerrillas. Likewise, in early 1865, Brigadier General John Sanborn banished from the District of Southwest Missouri 150 known wives of guerrillas because of their relations.[46]

In her study of Confederate refugees, Mary Elizabeth Massey notes that banishments were often used to "create a docile citizenry within federal lines . . . by ridding the area of hostile Southerners." The description certainly fits Ewing's General Orders No. 10 and No. 11. Massey also points out that selective banishments were used to subdue those who remained, which seems to characterize Sanborn's banishments.[47] To a certain extent this may have been true of the 1863 St. Louis banishments, but in this case the women sentenced to exile were not selected indiscriminately. All the women sent south from St. Louis faced charges of disloyalty against the Federal government.

Massey also argues that retaliation very often motivated banishments, particularly affecting wives of Confederate officers or women living in areas experiencing guerrilla raids, as in the case of General Orders No. 11, which came in response to William Quantrill's attack on Lawrence, Kansas. Many of the women who departed St. Louis per order of the military command were, in fact, wives of Confederate officers. Nevertheless, the banishment of the women departing St. Louis in 1863 represented retaliation for the deeds Union military personnel believed the women themselves committed. Indeed, many of the women freely admitted their guilt, showing no regret for their actions and no change of heart in their loyalties. Even the deprivations of banishment did not humble some of these women. Annie Martin and Ada Haynes continued to exhibit their disrespect for the Federal government by their violations of the orders that sent them south and their continued support for the Confederacy. Whatever relationship Marion Vail had to "influential Union men," she again came under suspicion of having committed illegal activities. According to a statement given against her in February 1865, Vail still openly expressed her Confederate sympathies, entertained unknown men who visited her Warren County home, and boasted of harboring Confederate officers and aiding bushwhackers. And, of course, Drucilla Sappington returned to St. Louis by March 1864, much to the pleasure of the Confederates receiving her communications.[48] At that time Missouri Confederate Sterling Price was planning his much-awaited advance on Missouri to liberate the state from Yankee rule.

By mid-1863, the war seemed to turn in favor of the Union. In the East, the Army of the Potomac stopped Robert E. Lee's advance into Pennsylvania, routing the Army of Northern Virginia after three days of pitched battle at the town of Gettysburg. Although Lee's damaged army escaped back into Virginia, the Confederate hero would be unable to launch another major invasion into the North. To the west, the Confederate stronghold at Vicksburg on the Mississippi River submitted to Ulysses S. Grant's demand for surrender after Grant's forces had besieged the city for six weeks. Five days later, rebels at Port Hudson in Louisiana capitulated, leaving the Mississippi River entirely in the hands of the Union and severing the Confederacy in half.

Meanwhile, if Franklin Dick and other Federal authorities in Missouri previously did not know what to do with disloyal women, by this point they had wisdom from experience and authority from Lieber's Code to inform them on an appropriate course of action. The war on Confederate women in Missouri had entered a new phase. The banishments of rebel women initiated by Dick during Samuel Curtis's regime continued when John Schofield returned to St. Louis to take command of the Department of the Missouri. When Schofield named James Broadhead as his provost marshal general, Confederate sympathizer Ann Lane expressed optimism that the crackdown on Southern partisan women would come to an end. "Broadhead is said to be a decent man," she opined. She did not think that he would punish women in such a way. Although Broadhead was a strong Unionist, Lane knew that he held conservative views and openly opposed emancipation. In fact, Broadhead's outspokenness caused the *Missouri Democrat* to criticize his appointment. Lane also may have based her impression of Broadhead on the part he played in securing the release of seventeen-year-old Jennie Knight upon her swearing an oath of allegiance. Arrested on March 20, 1863, Knight had been staying at the home of Margaret McLure and was suspected of being a part of the illicit mail network that McLure helped to operate. As U.S. district attorney, Broadhead wrote to Franklin Dick at least twice requesting the release of

Knight from confinement. She probably would have been banished had Dick not decided to set her free on her oath a week before the other women in McLure's home left for the South.[49]

Lane was wrong. Broadhead proved eager to maintain the flow of disloyal women beyond the lines, his aid to Jennie Knight notwithstanding. This is not to say that Schofield and Broadhead went about banishing all women that crossed them. The records indicate that banishment was utilized only in response to the most serious transgressions. From mid-May, the time of the first mass banishment of women from St. Louis, until the end of 1863, several dozen Confederate women came into military custody in the city without being exiled to the South. Records further indicate that the cases of these women were carefully investigated by Broadhead and his staff. Union authorities used their discretion in evaluating the women brought before them, and they meted out stern, albeit what they considered fair, punishment for disloyalty.

The recognition of disloyal women as partisans as delineated in Lieber's Code and the new threat of banishment in mid-1863 temporarily diminished but did not stamp out disloyal sentiments held by St. Louis's Confederate women. Ten days after Margaret McLure and her fellow travelers departed for the South, a Unionist woman informed her sister that "there is a good deal of secession feeling here. The Ladies show it by not wearing any thing blue. . . . Two of them came in the parlor [of the woman's boarding house] the other night with most [sic] beautiful bunches of flowers but all red, white and red. . . . That is the way they show their contempt for the old Flag." Evidently the effect of Henry Halleck's prior collaboration with the city's prostitutes to stop women from wearing red flowers as signs of Confederate loyalty had worn off. The letter writer added that wearing the red and white flowers and eschewing anything blue was "all they *dare* do," but she underestimated the determination of the rebellious females of the city.[50] Even the threat of banishment could not keep the rebel women from acting on their convictions.

Mrs. D. W. Bell, for instance, remained an "outspoken and Bitter Secessionist." The wife of a Union soldier and operator of a St. Louis embroidery shop, Bell was accused of making a silk flag that she sent beyond the lines to the Missouri Confederates. She boldly admitted to Union soldiers who came into her shop that "she was a secessionist from the top of her head down to her toes." Another witness reported that Bell declared that "if she had all the Lincolnites under her heal she would kill them as quick as she would a misquito." Furthermore, she announced to others that "she never *enjoyed* [?] so much in her life, as when Genl. Lyon was killed." Bell would be arrested in June 1863.[51]

A few weeks later, news of the fall of Vicksburg arrived in St. Louis, to the great satisfaction of Unionists. On July 10 the city witnessed a large celebration. The festivities, in turn, prompted several secessionist women to lash out against Unionists. According to testimony given by one Kate Merrick, Mary Fitzgerald "is a Rebel, during the 10th of July she was talking in a violent Rebel manner, singing Rebel songs, &c." Fitzgerald, a laborer at a restaurant, told Merrick that "she had seen a lot of 'Dirty Rags' hanging out," referring to the American flags Unionists had displayed to commemorate the victory at Vicksburg. Another witness, Mary Bagley, recalled these lyrics from one of Fitzgerald's songs: "Dixie the Land of Cotton / Secession forever, the Union never." Anna Hiegan gave even more damning testimony. Hiegan said that she "heard [Fitzgerald] say she would like to poison the Union soldier & if she got the chance she would do it." Mary Reed told that Fitzgerald "was talking Treason & said that should she hear any one say that a Rebel was not as good as a Dog, she would give them to understand that a rebel dog could bite." Despite Fitzgerald's threats, St. Louis's assistant provost marshal George W. Shain decided that her bark was worse than her bite. He recommended that she "be confined for a time" as appropriate punishment. Fitzgerald was held for four days and then released upon taking the oath of allegiance.[52]

Fitzgerald had been arrested with several co-workers. According to testimony against her, Joanna Murphy sang secessionist songs, with one person adding that she also "talked treason." Maggie Melvin compared the two warring presidents in verse: "Jeff. Davis Rides a White Horse / Abe Lincoln rides a mule / Jeff. Davis is a wise man / Abe Lincoln is a Fool." Another witness testified that Melvin "wished a Union woman might have twins by a Big Buck Nigger." Also outspoken in her support of the South, Louisa Stokes wore the red and white rosette associated with the Confederate cause, calling the two-toned color combination "her colors." Emma Martin, on the other hand, seemed to be guilty by association. All the statements in her file attested to her loyalty, and she would be released with no further action. Murphy, however, was required to take the oath like Fitzgerald's after a few nights behind bars.[53] Clearly, with the exception of Martin, these women held strong Confederate sentiments. Nevertheless, Union officials merited it sufficient to imprison briefly these lower-class women as an appropriate response to their indiscretions rather than banish them.

A similar fate awaited Eliza Campbell. On the day that the news of the surrender of Vicksburg arrived at St. Louis, according to Unionist Julia Gazzollo, Campbell threw water out a window drenching Gazzollo as she passed by. Gazzollo explained that Campbell had called her names and often sang rebel songs, the latter accusation to which another witness attested. In her defense, Campbell claimed that dousing Gazzollo had been an accident, yet she freely admitted that she "had sung secesh songs or parts of them." She proclaimed herself "Union, *provided*, they would keep the Nigger out of the question," reflecting the attitudes of many Missourians toward the Emancipation Proclamation. She was released on parole having given her oath.[54]

Union authorities in St. Louis remained ever vigilant against demonstrations of Confederate partisanship, especially around the city's military prisons. Such activities had long been identified as a punishable offense. On July 27, 1863, guards near the "female military prison," Edward Dobyns's former house, arrested four young women for displaying a Confederate flag and starting a secessionist demonstration. Upon questioning, Mary Devinney claimed that the flag, which was imprinted on a large envelope, had been given to her by "a young man who sells soda at the open stand on Olive street." The lad, William Carroll, was called in to the provost marshal's office for questioning. He said that someone in the crowd had playfully tossed the envelope to him, and he, in turn, threw it to a young lady at the stand, Mary Devinney. It all seemed like harmless flirtation, except that upon searching Carroll's room at his boarding house, investigators uncovered another smaller envelope bearing the Confederate flag. Devinney was released on parole, pending further investigation. Her three female friends arrested at the same time were "unconditionally released, it appearing that they committed no other fault than that of being in secesh company."[55] It seems that the provost marshal decided that Devinney was not as innocent as she first appeared, but there was yet no solid evidence against her.

Demonstrations of Confederate loyalty would not be tolerated by James Broadhead, but the provost marshal general used discretion in determining how to respond to such actions on a case-by-case basis. Many women who expressed or demonstrated Confederate sympathy usually faced a brief imprisonment—a few hours or a day or two—followed by the taking of the oath of allegiance to the Federal government. If they refused the oath, which was probably the case with Mary Simpson, they very well could face prolonged imprisonment. Simpson came into custody in mid-July 1863 on charges of disloyalty. "She said she was secesh," declared a neighbor, "and did not care who knew it." The neighbor had often heard Simpson use disloyal language, "very abusive of our government—she said all her friends were south and she wished to be there too." A twenty-two-year-old native of Alabama, Simpson admitted to being "secessionist," even though her brother served in a Union regiment. Simpson's offenses seem no worse than those of Mary Fitzgerald and her rebellious co-workers. It is doubtful, however, that a woman of such strong anti-Federal sentiment would swear an oath to that government. Such a refusal would explain her imprisonment. Two weeks after her arrest, she was still confined in the female prison, from where she unsuccessfully attempted to escape.[56]

Of course, Confederate women continued to commit violations of a more serious nature than disloyal demonstrations. In late September, Emma English of Lincoln County was arrested for corresponding with the enemy. She also allegedly was "cognizant of the precincts of murderers and robbers and beyond doubt implicated in the attempt to Bushwhack and to destroy Wright City, Warren Co. Mo. of recent date," a charge English vehemently denied. English, a school teacher, declined to answer most of the questions posed to her, but on some matters she was quite candid. In her interrogation, English admitted to having letters in her possession "written by persons in the Confederate States," but she refused to turn them over or to reveal from whom she received them. According to her inquisitor, "Miss English said that she was a Rebel from principle—that she despised the Government of the U.S. worse than anything, and next to it she despised Government officers." English refused to take the oath of allegiance because "being a Southern Sympathizer and a *'Rebel from Principle,'* it would be swearing to a lie." A notation on her file jacket recommended that English be banished to the South, but she eventually was allowed to go on parole to Wyoming County, Michigan, from where she reported periodically.[57]

According to two witnesses on her behalf, St. Louis boarding housekeeper Amelia Shoemaker would not "wrong the government [of the United States] by an act of disloyalty," despite her strong Southern sympathies. Nevertheless, other deponents painted a different picture. "She is a Rebel," told one witness, "and I know that she keeps Rebels & boards them & will not take any other kinds of Borders [sic]." Several witnesses saw her yelling words of encouragement to prisoners arriving from Vicksburg, while others asserted that she had clandestinely aided rebels in the city. Of more concern, Shoemaker had been overheard planning to put to the torch a nearby warehouse operated by the U.S. government. One witness even claimed to hear her swear that "she would break her sons [sic] neck if he went into the Union army."[58]

Like Shoemaker, other women dealt with by the provost marshal's office in St. Louis during John Schofield's tenure as commander in 1863 stood accused of materially aiding the Confederates. On June 4, 1863, Margery Callahan and Lulu Kinkhead were caught with Confederate flags and uniforms that they had made, and the two St. Louisans spent several weeks in prison. Kinkhead admitted her disloyalty and refused to take the oath, resulting in her banishment. Callahan, on the other hand, cooperated with her captors. She revealed the names of two Confederate spies and discussed the clandestine contraband mail network in St. Louis. Having taken the oath, Callahan gained release. According to the provost marshal, she had "done her part of the bargain" in providing the information. Historian Michael Fellman suggests that Margery Callahan proved to be a "survivor," betraying her loyalties to the Confederacy to avoid banishment. That might be the case, but Callahan's betrayal was only temporary. According to information received from two sources by the provost marshal's office in February 1865, Callahan had continued her covert activities after her release. In the spring of 1864, she allegedly passed through the lines with mail and money destined for Sterling Price's army. She also resumed her sewing activities, preparing several shipments of uniforms for smuggling through the lines.[59] Perhaps Callahan was a survivor in a different sense. She avoided banishment not to protect herself but rather to remain active in promoting the Confederate cause in her own way. She may have given information in exchange for her freedom, but the value of that information has yet to be proven. Whatever the case, for her cooperation, Union authorities had spared Callahan from exile.

Providing information on disloyal activities was no guarantee of mitigation when it came to sentencing. Mary Byrne and her daughter, a Mrs. Dye, stood accused of raising money and buying clothes for the Confederates. Arrested in the middle of May 1863, Byrne maintained her innocence. "We are two lone and unprotected females," Byrne insisted of her and her daughter. "We have know [sic] friends in the rebel army." Stressing their female vulnerability, Byrne implored, "I just bege protection from the flag for which my fore parrents fought [sic]." The forty-five-year-old, two-time widow who was characterized as a "notorious prostitute" proclaimed herself a "Constitutional Union Woman." "I am for the Union. Every way Except freeing the negroes." Early in her confinement Byrne befriended Marion Wall Vail, Absalom Grimes's trusted mail operative who now faced banishment. From her Byrne had learned the names of several Confederate mail couriers. She passed along the information to the provost marshal general and later informed another officer of when "two rebel spys" could be caught. "They are intamet [sic] friends of one of the prisoners now in confinement here," undoubtedly Marion Vail. The information she offered proved to be of little value; Byrne and her daughter were not banished to the South, but they were ordered to be exiled from the Department of the Missouri.[60]

Mary Grandstaff managed to avoid exile altogether. The Jackson County resident had been accused of feeding and harboring guerrillas and receiving stolen property, specifically "calico and other dry goods" taken from a store in Shawnee, Kansas. A military tribunal in Kansas City, Missouri, found Grandstaff guilty only of being in possession of the pilfered goods. Authorities transferred Grandstaff to St. Louis, from where she was to depart for the South. She spent several more weeks in custody there, but rather than being sent beyond the lines, according to a report of the provost marshal general's office published in the *Missouri Democrat*, Grandstaff earned release upon taking the oath and paying a one-thousand-dollar bond.[61] Evidently Grandstaff's sentence had been reconsidered by either James Broadhead or John Schofield and determined too harsh of a penalty.

The records of these 1863 arrests suggest that Union authorities in St. Louis were quick to arrest anyone, women included, suspected of disloyalty. But they also reveal that great care was taken in investigating the cases and leveling penalties deemed appropriate to the transgression. Furthermore, suspicion of wrongdoing was not enough to punish someone without proof, although caution had to be taken in such instances. Thus, Mary Devinney was released on bond until the truth could be ferreted out in her case. Another case of suspicion without proof involved Matilda Orme and her husband, Robert. The Ormes lived forty miles outside St. Louis city, where they rented out rooms. They had taken in a man named Smith, who according to reports was up to no good. Just what misdeeds Smith was suspected of, or who he even was, is not readily evident in the records. Nevertheless, it was enough to cast a shadow of suspicion on Smith's landlords. An investigation of the Ormes revealed no improper activities on their part. Perhaps to serve as a warning to be more careful about whom they rented to, James Broadhead released the Ormes on parole rather than releasing them outright and required them to report to his office once a week; after two months of making the weekly eighty-mile, round-trip journey to St. Louis to check in with Broadhead, the Ormes were given permission to report by mail.[62]

The case of Mary Byrne also exposes the concern given for the innocent, despite her initial banishment from the Department of the Missouri. Christmas Day, 1863, found Byrne in Cairo, Illinois, from where she wrote to Provost Marshal General Broadhead. She described her "desparate condition" and pleaded that her case be reinvestigated so that she could return to St. Louis. Byrne, a lowly prostitute, carried no weight in the community. Her letter could have easily been dismissed by Broadhead, as there were many more urgent matters at hand. An unsigned summary of the reconsideration of the charges revealed that the evidence used against Byrne bore weaknesses. All the witnesses against Byrne were rival prostitutes, "personal enemies" of the accused "and morally unworthy of evidence." They "let no opportunity escape to republish to associates the most inconceivable falsehoods concerning their [competitor's] views and participation in the rebellion." The author of the summary concluded that Byrne should be allowed to return to St. Louis upon taking the oath of allegiance and posting a $1,000 bond. Being held to such a bond would have been prohibitive for Byrne, and Broadhead probably recognized that fact. Besides, her guilt was highly questionable. Broadhead allowed Byrne to return to the city with only the one condition of taking the oath.[63]

In another case, Broadhead questioned a Mrs. McRea concerning allegations that she had been speaking out in favor of the Confederates. During her mid-June 1863 interrogation, McRea carefully refused to answer many of the queries posed to her, such as whether she had any relations in the Confederate army or had ever received correspondence from any of the rebels. She later reported to a friend that her inquisitors asked her if "she was in favor of emancipation in Missouri and if she wished the South crushed out," to which she gave no response. McRea, who traveled in the same social circles as Margaret McLure and her banished cohorts, certainly knew what the consequences might be for her failure to cooperate. Of course, she also knew what would have resulted from telling the truth. The records suggest her skillful evasion of the questions led to her release due to a lack of evidence against her.[64]

In contrast to McRea's guileful ability to avoid arrest, only the intervention of a prominent Unionist neighbor saved thirteen-year-old Katie O'Flaherty from arrest after a United States flag nailed to the porch of her Confederate-sympathizing family's house disappeared. The flag had been placed there by unknown Unionists to commemorate the Vicksburg victory and to belittle the disloyal inhabitants. The young rebel, who showed no restraint in insulting the soldiers who searched her house for the flag, had hidden the banner in a bundle of cloth scraps where it was never found. Even without the flag, O'Flaherty's verbal attack on the soldiers normally would have been enough proof of her disloyalty to warrant a trip to the provost marshal general's office. Three and a half decades later, she briefly mentioned the incident in an essay she published under her pen name, Kate Chopin, and took credit for tearing down the flag.[65]

That youth may have proved mitigating circumstances for O'Flaherty and Hannah Martin is probably true. Nevertheless, the year 1863 witnessed an escalation of the war against disloyal women in the Department of the Missouri. The adoption of Lieber's Code, the implementation of banishments to the South, and the continued arrests and imprisonments of rebellious women characterized this aspect of the hardening of the war against the Confederacy and its supporters. In Missouri, arguably nothing embodied this hardening of the war more than Brigadier General Thomas Ewing's General Orders No. 11, put into effect in August 1863 in response to the attack on Lawrence, Kansas, by the notorious Missouri guerrilla William Quantrill, which left one hundred and fifty of the town's residents dead. The order caused the evacuation of all inhabitants of the western Missouri counties of Jackson, Cass, Vernon, and Bates, a region suspected of containing many sympathizers and abettors of Quantrill and other guerrillas. Residents deemed loyal were later allowed to return to their homes, although few returned until after the war. Those who could not prove their loyalty, or did not want to, became refugees. This number included many women, and some of them would again encounter the wrath of the Federal government because of their rebellious activities.[66]

Further south along the Mississippi River, Confederate women also challenged Federal authority as the Union army occupied territory of the rebellious states. Many of the disloyal women would face arrest at the hands of Federal authorities, and some of them would be sent to the St. Louis area for confinement as prisoners. It would be their fate to be incarcerated just north of St. Louis on the Illinois side of the river at the former state penitentiary at Alton. The arrival of women at the Alton Prison marked the beginning of longer incarcerations for female rebels in the region's military prisons.

CHAPTER 4

"They Have Five Ladies . . . at Alton"

The year 1863 represented a turning point for the treatment of women in active support of the Confederate cause in the St. Louis area. Backed by Lieber's Code, the military command in St. Louis began using exile to the South as retribution for the actions Southern-sympathizing women took against Federal authority. In response to their rebelliousness, several dozen women arrested at the hands of the military faced banishment, and many more experienced this fate during the last two years of the war. Other women who came into custody had their cases handled without resorting to banishment. In most instances, the methods used to deal with rebellious women prior to the spring of 1863 sufficed: a period of incarceration followed by the imposition of a loyalty oath and a bond to guarantee future good behavior. Banishment awaited those women for whom the oath and bond would not do. Nevertheless, in 1863, the St. Louis region's military prisons began to confine women for longer periods of time, particularly the military prison in Alton, Illinois. On the night of January 23, 1863, Clara Judd arrived at Alton, per the order of Major General William Rosecrans, commanding the Department of the Cumberland in Tennessee.[1] Judd became the first woman confined to the Alton Military Prison. She would not be the last.

When the former penitentiary at Alton began operation as a military prisoner of war camp, Major General Henry Halleck envisioned that the site would be used as "a place of confinement for prisoners of war and as a prison for those who may be sentenced by courts martial or military commissions to close confinement or hard labor for offenses in violation of the laws of war."[2] Halleck's inclusion of those sentenced by military commission shows that at this early date he intended Alton to hold civilian as well as military prisoners. Eventually the prison held female civilian prisoners as well as males. Unlike the typical women confined in St. Louis to this point, the Alton women could not expect a quick release or even banishment to the South. These women were destined to remain in custody for a good long time.

The location had a rich history before becoming a military prison. In 1831 the prison facility at Alton opened as the first state penitentiary in Illinois.[3] Located on the down slope of a bluff overlooking the Mississippi River, the original penitentiary building sat on a 92,800 square foot plot of land enclosed by a thick stone wall. Cells in the stone structure, twenty-four in all, measured seven by four and a half feet. Over the next decade, the state legislature added thirty-two additional cells and a number of workshops to employ the convicts. In 1839 the state turned control of the operation of the prison over to a private lessee, responsible for feeding and clothing the inmates. In return, the lessee contracted out the prisoners as laborers and collected the money. Under this system, the lessee had little incentive to maintain or improve the prison's facilities, which fell into disrepair. In addition, the prison's location on a slope and its proximity to the river created serious drainage problems. In an investigation of the penitentiary conducted by Dorothea Dix, the well-known humanitarian reformer concluded that no amount of money could revitalize the prison. She therefore recommended that a new location be found for the state penitentiary.

The state legislature kept the Alton prison open, but over the next few years lawmakers authorized the purchase of more land and expanded the number of cells to two hundred and fifty six. The legislature also called for the grounds to be macadamized and for a new warden's house to be built. The completion of this latter improvement allowed the old warden's house to be used as a prison hospital, something the facility sorely lacked. Despite the upgrades, the penitentiary facilities continued to suffer neglect under the leasing system. In 1857 a legislative committee reached the same conclusion Dorothea Dix had a decade earlier: because of the poor state of the prison, it should be closed.

To replace the Alton facility, the committee recommended the erection of a new penitentiary elsewhere. It took three years to complete the new prison at Joliet. In the meantime, conditions at Alton worsened. Along with the general deterioration of the facilities, a fire destroyed nearly all the workshops before the last of the prisoners was removed in July 1860. For the next year and a half, the empty Alton prison remained under lease to Samuel A. Buckmaster, but it would soon find a new life as a military prisoner-of-war camp. By late 1861, the two military prisons in St. Louis—the Gratiot Street Prison and the Myrtle Street Prison—held far more prisoners than they could handle. To ease the pressure, then commander of the Department of the Missouri Henry Halleck requested permission from the War Department to ask Illinois governor Richard Yates if the former penitentiary could be fitted as a military prison.[4]

With permission granted by Yates, and Buckmaster satisfied by a lucrative contract to maintain the prison and feed and clothe the inmates, the Alton prison began receiving military prisoners on February 9, 1862. Still, the prison facilities remained insufficient. For instance, the prison commander had to rent buildings adjacent to the facility to serve as storehouses and a quartermaster's department, and the prisoners themselves were put to work cleaning the prison. Furthermore, requisitions had to be submitted for many "needful articles." By the end of June, the prison, which had held fewer than four hundred prisoners at any given time as a state penitentiary, housed almost eight hundred. By the end of January 1863, the prison reported a population of 1,501, including one from Winchester, Tennessee—Clara Judd.[5]

A native of New York, Clara Judd gave a somewhat confusing account of the events leading to her December 19, 1862, arrest at Mitchellville, Tennessee. In a statement given in May 1863, Judd revealed the rather detailed and elaborate stories accused women wove when confronted by military authorities.[6] Prior to moving to the South, Judd had lived in the Minnesota territory with her husband, Burritt S. Judd, and their children. Her parents and at least one sister also lived in the territory at that time. The 1860 census shows that the Judds had been rather mobile, living in Arkansas, Connecticut, and Ohio before settling in Minnesota in 1852. In 1859 the family again moved, this time to Sewanee, Tennessee, and then to Winchester, west of Chattanooga about fifteen miles north of the Alabama border. While Burritt Judd was also a skilled carpenter, he had been ordained a minister in the Episcopal church and held services for a congregation in Winchester.[7] While in custody, Clara often stressed that she had been the wife of a minister.

By the time of this last move, the Judd family had grown to eight children, but tragedy struck in 1861 when Burritt succumbed to injuries he received in an accidental fall. Burritt died on April 12, the same day as the attack on Fort Sumter. Because Tennessee did not secede until several weeks after Fort Sumter, Judd was still in correspondence with "friends in the North," who encouraged her to return to Minnesota.[8] Other matters that Judd had to attend to hindered her from following that path, and soon the war cut off correspondence between her and her Northern friends and complicated the possibility of returning to Minnesota. For the time being, the widow Judd remained in Winchester. According to Judd's statement, through the rest of 1861 and most of 1862, she and her children made do with what they had. To protect them from the draft, she obtained jobs for her three oldest sons in a government factory where their work would provide them with an exemption, a plausible statement considering their carpentry skills. Shortly after, with the state threatened by the oncoming Union army, Confederate authorities moved the factory from Tennessee to Atlanta. Judd next indicated that in each of the five instances that Federal troops had visited Winchester before her arrest, she opened her house to them, but she had never offered her hospitality to Confederates when they controlled the area.

On the advice of a Union officer she encountered during one of their occupations, Judd said that she decided to bring her youngest children to Minnesota. She left her twelve-year-old son[9] behind to tend to the house and departed for the North on August 11, 1862. It had been her intention, she asserted, to return to the South, retrieve her sons from Atlanta, and take the entire family to the Nevada Territory to escape the impact of the war and protect her older sons from Confederate conscription.[10] Judd claimed that when she left Winchester, she planned to be gone for four weeks, but her return had been slowed first by hostile Indians in Minnesota, then by an anticipated attack on Louisville, Kentucky, and finally by sickness, which left her incapacitated for six weeks at New Albany, Indiana, just north of Louisville on the Ohio River. Delayed further in Kentucky, Judd alleged that she obtained money in Louisville and then returned to New Albany to purchase some needed clothing for herself and a "hand knitting-machine which [she] had been talking of getting for several years."

Judd passed back through Confederate lines and finally returned to Winchester, her statement continued, only to find her house ransacked and the son she left behind gone to Atlanta to join his brothers in work. She also discovered that she would not be able to get her sons from Atlanta. Of course, the manpower shortage in the Confederacy would have made the prospects of Confederate officials willingly allowing four young men at or near the age of service to pass through their lines to the North rather dim, so Judd set out for Nashville, headquarters of the Union Department of the Cumberland, to obtain a pass allowing her to return to Louisville. Just beyond Murphreesboro, Judd reached the fringes of the Confederate army. There a Confederate officer under a flag of truce attempted to pass her to the other side, but Judd was told by the Federal officers she encountered that she would have to wait there before obtaining permission to go on to the headquarters.[11]

While waiting, Judd explained, she met a man named Mr. Forsythe, whom she identified as a "prisoner from Murphreesborough." Forsythe claimed that he had been a prisoner of the Confederate army but now was free on parole. The two quickly became acquainted, and Judd told Forsythe of her intentions to get a pass. Forsythe responded that he would "see [departmental commander William] Rosecrans about [her] pass." When Judd later asked him about the influence he claimed over Rosecrans, Forsythe explained that he and the major general had at one time been neighbors. Nevertheless, he assured Judd, he was a "Southern man as strong as any dared to be," despite his Connecticut upbringing.

The next day, Judd finally passed through the lines and went to Nashville, where she met with the provost marshal. She related to him everything she had seen while in the South; at that time, she did not receive her pass. Judd then went to the hotel where she believed Mr. Forsythe was lodging. She explained that she failed to find him there, and as the hotel was full, she sought lodging elsewhere. On the following morning, Judd received her pass to Louisville but then learned that because of a battle that supposedly raged near that city, she would not be able to leave then. It is not clear to what, if any, battle she referred. Another day passed and she decided to go to Mitchellville, Kentucky, where she had left some baggage during her return from Minnesota, to retrieve some clothes. Because Forsythe had claimed he was a merchant and would probably have access to a wagon, she contacted him to ask if he could provide her with a "private conveyance" there.

If Judd's statement is a bit convoluted and her intentions unclear to this point, it only gets worse, but it appears that her eventual intention was to make her way back through the lines to Atlanta. Forsythe met with Judd and told her that he intended to go to Louisville the next day. At this point she said she revealed to Forsythe her urgency in carrying out her plans; she had learned that Confederate cavalry commander John Hunt Morgan soon planned to "interrupt" the railroad they would have to take. She indicated that she feared being "left South" if Morgan succeeded in driving out the Federals from the area because she owed people in the North money that she would be unable to repay on time. She never noted how she intended to pay her lenders back. Later she claimed that it tempted her to let herself be caught behind the lines, protecting her from those to whom she was indebted in New Albany.

Forsythe urged Judd to get a pass allowing her to return to Gallatin, Tennessee, north of Nashville, after she completed her business in Louisville. Supposedly Forsythe informed Judd that Rosecrans had given him a pass to sell some merchandise in Murphreesboro. From Gallatin, he continued, Judd could make her way to join him. According to Judd, Forsythe, a widower, had confided in her that he would "like to become better acquainted with" her. With Forsythe's help Judd had her pass changed accordingly and the next day the two left by rail for Louisville. Upon arriving, Judd claimed that Forsythe warned her not to purchase anything contraband; she replied that as long as she remained in Federal lines, she understood that nothing was contraband. Forsythe then urged her to buy medicines, offering the money she lacked to do so. She declined. The two next went to New Albany where Judd planned to pay back her debt. The lawyer from whom Judd had borrowed money was not there, and so Forsythe made arrangements that he would repay the debt in three weeks through business contacts in Louisville. After making these arrangements, Forsythe told Judd to use the money with which she had planned to repay the lawyer to purchase drugs. He further told her that he would later send her whatever drugs she wanted and that she had no need to worry. Judd asserted that she assumed that what Forsythe had proposed had been "understood between him and Rosecrans," even his stated plans to open a commission store in Atlanta once Judd made her way there.

Judd proceeded to order various medicines in New Albany. She added that she found it odd that Forsythe chose not to go with her when she did her shopping. Judd and her traveling companion did not return to Louisville until after midnight, too late to pick up the knitting machine she had ordered previously. Nor could she get it the following day, being Sunday, but she did retrieve the medicines she had ordered in New Albany the previous day. The drugs had been packed in a carpetbag delivered to some prearranged place in the city. Forsythe went with her that Sunday and carried the drug-laden bag as well as some other items Judd had bought until they returned to Judd's place of lodging. Judd explained that while she lit the lamps in her room Forsythe placed the bag and her other packages in the room and left for the night. When she awoke the next morning, Judd looked for the bag, but it was not there. She called for the proprietor who told her that a guard had found the bag in the hall outside her door in the night. Judd now suspected that Forsythe had taken the bag with him when he parted company that night and that it had been searched, but when she retrieved it, the bag appeared not to have been opened.

It is not clear whether Judd and Forsythe left for Gallatin on Monday or on Tuesday, but before their departure on the Louisville and Nashville Railroad Judd had obtained the knitting machine. At Bowling Green, Kentucky, detectives from Nashville boarded the train, but it was not until the train reached Mitchellville, just south of the Kentucky line, that they moved to arrest Judd. She was charged with "attempting to carry through the lines articles contraband of war such as quinine, morphine, nitrate of silver, besides other goods, and one knitting-machine" and being in possession of "a pass obtained under false pretenses."[12]

Judd's earlier suspicion of Forsythe had been well founded. He was not a "Southern man as strong as any dared to be" as he claimed, but rather a strong Union man. More importantly, he worked for the provost marshal's office in Nashville. Forsythe had become wary of Judd while waiting to pass through the lines with her after he overheard a Confederate officer tell Judd that if she failed to get permission to cross the lines he could instruct her on how to slip into Federal-occupied territory without permission. Forsythe related this information to his superiors and then volunteered to keep a close eye on her movements.[13] Judd protested the accusations, claiming that Forsythe had sworn falsely against her. She painted Forsythe as a spurned suitor out for revenge, but to no avail. Further damning Judd was the fact that Morgan's cavalry had, in fact, made a raid on the Louisville and Nashville Railroad north of Gallatin shortly after she should have arrived there.[14] Judd again denied any wrongdoing. She insisted that had she not been delayed, she would have come and gone from Gallatin before the attack. She knew nothing more than what she said she had learned from two of Morgan's adjutants while still behind Confederate lines, and with the exception of Confederate general Leonidas Polk, an old acquaintance, she knew no rebel officers higher in rank than lieutenant colonel. "I never had anything to do with political affairs," Judd insisted, "neither do I wish to have."

These were the facts that Judd stood by in her May 1863 statement, but shortly after her arrest Department of the Cumberland provost judge John Fitch gave a somewhat different account. Fitch passed along the summary of his investigation to the department's provost marshal general on January 13, 1863.[15] At least some of the information came from Judd herself, but some probably also came from Forsythe. Fitch briefly recounted Judd's trip to Minnesota and her return to Winchester. He mentioned Judd's sons in Atlanta and then noted that after returning to Winchester, Judd next went to Atlanta, where she supposedly received money from her oldest son and funds from other people who desired her to "purchase articles from the North for them." In her May statement, Judd never mentioned actually going to Atlanta. It was on the train from Atlanta to Murphreesboro that Judd met some Confederate officers from whom she learned of Morgan's plans. After reaching Murphreesboro, Fitch continued, Judd then returned back through the lines, claiming that she intended to return to Minnesota to be with her youngest children. Instead, traveling with Forsythe to Louisville and elsewhere, Judd obtained the contraband articles and then set out for Gallatin to "set up her knitting-machine and manufacture stockings, &c., for a living." There she would remain, holding on to the goods she had purchased "in expectation that the enemy would occupy the country and that she would then fall into their lines." About Morgan's raid, Fitch added, Judd had been "tolerably well informed."

In an account written for publication later in 1863, Fitch strayed little from this January recounting, other than identifying Forsythe as a "Mr. Blythe" and elaborating on certain points. For instance, Fitch noted that as soon as she came to believe that she could trust Forsythe, Judd candidly told him of her plans to purchase medicines and other contraband goods for the Confederates. She also admitted to Forsythe to being a spy for Morgan. Fitch further suggested that it was Judd who became smitten with Forsythe, and not vice versa, "devot[ing] herself to him as only women do to those whom they love." Fitch summarized the effect Judd's arrest had on the command in Nashville:

> The circumstances, when known, created not a little excitement in army circles, and the case was personally examined by the general commanding and his staff. The crime was the highest known to military law; the importance of the consequences in the success or defeat of the scheme, almost incalculable. In short, it was one of those little pivots on which the fortune of a campaign or the fate of an army might turn. For such an offense the only adequate punishment was death; but the person implicit was a woman; and the reverence for the sex which brave men ever feel would not allow the application of so extreme a penalty. To pass her lightly by, however, could not be reconciled with a sense of duty.[16]

In Fitch's opinion, Judd was "probably a spy as well as a smuggler" and a "dangerous person to remain in these lines." Judd's gender may have shielded her from execution, but not from punishment. Fitch recommended that she be committed to the Alton Prison, "as there is at present no proper tribunal for her especial trial or proper place of imprisonment at Nashville." While Fitch noted "cases of this kind being of frequent occurrence by females," it appears that up until this point no harsh action had been taken against rebellious women in the department. Fitch continued, "Examples should be made." Thus, he recommended Judd's extended confinement. William Rosecrans concurred, and Judd was sent to Alton to be held "during the present war or until tried, unless sooner released by the commanding general of the department."[17]

When Clara Judd arrived at the Alton Prison on the night of January 23, 1863, her presence at the prison immediately caused troubles, ironically concerning an issue of domesticity. Prisoners were expected to cook their meals themselves, usually in groups called messes. As a woman, Judd could not be kept with the other prisoners, yet the prison contained no room to hold her where she could cook her food "without a great expense," according to Colonel Jesse Hildebrand, who commanded the prison. For the time being, he boarded her at the same house where he and two other officers stayed at two dollars per week.[18] Judd was later moved within the walls of the prison facility itself.

General William Rosecrans had sent Clara Judd to Alton in part to serve as an example to other Confederate women that he would not tolerate their partisan activities against the Federal government, but also because he was unsure what to do with her, like Franklin Dick. Shortly after, Rosecrans wrote to General-in-Chief Henry Halleck asking for a sterner policy against the disloyal, to which Halleck responded with his definition of military treason.[19] Until the adoption of General Orders No. 100, Judd remained the only woman confined to Alton by Rosecrans, or anyone else for that matter. After the imposition of the new guidelines for the treatment of civilians by the army, the number of women at Alton began to rise. By June 1863, Confederate prisoner of war Edward Herndon Scott of the Sixth Missouri Infantry could inform his father, "They have five ladies, and a child . . . at Alton also as prisoners."[20]

Besides Judd, one of the women Scott referred to was Mollie Hyde, who was sent to Alton from Nashville by Rosecrans in mid-May. Described by John Fitch as "a young, ardent, handsome, and smart rebel lady, mother of two children, and whose husband was in the rebel army," Hyde had been charged with "spying and other misdeeds" and had been sent to the prison "to be confined during the war or until released by competent authorities." A United States detective named Randolph, who had gained Hyde's trust much like Forsythe had Judd's, claimed that Hyde admitted to working for John Hunt Morgan. Randolph also reported, according to Fitch, that Hyde "regretted nothing that she had done for the Confederacy, for her whole heart was with the South, and she would remain as true as steel."[21] Hyde was joined by Mary Nicholson, who arrived from Memphis on May 30 by order of Brigadier General Stephen A. Hurlbut to serve a four-month sentence for an unspecified charge, after which she was to be "sent beyond the lines of the United States." Nicholson claimed British citizenship, which may explain why Hurlbut remitted her sentence early and then ordered her to leave the country.[22] Five days after Nicholson arrived, Ann Trainor entered the Alton facility. Trainor had been arrested with her husband near Nashville on March 25, 1863, and accused of spying. She remained in Alton Prison until October 1863, when she was returned to Nashville to stand trial.[23] The identity of the fifth woman in Alton to whom Scott referred cannot be determined, but she may have been Molly Hyde's sister, a "Mrs. Payne," who was also arrested in Nashville with Hyde. Payne had been involved with the contraband mail business, "superintend[ing] generally the Nashville terminus of their grape-vine line of communications." John Fitch's published account, however, does not mention Payne going to Alton.[24] To whom the child mentioned by Edward Herndon Scott belonged is unknown.

Although they were not present in large numbers in 1863 and into 1864, female prisoners continued to arrive at the Alton Military Prison. Most came from Union-occupied areas of Tennessee. For instance, on July 13, 1863, Barbara Ann Donovan, or Duvana, and Elvira Mitchell arrived from Memphis. The prison records do not mention the charges against them, but they do note that both had been "sentenced to close confinement in Alton Military Prison During the War." The Stillman sisters, Julia and Eliza, received one-year sentences along with a five-hundred-dollar fine each for smuggling and carrying a forged permit, charges they both denied. They claimed they received their permit from a Treasury Department agent for the supplies and safe passage back from Memphis to their home in Germantown, Tennessee.[25]

Ann Nichols and Betty Conklin both admitted to having "grey uniform cloth in their possession," destined "for the use of rebel officers." The women attempted to smuggle the material by fashioning it into petticoats; when unraveled, the cloth measured a total of 150 yards in length. In early January 1864, the women each received one-year sentences, but despite their willingness to confess, they refused to reveal from whom they obtained the contraband cloth. In late August 1864, a doctor examining Nichols found her "laboring under consumption" and recommended her release. The prison commander at Alton agreed, noting that "she is little more than a skeleton now," and sent the appropriate request to Major General C. C. Washburn, in whose hands Nichols's fate rested. Washburn responded: "When Ann Nichols will disclose the names of the parties from whom she obtained the within inventories: Grey Cloth, an application for her pardon will receive favorable attention at these headquarters." Evidently, concerns for her broken health outweighed her loyalty to the Confederacy. Nichols left the prison ten days after Washburn made his offer.[26] Had Nichols and Conklin told who provided them with the cloth at the start, they may have never been sent to the prison in the first place.

At least two female prisoners were sent to Alton after being arrested in Kentucky in 1863, although it appears that they, too, had had their cases heard in Nashville, Tennessee. Arrested in Macon, Sarah B. Keys had been "charged with harboring guerrillas, going about the country with them—disguised in male attire—the bosom companion of Wm. Callahan, a notorious Guerrilla Rober [sic] and Horse thief." One report related how disguised as a "negro man," Keys had helped the guerrillas in robbing the house of a discharged Kentucky Union soldier. According to Major E. L. Motley, the provost marshal of Bowling Green, Kentucky, Keys was "a rebel—a prostitute and a dangerous woman." Keys arrived at Alton on July 10, 1863, the same day as Mollie Jumper, a "free Col'd woman." Identified as "Polly" in one document, Jumper had been arrested for "Belonging to a Guerrilla band." Neither the prison records nor Keys's nor Jumper's provost marshal files implicated the two as associates, but the fact that they were released and sent back to Tennessee by the same order of September 23, 1863, suggests that there may have been a connection between the two.[27]

As for Alton Military Prison's first female prisoner, Clara Judd remained in the Illinois facility for seven months before her release on parole by order of the Department of War because of her declining state of health. Her release happened despite the protest of Commissary General of Prisoners William Hoffman and without the knowledge of William Rosecrans, who was in the field with the Army of the Cumberland. Still insisting on her innocence, Judd gained her freedom provided she would immediately go to Minnesota for the duration of the war. Perhaps authorities should have listened to Hoffman. After leaving the prison, Judd went to St. Louis where she was supposed to make arrangements to travel to Minnesota. Instead, she booked passage on a steamer to Memphis. When Missouri's provost marshal general James Broadhead learned of this deception, he promptly ordered Judd's arrest. Judd was apprehended before she could leave the city. Although it is unclear what reason she gave for booking passage for Memphis, by August 25, about three weeks after her original release orders were given, Clara Judd arrived in Minnesota.[28]

Upon her return to Minnesota, Judd underwent a vicious attack by the *Valley Herald*, a Republican newspaper published in the town of Chaska. The paper asserted that "knowing her antecedents, the people here at once pronounced the verdict of guilty, which verdict in this community still remains in full force, not set aside, annulled, or its validity impeached." The editorial did not elaborate on just what the "antecedents" were, but evidently Judd or her now deceased husband or both once had been at the center of some unpleasant local controversy. The *Herald*'s harangue continued:

> She is an avowed public enemy to each and every citizen who has a father, brother, husband or son, bearing the banner of our nationality over territories wrenched from the Union by shameless traitors. With an air of boldness and vindictiveness, unbecoming her sex, she denounces the Government and all its adherents, and boasts that if she was engaged in treasonable acts, her fertile brain furnishes ample means of secresy [sic] and escape. Although she has been released, and returned here a citizen free from military restraint, the mark of Cain is upon her, and none can know her to respect her so long as sentiments of treason are the burden of her soul.

The editorial finally noted that while Judd "accuses the Government of stealing everything she owned," she arrived in Minnesota with "two large trunks well packed, together with other cases of goods." These last comments not only seem to refute her claims but also to carry with them a hint of suspicion as to what might be in her luggage and what she intended to do with the mysterious contents.[29]

Another local paper, the Shakopee *Argys*, came to Judd's defense. The Democratic Party organ condemned the "ungentlemanly and malacious [*sic*] attack" upon "a poor defenceless [*sic*] woman." Oddly, the paper added a word of thanks to Judd's mother for the "most delicious plums" she produced. Not to go unchallenged, the editors of the *Herald* defended their assessment of Judd and accused the "Argoose" of receiving bribes of plums to defend Judd.[30]

The issue did not end there. In December 1863, the *Valley Herald* published an extensive account of the events leading to Judd's arrest and challenged the *Argys* to continue its defense of Judd in light of the report. The *Herald* noted that Judd still "flaunts her treasonable sentiments when and to whom she chooses." The paper also added with an air of accusation that Judd recently had adopted an alias, Mrs. Jennie Smith, although "what schemes she and her correspondents are now concocting remain to be developed."[31]

Clara Judd's name resurfaced in official correspondence in a November 30, 1864, communication received by Joseph Darr, then serving as provost marshal general of the Department of the Missouri. It came from the headquarters of William Rosecrans, now in command of the same department. Rosecrans had learned through a letter that Judd was back in Nashville. Judd had been detected associating with a John A. Stuart, who concealed her in his boarding house room (she entered the establishment dressed as a man) until he discovered that she was being sought. Stuart then "sent her to a House of ill fame (in the proper clothing for her sex) where she staid under the name 'Ida Robinson.'" The general ordered Darr "to take such steps as will, if possible, lead to the arrest of . . . Mrs. Judd. . . . She is a spy of the worst description." Darr informed General George Thomas, commanding at Nashville, of Judd's presence in that city, and accordingly his men arrested her on November 17. Somehow she managed to escape and she eluded arrest for several months. Nevertheless, on April 1, 1865, the editors of the *Valley Herald* took pleasure in reporting that "the notorious female spy Mrs. B. S. Judd . . . has recently been caught at her old tricks again in Kentucky." The waning days of the war found her confined in a female military prison in Louisville from where she was ordered "to be sent north of the Ohio River not to return during the war under penalty of death."[32]

For someone who claimed to be guiltless, Clara Judd spent a considerable amount of time in the custody of military authorities during the war. Perhaps she was simply a victim of circumstances, or as she once suggested, a victim of a rejected suitor who sought revenge for spurning his advances. Or perhaps Judd's protestations were simply a deception designed to win her her freedom to continue her work for the Confederate cause. Judd's record after leaving Alton would suggest so. For any women conducting the type of covert activities of which Judd was accused, deception would have to play a key role in order to be successful. Clara Judd got caught. How many Confederate women who were involved in spying and smuggling avoided detection will never be known. From his experience with Judd, Mollie Hyde, and the other rebellious women he ordered sent to Alton, William Rosecrans would learn of the dangers that Confederate women's partisan activities posed to Union victory. He carried this knowledge with him to St. Louis, where he took command of the Department of the Missouri in early 1864. Up until then, women landing in Alton came from Tennessee, Kentucky, and other states further south. Not until 1864 did Alton begin receiving female prisoners convicted of serious offenses from St. Louis and elsewhere in Missouri.[33] At the same time, the number of women in the prison increased dramatically.

CHAPTER 5

"Rebel Women . . . Are Engaged in the Treasonable Work"

T he war against the South escalated in 1864 with the appointment of Ulysses S. Grant to command the entire Union army. He launched a strategy designed to apply continuous and coordinated pressure on the Confederate army on all major fronts. Because the regular Confederate army had been driven from Missouri in 1862, Grant did not consider the border state a key target in his strategy. In fact, to Grant, the war in Missouri seemed irrelevant, and rather than strengthen the presence of the Union army there, Grant drew men and resources away from the state to be used elsewhere. Nevertheless, the conflict was not irrelevant for the Unionists in the state and for Major General William Rosecrans, who replaced John Schofield as commander of the Department of the Missouri in January 1864. Rosecrans was no stranger to disloyal civilians, having encountered many when he commanded in Tennessee, including women like Clara Judd. Rosecrans's confrontation with a disloyal civilian population in Tennessee paled in comparison to what he faced in Missouri.

Missouri continuously remained a hotbed of rebel guerrilla activity—in fact, it expanded starting in early 1864—and control of large portions of the state by the Federals remained tenuous at best. Confederate guerrillas enjoyed the backing of the state's many disloyal civilians, who often gave aid and comfort to them, despite the consequences. Guerrilla partisans could not survive without the aid of like-minded civilians connected to them by kinship and community, including and especially women, who gave them support, information, and protection and who supplied them with food and other necessities. These women operated the guerrilla supply line, but unlike the supply line for the regular army, which existed behind the front lines, the women's supply line operated out in the open. Indeed, their place often was the front line, exposed to the enemy much more than the guerrilla menfolk who revealed themselves by choice or when necessary. The safety of the guerrillas often depended on what information the women gave, or did not give, to Union forces. While Confederate guerrillas saw themselves as the defenders of their womenfolk, this dynamic between men and women was one of mutual or reciprocal protection.[1]

Confederate-sympathizing women embraced this role, especially in Missouri, where in 1864 at least two hundred women were charged with disloyal activities by the provost marshal general in St. Louis. About 60 percent of them were arrested outside of the St. Louis area in regions of Missouri where rebellious sentiment thrived. The arrest of women had become commonplace, and the impact of Lieber's Code felt, as many of the accused, first and foremost, faced the charge of violation of the laws of war; implicitly, if not explicitly, they were accused of Henry Halleck's war treason. Union soldiers in the field, such as Captain W. T. Leeper, sought justice against them. On February 1, 1864, Leeper reported from the town of Patterson in the southeast corner of the state: "I become more than ever convinced that many of the people between here and Arkansas will either have to be killed or moved out of the State. Many men and women who are at home do us more damage than the regular soldier; they feed, harbor, and conceal the guerrillas." These dangerous people included "our good, loyal friend Mrs. Byrne," who, Leeper believed, "has been a regular spy since the commencement of the war." If she were a man, he concluded, "and guilty of the crimes that she is, he would not live here twenty-four hours." Whether Leeper would have Mrs. Byrne killed or removed from the state is not clear; nevertheless, he clearly felt frustrated by the disloyal activities of Byrne and intended to take strong action against her, as well as against any other women giving aid to the enemy.[2]

To be sure, many partisan women in rural Missouri had been arrested prior to 1864, yet the threat of arrest, imprisonment, and banishment did little to quell the rebelliousness of the state's disloyal females. Local provost marshals dealt with most themselves, while sending a small number to St. Louis to have their cases heard. While the number of arrests of women in the St. Louis area noticeably grew in the first half of 1864, the flow of accused women arriving in St. Louis from out-state began to escalate dramatically starting in July. As a result, the number of women in military prisons in the St. Louis area began to swell as well.

By spring, William Rosecrans distinctly felt the drain of men from his command caused by Grant's reallocation of resources to confront the major Confederate armies in operation elsewhere, much to Rosecrans's consternation.

The fact that Grant strongly disliked Rosecrans did not help the situation.[3] Despite the loss of troops, or perhaps because of it, Rosecrans escalated the campaign to control and ultimately crush guerrilla activity in the state. As a result, more and more civilians came under arrest for assisting the enemy as the year progressed. Rosecrans had reasons for concern. In June, he informed Secretary of War Edwin Stanton that "reports of rebels and guerrillas drifting in from the south" continued to arrive in his office from "all districts of the department," suggesting that the rebels were setting the stage for a confrontation. After the withdrawal of regular Confederate troops from Missouri in 1862, rebel supporters in the state had been anticipating a triumphal return of its men in gray under the command of Missourian Sterling Price. Rosecrans took the threat of an organized Confederate raid to heart. "The consequences of a powerful raid would be very serious," he feared, and such a raid would come "as soon as corn is fit to sustain man and beast." Indeed, according to Rosecrans, guerrilla activities in the state received "additional life and animation from the hope of rebel raids."[4]

This threat of a Confederate invasion was not the only concern in 1864. The day before Rosecrans apprised Stanton of the reports of rebel activity, the *Missouri Democrat* warned that "the traitors in our city and State are not of the acquiescing, unenterprising kind, but will bear incessant and sharp watching." The editors concluded that the army needed to maintain martial law in St. Louis and the rest of the state.[5] Rosecrans also remained concerned about clandestine threats against Federal rule posed by the city's and state's disloyal element. Another potential menace came in the form of a perceived pro-Confederate conspiracy plotted by a secretive group known as the Order of American Knights. In early March 1864, Colonel John P. Sanderson became the provost marshal general of the Department of the Missouri after James Broadhead resigned. Sanderson quickly instituted an investigation of covert disloyal activities that ultimately would implicate dozens of pro-Confederate sympathizers, including some women. Intelligence gathered through the investigation further fueled Rosecrans's fears of a Confederate attack on Missouri. Fears became reality in the early days of the Fall, when Price launched his long-awaited invasion of liberation.[6] Under these circumstances, the number of women arrested in Missouri escalated dramatically during the second half of 1864.

During the year's first half, however, the arrest and imprisonment of women in St. Louis remained slow but steady, with about three dozen women arriving in the area's female military prisons between January and June. Nevertheless, newly appointed Provost Marshal General Sanderson learned quickly not to expect disloyal women to be passive and respectful. Just days after Sanderson arrived in St. Louis, an accused female smuggler verbally accosted him as he toured the prison where she was held. She demanded that he release her, but to no avail.[7]

While most of the women coming into custody in St. Louis during these months lived in or near the city, a few resided in rural parts of the state. For instance, the Bond sisters, Ruth and Sarah from Miller County, faced accusations of feeding bushwhackers. A neighbor, Henry Jenkins, claimed to hear Sarah "say that she had fed bushwhackers & she would do it again in Spite of Hell." Meanwhile, another neighbor attested that the Bond sisters actually had been victims of robbery at the hands of guerrillas wearing blue uniforms.[8]

The case against Eliza and Rachel Haynie proved to be much more solid. In June 1864, a scouting party from the Fourth Cavalry of the Missouri State Militia confronted four disloyal women in Saline County after spotting two suspicious-looking men scurrying away from their back door and into the brush. The soldiers also found a collection of "rebel mail" and some merchandise that had been reported stolen nearby. According to Captain W. L. Parker, who led the expedition, the women had provided food to the bushwhackers. To make matters worse, the four admitted that they would do it again, and, in Parker's words, they "gloried in bushwhackers." Captain Parker never defined how the Haynies went about glorying in bushwhackers, but he did order the arrest of all four women. Two of them, Eliza Haynie and her daughter Rachel, were sent to St. Louis to have their case heard. A formal court martial found the two guilty of "harboring and feeding guerrillas. . . . aiding and abetting the enemies of the United States," and "receiving stolen property" and sentenced them "to be confined to some military prison during the present rebellion." Thus, the Haynies found themselves imprisoned in the Alton Prison, where they remained until February 1865.[9]

While the accusations against the Bond sisters left much doubt about their guilt, the Haynies themselves provided ample evidence of their disloyalty. They were not alone. Many Confederate women continued to take ownership of the political motivations that challenged the Federal government, in spite of the consequences. Arrested in July 1864 for "uttering disloyal sentiments," Mollie Goggin of Cooper County admitted to being a rebel and to giving aid and comfort to the Confederates whenever possible. Goggin revealed that "she had never take the oath of allegiance, and never would take it." She also disclosed that "it would be a pleasure to be sent South." A military commission instead sent Goggin to Alton Prison. Nannie Douthitt of Pocahontas County, Arkansas, pled guilty to corresponding with the enemy and was ordered "confined during the war." Her interrogator noted that she was "rather candid and discloses being a spy." In a letter intended for Confederate major Tim Reeves, she gave the following words of encouragement: "May success, glory and honor crown your every exertion in promoting the interests of the South, adding one link to the gaining of independence." Unlike Goggin, Douthitt took the oath of allegiance, but only with a sense of great shame and a feeling that it had been forced on her. From prison she admitted that "she had done a great deal [in Arkansas] for the rebel cause & that if she was fortunate enough to get out of prison she would make her time good in serving the rebels."[10]

Even more sensational—and sensationalized by the press—was the case of Nina Hough. The wife of Warwick Hough, the one-time adjutant general of the State of Missouri under Claiborne Jackson who became an officer in the Confederate army, Mrs. Hough had resided in the Confederate South since the early days of the war when her husband enlisted. During that time, she had at least one and perhaps two children, with whom she appears to have been traveling when arrested. In late June, Mrs. Hough passed through the lines and made her way to Memphis. From there she went by steamboat to Cairo, Illinois, before heading to St. Louis. At no time did she present herself to Union army authorities, as was required, although she did have a pass that she claimed had been obtained from an assistant provost marshal by a cousin in Memphis. Once in St. Louis, she attempted to board a train to Jefferson City but was arrested before the train departed. Examiners found in her possession a pass signed by Confederate general Robert E. Lee allowing her passage through the rebel lines; presumably she planned to use the pass to return to Confederate-occupied territory. Hough claimed that she came to Missouri to visit her ailing mother in Boonville and that she had no other business, but Provost Marshal General Sanderson found that claim dubious. Throughout her examination, according to Sanderson, Hough remained indignant, evasive, and defiant. More startling, investigators discovered in her baggage a piece of human skull, about an inch and a half by an inch and a half in size, marked with the words "December 21, 1861, Wilson's Creek." When questioned about the relic, Hough admitted that she believed it came from a Union soldier killed in the battle, "but never thought any more about it," except that she "designed to keep it as a memento of the battle." Considering the "spirit and temper manifested" by her as well as the morbid souvenir in her possession, Sanderson recommended to William Rosecrans that she be treated the way his predecessor Franklin Dick handled such influential yet disloyal women: banishment to the South. Rosecrans concurred.[11]

The Union army in Missouri continued to grapple with the disruptions caused by irregular rebel activities through 1864. The situation became more dire in the fall, when Confederate forces under the command of Sterling

Price launched their long-expected invasion. In the weeks preceding Price's campaign, Confederate scouts scoured the Missouri countryside recruiting soldiers and encouraging rebel supporters to aid Price's army when it arrived. Preparations for the incursion stimulated a flurry of guerrilla activities in the state, elevating concerns among Federal authorities as well as taxing their resources. These actions involved both the irregular rebel fighters and those who supported them. In his official report on the campaign against Price, General Rosecrans observed that "previous to and pending [the invasion] the guerrilla warfare in north Missouri had been waging with redoubled fury. . . . Women's fingers were busy making clothes for rebel soldiers out of goods plundered by the guerrillas; women's tongues were busy telling Union neighbors *'their time was now coming.'"*[12] Consequently, in the weeks before the arrival of Price's invading force, many Missouri rural women faced arrest, charged with aiding guerrillas. A large number of them were sent to St. Louis to have their cases heard. For example, Mary Harlow of Lafayette County in western Missouri faced charges of "violations of the laws of war, and harboring and feeding bushwhackers." One neighbor testifying against her claimed, "I know her to be a rebble [*sic*] and I also know her to be giving aid and comfort to bushwhackers ever since thare [*sic*] was any in Her counterey [*sic*]." Likewise, sisters Dorotha and Sarah J. Durritt, who lived in the southwest corner of Johnson County stood charged with "harboring, feeding and giving comfort to Guerrillas or Bushwhackers." "I am intimately acquainted with Dorotha and Sarah J. Durritt," asserted assistant provost marshal Captain R. L. Ferguson. "They are very active Rebels and free to express their sympathies with the Bushwhackers and Guerrillas. The House of Mrs. Durritt is in my opinion a place of resort for bushwhackers and that they secure all the aid and protection from Dorotha and [blank] Durritt that is possible for them to give." Other witnesses and the testimonies of the Durritt women only corroborated Captain Ferguson's assessment.[13]

Seventy-year-old Sarah Moss of Wayne County also faced charges of harboring and feeding bushwhackers and horse thieves. She admitted to feeding her two sons, both in Confederate service, when they showed up unexpectedly at her door. She also acknowledged that the men were not wearing uniforms when they arrived, an offense punishable by execution if captured behind lines. On the other hand, Moss denied making a suit of clothes for another Confederate. Nancy Longacre and her fourteen-year-old daughter Martha, also of Johnson County, were arrested after neighbors accused them of being in communication with and aiding bushwhackers.[14] There were dozens more.

The arrival of Price and his men appears to have interfered with the arrest of rebellious women outside of the St. Louis area. His army began entering

Missouri near the bootheel region in mid-September 1864, and soon after, the flow of accused women arriving in St. Louis slowed to a trickle. Price's Confederates pushed northward and came within forty miles of St. Louis before veering to the west toward Jefferson City, the state capital. Unknown to Price, his forces outnumbered the St. Louis's defenders, and he may have met with success had he tried to occupy the river city. Price then reached within two miles of Jefferson City, but again he overestimated the opposition he faced and decided to continue westward toward the Kansas border. Although Price accumulated recruits from among Missouri's disloyal population, his army eventually met with defeat after clashing with the combined might of Union forces defending the border region and another concentration of Federal troops pursuing him and his men across the state at the Battle of Westport, south of Kansas City and Independence, Missouri, on October 23, 1864. After that, Price's army withdrew southward, making its way across the Missouri border and then beyond Union lines.[15]

The Battle of Westport and subsequent withdrawal of Price's command effectively ended any organized military threat to Federal control in Missouri. Nevertheless, guerrilla activity in the state continued, and so did the arrest of women suspected of abetting Confederate bushwhackers. By November, the flow of arrested women from outstate brought before Missouri's provost marshal general resumed. The disruptions caused by Price's invasion also may have been the catalyst for the punishment meted out to a group of ten women arrested in western Missouri, including the Durritts and Mary Ann Harlow, who were sent to St. Louis just before the incursion began. Having deemed them "guilty of violation of the laws of war, and harboring and feeding guerrillas," General Rosecrans ordered the women "released from custody . . . upon the condition that they take up residence in any of the free states, North and East of Springfield, Ills." Perhaps coincidental, all but one of the women resided in the region where Price was operating at that moment in time. In a rare gendered attack on these prisoners, the order, Special Orders No. 288, noted that Rosecrans took "these actions in the case of these persons, because the time of the Military Courts is occupied with a more respectable class of prisoners; and he is not without hope that removed from temptation, and deprived of the opportunity of indulging their taste for the society of murderers, thieves, and guerrillas, they may become, if not loyal and good citizens, at least more creditable specimens of their sex."[16]

Such a banishment appears to have been used other times. Two weeks after issuing Special Orders No. 288, Rosecrans decided to banish Clarinda J. Mayfield and Susan Waitman in a similar way after finding them guilty of aiding the rebels, only to find out that they had escaped from the St. Charles Street

Female Prison. Rosecrans had more success banishing Charity Ward and her daughter Mollie. They had kept a boarding house in Springfield, Missouri, before moving their business to St. Louis, and had used their establishment to harbor spies. The order banishing the Wards noted that they were "unfit to remain in the Dept." but stated nothing specifically related to their gender. In response, both women attested in writing that upon their honor, they "will remain without the limits of the Department of the Missouri, and will not return during the War."[17] Whatever Rosecrans thought of the shortcomings of these women as "specimens of their sex," his primary concern remained stemming their treasonous activities.

Meanwhile, throughout 1864, arrests continued in the immediate St. Louis area. Emeline Stewart, Elizabeth Price, and Mary Rudder, for example, all faced the charge of corresponding with the enemy. Authorities detained four women from Tennessee after it had been determined that they had obtained "a larger quantity of goods than allowed by the trade regulations" while on a shopping excursion to the city, and arrested a women named Smith and her two daughters on charges related to spying or assisting spies. Sue Drake, who openly "declared herself to be a rebel sympathizer," illegally passed through the lines after being allowed to leave the Department of the Missouri for the Confederate South. Likewise, Martha Williams had returned to Missouri by way of St. Louis without permission. A resident of Cass County, she initially had been banished from the state through General Thomas Ewing's notorious General Order No. 11. Delia Davidson used "disrespectful language towards the President of the United States and Officers of the Army." According to a witness, Davidson claimed that "the secesh men were as good as the Union men[;] that there was no Union officer who were officers to serve their country[;] that it was only for the good of their pockets to get Uncle Sam's greenbacks[.] It was not because they were Union for they did not care any thing more about the government than she did. They thought because they got 'Old Abe' Lincoln for President they thought they could do as they pleased, but she was not a going to stoop to Abe Lincoln or his officers that they all ought to be hung."[18]

A number of women from areas further south that had fallen under Union army control arrived in St. Louis, then were forwarded to the Alton Prison. Among them, Ann Nichols and Betty Conklin, arrested in their hometown of Memphis, confessed to smuggling. In Alton they joined fellow Tennesseans Elvira Mitchell and Eliza Stillman, also convicted of smuggling. Mary E. Kirby, arrested in Baton Rouge, Louisiana, had been a rebel mail carrier. And Clarinda Rasure, alias Madam Julia Dean, a brothel proprietor from Louisville, Kentucky, had purchased and passed along counterfeit currency.

Her mistake was that she sent at least some of the bogus greenbacks to her son, Lieutenant David Rasure of the Second Missouri Artillery, U.S.[19]

A close examination of the records reveals that as vigilant as the Federals were in trying to root out disloyalty and treason, they did not assume guilt and continued to take great pains to investigate the alleged actions of the accused. Federal officials remained quick to arrest, but with the growing number of cases, adjudication moved more slowly. Nevertheless, authorities still sought justice. For example, Harriet Snead and Anna Polk, whose cases received much attention in the pro-Union *Missouri Democrat*, had been living behind Confederate lines, but in mid-1864, they came north without permission. Despite being arrested separately—Snead in St. Louis and Polk in Cairo, Illinois—evidence suggests that they knew each other. Each of them also had with them letters destined for people living in the Confederate states. Snead, the wife of a rebel officer serving on Price's staff and recently elected to the Confederate Congress in Richmond, admitted that she carried the prohibited items and refused to take the oath of allegiance. General Rosecrans ordered her banished back beyond the lines. Polk, who said she was the wife of a farmer presently living in Arkansas behind Confederate lines with their children, proved more convincingly that she intended no harm and posed no threat. "Having satisfied the General commanding that her intentions were not bad, and that the forbidden letters and articles were imposed upon her care by the selfishness of others less honorable," Rosecrans ordered that Polk "be released from custody on taking the oath of allegiance, and [be] permitted to remain within our lines, and, with the consent of the proper military commander, to go beyond them to get her children, and return without unreasonable delay."[20]

Of course, Rosecrans's judgement was not foolproof. John Polk was not a simple farmer; in fact, he had served under Sterling Price. He was also related to Trusten Polk, a former U.S. Senator now on Price's staff. In August 1864, Trusten Polk wrote to Thomas Snead, Harriet's husband, of Mrs. Polk's anticipated arrival in Price's camp from St. Louis after her release. He noted that because of this delay, the general had held off dispatching his trusted messenger, presumably because Price expected that Mrs. Polk carried information that he would then pass along to others.[21]

Whether or not Rosecrans had been duped, he did not automatically judge Mrs. Polk in violation of military law. He may have exercised discretion because of the attention the case received, but the Bond sisters, whose arrest gained hardly any public notice, also were not presumed guilty. Upon reviewing the evidence, Provost Marshal General Sanderson noted in their file that "this case in its present shape is wanting in Material upon which to found even an opinion!" Due to the hearsay nature of the accusations against the Bonds and the testimony that cast the sisters as victims, Sanderson decided to release the two provided they take the oath of allegiance and pay a $500 bond.[22] Questionable evidence also accounted for the release of Isabella and Melissa Fox of Chariton County. Neighbors attested to the "reputations" of the two and their "general impressions" of the women, and two even referred to seventeen-year-old Melissa as lewd. Nevertheless, the witnesses gave no damning evidence to contradict what the Foxes admitted: on three occasions they had fed bushwhackers, but only because the women feared what might happen if they refused. Authorities decided to release the two upon giving their oath of allegiance, their record noting "the testimony against them being insufficient to convict."[23] Likewise, America and Josephine Huckshorn, relatives of the Foxes, gained their release after an investigation, "the evidence in their case proving them undoubtedly loyal." With the number of civilian arrests escalating, Union authorities continued to resist rushing to judgment in these cases.[24]

To a certain extent, age and infirmity mitigated the penance given Susan M. Bass of Howard County for harboring and feeding guerrillas in 1864. While other women from central Missouri faced banishment for the same offense, authorities decided to release Bass from custody on a $2,000 bond and an order to report weekly in person or in writing to the provost marshal general's office in St. Louis. Furthermore, she was told that she still could be called for trial. In response to a request from her doctor asking for her unconditional release from these obligations due to her physical condition, however, an investigator reported, "There is no ground in my opinion for exercising clemency in this case. The woman declares herself to be a 'southern woman' and all her people 'to be southern people,' which means that she is a rebel sympathizer. She harbored and boarded bushwhackers and their wives and concubines during the most bloody part of the past year." Bass continued to remain under her obligation until May 29, 1865. Meanwhile, a group of nineteen women arrested for aiding guerrillas in neighboring Chariton County, at about the same time as Bass's arrest, received orders to report to St. Louis for banishment beyond the lines until the end of the rebellion.[25]

Besides guerrilla strife, threats to the security of Missouri in 1864 came in another form. While the Union army continued to ferret out disloyal civilians giving aid to the rebellion, Provost Marshal General John P. Sanderson became embroiled in an investigation of a broader kind. Since the early days of the war Federal authorities suspected that Confederate sympathizers had been creating a covert network, or networks, throughout the North designed to aid the Southern rebels and perhaps even to overthrow the government in Washington. Going by names such as the Knights of the Golden Circle, the Order of American Knights, and the Sons of Liberty, these groups did exist, but they proved to be much smaller and much more ineffective than the Lincoln administration feared. Nevertheless, with opposition to war policies, such as conscription and emancipation, growing and a small but vocal group of "Peace Democrats" trying to channel that Northern opposition against the war, government and army officials took such groups quite seriously.[26]

William Rosecrans had specifically requested the services of Sanderson in a letter to Abraham Lincoln. Colonel Sanderson, a native of Pennsylvania and Republican Party politico, had served under Rosecrans in Tennessee. In explaining his selection to the president, the general asserted that he wanted "an able officer not identified with local parties" in St. Louis, hoping that the new provost marshal general, unlike James Broadhead, could stay remote from the factionalism that plagued St. Louis's Unionists. Despite opposition from Secretary of War Stanton, Sanderson received the appointment. Shortly after taking over his new role, Sanderson began investigating a conspiracy in the state that he believed intended, among other purposes, to aid the anticipated invasion of Sterling Price.[27]

Created in the 1850s by native New Yorker Phineas C. Wright as a vehicle for promoting states' rights, the Order of American Knights (OAK) remained little more than an idea until early 1863, when Wright, now living in St. Louis and representing himself as a Peace Democrat, began piecing together an organization designed to counteract pro-Union sentiments, to condemn Lincoln's war policies, and to resist the war against the Southern confederacy in other ways. Wright managed to create branches of the organization in Illinois, Indiana, and New York, but actual membership remained limited. In fact, in early 1864, support for Wright and his organization began to fall apart, much of the OAK's small membership joining another clandestine group, the Sons of Liberty. Wright himself was arrested in late April and remained in custody until well after the war ended.[28] Nevertheless, Provost Marshal General Sanderson became convinced that the OAK posed a serious threat to Federal authority.

By June, Sanderson had compiled a thousand-page report, complete with testimony and other written documentation, on the clandestine activities of the Order, and turned it over to General Rosecrans. According to the report, the "object and aim" of the OAK was "the overthrow of the Federal Government, and the creation of a Northwestern Confederacy." Of course, aiding the Southern confederacy remained central to their purposes, so much so that Sanderson took that goal for granted. To this end, the Missouri conspirators planned to aid Sterling Price when he returned to reclaim Missouri for the Confederates.[29]

During the investigation, Sanderson and his subordinates arrested or questioned dozens of suspects. At least two of those taken into custody were women, Martha Cassell and Missouri Wood. Sanderson asserted in his report that "in many instances, rebel women—some of them of character and standing in society, and not a few of them outwardly professing to be loyal—are engaged in the treasonable work" of carrying mail to and from Price's army. They included Cassell and Wood.[30]

Of fair complexion with black hair and eyes, Martha Cassell lived in Marion County. Charges brought against her, to which she pled guilty, included "corresponding with and encouraging rebel enemies of the United States." Specifically, Cassell had been receiving letters from L. Rodgers and J. M. Kaylor, two "notorious rebels" who according to a *Missouri Democrat* account had been "lurking around in Clark county, Illinois, for the avowed purpose to incite rebellion, revolution and bloodshed in that county, and the destruction of the lives and property of the citizens of said county." According to one source, Rodgers claimed in a letter to Cassell that he intended to "see a Civil War and wide destruction sweep the north . . . [and] . . . to avenge the insults and indignities heaped upon the people of Missouri." Just how Cassell came to the attention of Sanderson or any other Union official is unclear, although certainly ambitions such as those professed by Rodgers in his letter corresponded with the activities in which Sanderson believed the OAK engaged. Nevertheless, Cassell not only admitted to receiving the letter, but also took responsibility for encouraging Rodgers in his goals. Of course, that did not stop her from complaining of "being subjected to a system of petty tyrany [sic]." With Cassell's guilt proven by her own admission, in August the military court that heard her case sentenced her to confinement in the Missouri State Penitentiary for the duration of the war.[31]

Thirty-year-old Missouri Wood was the daughter of former St. Louis recorder Solomon P. Ketchum. Sanderson's report gives little specific information about Wood, but one newspaper account reveals that she faced charges of carrying rebel mail and hiding Confederate spies, while another referred to her as a spy. Testimony taken by the provost marshal relates her comings and goings from St. Louis and other suspicious behavior. Unlike Cassell, Wood refused to admit guilt, thus prompting a thorough investigation. Wood came into custody no later than mid-June 1864, and while a case was built against her, she remained under lock and key at the St. Charles Street Female Prison. That is, she remained confined until she escaped on September 25. Martha

Cassell's stay in prison ended prematurely, as well, for in late October 1864, she received a pardon from President Lincoln.[32]

Colonel Sanderson asserted in his report on the OAK that the investigations of Cassell and Wood had led to the uncovering of other women who were working for the clandestine organization. While he mentions no others by name, one woman whose account parallels that of Martha Cassell's is Pauline White of Wayne County. White had taken the oath of allegiance in October 1863 and faced charges of violating that oath because she, like Cassell, had been corresponding with and sending information to the rebels. Arrested about the same time as Cassell, White denied any wrongdoing, although she pled guilty to the charges against her. She received the same punishment as Cassell did: to spend the duration of the war in the Missouri State Penitentiary, a sentence received by only a handful of women. In fact, White learned her fate on the same day as Cassell and they arrived at the penitentiary together. The parallels between the two may be coincidental, but there is one significant difference: Pauline White remained behind bars for the duration of the war, when she received pardon from President Andrew Johnson.[33]

Sanderson's OAK report made its way to Judge Advocate General Joseph Holt, who used it to shape his October 8, 1864, report to Secretary of War Edwin Stanton concerning secret societies and conspiracies in the western states. Holt's report mentioned the "notorious" mail carriers Martha Cassell and Missouri Wood and the importance of having them under lock and key (even though Wood, by then, had been on the lam for two weeks). It also described the types of witnesses and sources used in the investigations of these disloyal activities: information gathered by detectives and scouts; captured and deserted rebel soldiers and officers; citizens under arrest; members of the organizations who gave confessions; and so forth. One source, in particular, the importance of whom Holt could not stress enough, was "the female witness, Mary Ann Pitman." According to Holt, Pitman's "testimony is . . . particularly valuable, and being a person of unusual intelligence, and force of character, her statements are succinct, pointed, and emphatic. They are also especially useful as fully corroborating those of other witnesses regarded as most trustworthy."[34]

Aiding the enemy, spying, smuggling, and other manifestations of disloyalty remained common charges brought against civilians dealt with by Union authorities, male and female alike. The records show that the punishment meted out for men and women deemed guilty of disloyal activities was usually similar. In his study of wartime civil liberties, Mark Neely offers that except for civilian prisoners found guilty of serious offenses and sent to prisons like Alton to carry out their long-term sentences, most civilians remained in custody for only a few weeks, although it is unclear how he came to that conclusion.[35] For the 111 Missouri women arrested in 1864 and not sent to Alton for whom at least a ballpark estimate for the length of their incarceration can be made, the average time in custody was at least sixty-one days, with the median at fifty-five days, in other words, eight to nine weeks. For some of these women, release from custody only preceded their banishment to the South.

Ulysses S. Grant's decision to give the conflict in Missouri low priority left the Union army there at a decided disadvantage. While department commander William Rosecrans lacked the personnel he believed necessary to crush Missouri's disloyalty, he took compensatory measures that included the continued arrest, imprisonment, and banishment of civilians, including women, who aided the enemy. Had Rosecrans been given the support he believed he needed to eradicate the guerrilla threat, then, perhaps, the war on women would have abated. That was not the case.

The events of 1864 brought to light one of this story's most enigmatic characters, indeed one of the most enigmatic characters of the entire war—Mary Ann Pitman. She played an important role in the investigation of the Order of American Knights and then offered her services as a spy for the Federal government. Through the end of the war, she participated in a number of covert investigations, including some within the prisons holding Confederate women. Her unique story merits further attention.

CHAPTER 6

"Thompson, Charles (Alias Mary Ann Pittman), Transferred to St. Louis"

On November 3, 1864, Griffin Frost, a prisoner in the Alton Military prison, noted in his journal the arrival two nights earlier of a "female, dressed in male attire, and calling herself Mollie Hays." Frost, a captain in the Confederate Second Missouri Infantry, was a keen observer of prison life and a harsh critic of the practice of arresting and confining women by the Federal authorities. He added further that he had heard she was "a very hard case," although he did not elaborate on his meaning. Two days later, Frost saw "the *female man*" as he referred to her as she walked to dinner. The woman's coarse features and masculine attire disturbed Frost; indeed, he found her "by no means a pleasing object to look upon."[1]

Frost made no attempt to communicate with Mollie Hayes (as the name was usually spelled) despite his gregarious nature and his friendship with other women confined in Alton, and there is no evidence that the prison's female community welcomed her. Perhaps the women and Frost deemed the extent to which Hayes went too extreme, even for the sake of the Confederate cause. Frost relates little more about Hayes, and the prison records show no one by that name. Other records reveal that Hayes was, in fact, Mary Ann Pitman, Missouri provost marshal general John Sanderson's star witness in his investigation of the Order of American Knights. Her revelations may have been true, or she may have been a Civil War-era Keyser Söze,[2] and her testimony part truth, part the truths that Sanderson believed to be true, part the truths that Sanderson *wanted* to believe were true, that he then tied together with lies that made it all seem plausible. When Pitman arrived at Alton, a clerk there entered into the Register of Civilian Prisoners the name "Thompson, Charles," but then added "(alias Mary Ann Pittman)." Mollie Hayes and

Charles Thompson would be two of several aliases Pitman used as she went from being a female civilian to a Confederate soldier to a rebel smuggler and spy, then transitioned to a prisoner of war, an informant against the OAK, and finally a spy for the Union army. She also went by the names Mary M. Pitman; Mollie Turpin; Mary Simpson or Simmons; Ione Smith; Lieutenant Rawley; and perhaps Thomas H. (or T. H.) Phillips. Pitman's wartime tale reveals a woman who passed from one identity to another, playing several different roles depending on circumstances, at times out of choice, at others out of necessity, and sometimes a bit of both.[3] During the war, she negotiated the boundaries between female and male, Confederate and Union, soldier and civilian, civilian and spy with dexterity and skill. While the facts of her activities early in the war are sketchy and hard to verify, what she did in the last year of the war is well documented and captivating.

During her initial incarceration, Mary Ann Pitman produced three statements in the form of examinations by Sanderson describing her background and wartime activities. While there are differences in each of the narratives, the story Pitman weaves is both compelling and convincing. Sanderson's first examination of Pitman, executed on May 24, 1864, in St. Louis, focused primarily on her smuggling activities in the city. Through her answers, Pitman revealed some information about her background.[4] Pitman claimed that before joining Nathan Bedford Forrest's command, she had led an independent company of about sixty Confederates using the name "Lieutenant Rawley." She then joined "Stewart's Regiment, Richardson's Brigade" under Forrest.[5] She served in this capacity for about a year, when Forrest "detailed [her] for this business." To this point, Pitman infers, Forrest assumed that she was a he. Although she did not divulge what this first mission entailed, Pitman decided that "it was prudent to wear a female dress." But first she would let the general know. "After I had changed my dress I went to him and asked if he knew me, and he said that he did not," she explained. "Then I told him if he would give me his honor as a gentleman not to tell who I was I would tell him. He did, and I don't think he ever told it." She added, "I very frequently had to transact business that required me to wear a female dress." Sanderson asked her if she was aware that Forrest employed any others in this way, to which she responded, "I don't know. Perhaps he had. I did not ask him, for if I had, he would have told me it was none of my business." Pitman insisted that Forrest never told anyone that she and Rawley were one and the same. She never would expect him to expose the identity of anyone else in her shoes.

Most of this examination related to Pitman's three trips to St. Louis in early 1864. By this time Pitman had already conducted a number of missions for Forrest in western Tennessee. Between the end of January and the beginning of March, she made three trips to the river city. Each time she obtained needed supplies from John Beauvais, a local merchant sympathetic to the Confederacy. Her purchases included tens of thousands of musket and pistol caps, cartridges, several pistols, and—specifically for Forrest himself—an officer's belt, a gun cloak, and leggings. Each time she successfully left the city on a steamer headed south, having obtained the aid of either sympathetic or bribable crew members on the vessel. She then passed the goods along to other operatives who made sure they got to Forrest's troops.

Pitman named several men with whom she had dealings in St. Louis and elsewhere and described their clandestine activities. Sanderson asked her if she had met a "Mrs. Haines" in her travels, to which Pitman responded that she did not know. He may have been asking about Ada Haynes, who had been banished to the South, then caught after returned through the lines and in Sanderson's custody at the time.[6] Pitman also revealed that the Confederates were getting greenbacks directly from the Treasury Department, although she did not give specifics. When asked about knowledge of "any Secret Order, by which its members recognize each other," she denied knowing anything, but added that if she were a member of such a group, she would not tell, even though she had given so much other information. After implying that she did, in fact, belong to such an organization, she averred, "Do you think there would be any honor about it if I were to tell you?" Sanderson responded:

> That is an obligation like all other obligations, whether in war or in peace, that is not of a judicial or official character. It is not binding upon conscience. It is neither binding upon earth nor in heaven, and is only binding upon the mere technical point of "honor." The fates of war have decreed a different destiny for you. You are perfectly justifiable in using any information you have to your advantage. In doing so you would have a perfect right to impose terms and conditions upon me. If by doing so, certain persons whom you were under obligations to, were likely to be injured, you would have a perfect right to say that, "Any thing I say cannot work to the prejudice of such parties as I indicate"; but, as for any moral, or religious, or legal obligation I don't recognize it. The law of the country don't recognize it. I may say this to you; however: I know all about it, but I want confirmatory evidence of the fact. When I put these questions it was rather in a spirit of joking. I would not have you answer them to-night. Any terms of that character I unquestionably would obligate myself to fulfill. But, so far as your personal condition is concerned, you certainly cannot better serve yourself than on that very point.

Pitman gave no reply to this statement, but Sanderson hoped that it gave her something to consider concerning her covert connections.

A week later, Sanderson questioned Pitman again concerning a very different issue.[7] Captured on April 1 in West Tennessee near Union-occupied Fort Pillow, Pitman had been confined at the fort for ten days until being sent to Memphis. Two days later, men under Forrest's command attacked the fort, leading to one of the war's most tragic atrocities, the Fort Pillow Massacre.[8] In the course of this interview, Pitman gave more information concerning her joining the Confederate army. When asked bluntly why she did it, she replied, "I thought I ought to help to defend my country." She entered the army in Union City, Tennessee, where she was unknown and in disguise as a man. "None of my folks knew where I was" except for two unidentified men. "If my mother had been alive I would not have told her, as there are few women who can keep a secret—but I had no mother, no brothers, no sisters, and am the only one in the family that is living." When asked, Pitman admitted to being at the Battle of Chickamauga with Forrest in September 1863. Sanderson had also been there in what became a major debacle for General Rosecrans.

Pitman told of her capture at a farm house a few miles away from Fort Pillow. She said that she had been told that Union soldiers were approaching to arrest her, and that she did not care if they did. Nevertheless, she managed to send word to Forrest that "Lieutenant Rawley" had been captured. Strangely, Pitman contended that once she arrived at Fort Pillow, she offered to betray Forrest, who she said would be waiting for her at a prearranged location with her horse and uniform that night. She told fort commander Colonel Lionel Booth that if he sent her along with ten men—she did not propose that she would command them herself—that they could capture Forrest. Booth declined. In custody in Fort Pillow, Pitman was allowed her freedom in the fort by the colonel. One day while standing one hundred yards from the fort's headquarters—she claimed that it was the day after her arrest, but evidence suggests that it was nine days later—a civilian approached her, asked if she was Lieutenant Rawley, and told her that Forrest would attack Fort Pillow in a few days in an attempt to liberate her. Soon after, the message carrier received a pass from Booth allowing him to leave. Pitman was present at the time of the exchange, but said nothing. A few days earlier, she had had a confrontation with the colonel and he told her to mind her own business, that he knew best how to run his post. After the man left, Pitman revealed to Booth what had been said to her about Forrest. Booth was confident that the fort was well enough defended should it be attacked, but he decided it best to send Pitman from the fort as soon as possible. She left that evening on a steamer headed for Memphis. Two days later, Forrest's men attacked Fort Pillow. It should be noted that of the historians who have written about the Battle of Fort Pillow, none tie it to an effort by Forrest to free Mary Ann Pitman.[9]

During this examination, Pitman discussed a number of other things. She talked about the morale of the Confederate soldiers, their willingness to fight to the end to establish the Confederacy, and their unwillingness to accept peace without slavery. She, however, had other thoughts. "If they will just free those negroes, and not put them on an equality with white people, I say just free them." When Sanderson brought up "that Order we were talking about" in the last interrogation, Pitman again declined to answer. When pressed, she admitted that "There is a great many of your own officers that do belong to it." In fact, she had captured one once, but upon recognizing him she let him go so he could continue his work for the Confederacy. Sanderson kept it up. He told her that he wished she did not feel the way she did about "this subject" because he would like to see her "placed in the best possible position for a prompt and forcible appeal to the Government." If she wished to be a good citizen of the United States, she should reveal all she knows. "The concealment of the objects and purposes of that Organization is inconsistent with good citizenship." He also reasoned that because she wished to have nothing more to do with the Confederacy, she owed nothing to it or those that supported it. Pitman held her ground. Nevertheless, Sanderson began asking specific questions about the organization. Was it of Southern origin? Who led it in the North? In the South? Is there communication between the two halves of the group? He also began to reveal information that he had or that he believed about the organization. No matter what he said, Pitman still refused to divulge information about the secret organization.

What happened during the next three weeks went unrecorded, but evidently Mary Ann Pitman had a change of heart. On June 20, Sanderson conducted another examination; this one would be included with his report on the Order of the American Knights.[10] In the opening statement of the examination, she began by discussing herself, asserting that she had resided in Chestnut Bluff, Tennessee, before the war. She added that she raised the independent company of soldiers at the war's outset with one other, a Lieutenant Craig, before the company joined "Freeman's regiment," probably referring to Thomas Freeman's Twenty-Second Tennessee Infantry.[11] She then joined Forrest's ranks, later beginning her covert activities for the general. Pitman went on to relate much of the same information she gave in her first two examinations concerning her trips to St. Louis and her capture followed by her experience at Fort Pillow.

Then Pitman gave her most articulate expression of her decision to abandon the Confederacy:

Before my capture my mind and feeling had undergone a very material change from what they were when I started out in the war as to
the character of the Northern people and soldiers and the merits of
the controversy involved. I started out with the most intense feelings
of prejudice against the Northern people. I regarded all I had heard as
to their views, character, and purpose to be true, but my intercourse
with such as came into our possession during my service in the Confederate Army, and especially my trip to Saint Louis, convinced me
of my error in this respect. I found the Union officers and soldiers
not to be the desperadoes which I had been taught the believe them
to be. At St. Louis I found business flourishing, people thriving, and
everything so entirely different from the condition of things in the
South and from what I had supposed to be that my observations
could not help but make an impression upon my mind.

Although not enough to prompt her to desert, "a dishonorable act," it did
affect her. "This was the condition of my mind when I was captured, and I accordingly immediately resolved to perform an honorable part, and do nothing
to discredit or disgrace my name. While satisfied that I had been performing
services which placed my life at the mercy of the Federal Government," she
concluded, "I felt it to be my duty to tell the truth and do what I could to atone
for the past, and resolve to throw myself upon the Government."

With that said, Pitman went on to answer a series of questions about the
secret organization that she previously had refused to discuss. She revealed
that the organization went by different names in different regions of the country, that there was a northern section and a southern section, and that she
was a member. She acknowledged that members included Jefferson Davis
and many Confederate officers, but the heads of each section, the "supreme
commanders," were Ohio senator Clement Vallandigham in the North and
general Sterling Price in the South. Her revelations continued. Members
included Northern officers and soldiers. Information passed back and forth
between the northern branch and the southern, including information on
Union army strategy. Southern operatives had methods of obtaining greenbacks at a huge discount directly from operatives from the North working in
the Treasury Department in Washington. Plans existed to coordinate attacks
by the Confederate army with riots and demonstrations in the North. And
so on.

At the conclusion of this statement, Pitman affirmed, "I am not only willing, but anxious, to give you all the information I can that may be of benefit
to the Government. I am myself profoundly disgusted with the order and

wish I had never been in it and had no knowledge of it; but I took an oath, on becoming a member," she admitted, "and I cannot shake off that oath entirely from my conscience." Sanderson's persuasion, his convincing and cajoling, seemed to have impacted Pitman, but there were still limits to what she would expose. "I am willing to give you all the essential information I can, and have done so, but I cannot give names, signs, &c., because having given you the information I have, you have a sufficient key to unravel the rest and protect the Government against injury from it."

Besides the formal examinations conducted by Sanderson, two other narratives produced during the war contain additional information about Pitman's background. In these accounts her life story received elaboration and perhaps embellishment. The first, a "History of Mary Ann Pitman's Case," was produced by Provost Marshal General Joseph Darr, who replaced J. P. Sanderson upon his death in October 1864. Like Sanderson, Darr had great trust in Pitman, so much so that at this time he recommended her as a detective. With his recommendation Darr included Pitman's history.[12] The information it contained no doubt came from Pitman herself. According to Darr's account, Pitman was born and raised in Tennessee, the daughter of a farmer; it did not state whether her father or any other relatives remained alive. The history then related how she enlisted at the war's outset and how, dressed as a man and using the name Rawley, she raised a company of men. So far the tale differed little from what she had told before, except that the "company was engaged for some time in guerrilla operations" before joining Forrest's men. Pitman claimed to have been "present at all the battles fought by his command, no one being aware of her true character." The narrative then retold the events of Lieutenant Rawley's being called on by General Forrest for special service; Rawley donning female apparel and introducing herself to the general as a woman, Mary Ann Pitman; Forrest agreeing not to reveal the true identity of Pitman; and the birth of Mollie Hayes as a spy and smuggler for the Confederate army.

The "history" then reiterated the well-known accounts of Pitman's three trips to St. Louis as Mollie Hayes; her capture near Fort Pillow and the events that took place at the fort until she was sent to Memphis, just before Forrest's attack; her change of heart about the Confederacy and her decision to reveal what she could to Provost Marshal General Sanderson for the sake of the United States government. It strayed little from what was already known about the woman. Five months later, with the war winding down, Pitman prepared yet another chronicle of her life and experience, which she used to request $10,000 for her activities in the service of the United States Army.[13] This time, with her freedom secure, the war nearly over, and money on the line, Pitman definitely padded her story with information not appearing in previous narratives. Dated March 29, 1865, and notarized in St. Louis County, the document told that Pitman was born in Livingston County, Kentucky, and not in Tennessee, in May 1844. She, and presumably her family, moved to Dyer County, Tennessee, about ten years later. She made no direct mention of her family, which, in her second statement, she claimed to be dead. No information can be found to confirm that this was true at the time of Pitman's enlistment, but the 1860 census reveals a fifty-year-old laborer named A. Pittman living on the farm of T. Buchanan in Dyer County, Tennessee, with his wife and a daughter, the latter identified as twenty-eight-year-old M. Pittman. Both father and daughter were born in Kentucky. As for the twelve-year age discrepancy between the statement and the census, Pitman would not have been the first person, male or female, to lie about his or her age during the war.[14]

Pitman next disclosed how she enlisted, disguised as a man, and then raised a company of volunteers, of which she became the second lieutenant, making no mention of Lieutenant Craig, and having the company assigned to Colonel Freeman's regiment. There is no record for a soldier named Rawley in Freeman's Twenty-Second Tennessee Infantry, but according to historian Andrew Ward, Pitman used the name Thomas Phillips, taking the place of the real Thomas Phillips of Dyer County. There is a service record for a T. H. Phillips, about Pitman's age, who rose to the rank of second lieutenant. Ironically, it appears that in 1864 the real Phillips joined the Confederate army as a member of the Fifteenth Tennessee Cavalry, the other unit in which Pitman claimed membership. The Twenty-Second Tennessee also had a W. H. Craig, first lieutenant, in the same company as the Phillips that may have been Pitman.[15] What cannot be found is any record of or reference to a Charles Thompson, the name used as Pitman's alias when she first arrived at the Alton Prison, before her arrival at the prison.

The story continued. As a member of this regiment Pitman fought at the Battle of Shiloh, only this time she was "wounded in the side," something that remained untold until now. Because of her injury, she now claimed, "I deserted for fear of my sex being detected." After she recovered, she took command of another independent company, still in the guise of a man. For some reason, Nathan Bedford Forrest opposed Pitman's, actually Lieutenant Rawley's, "course in commanding this band," for he did not know her true identity yet, and at his insistence the company joined his unit. In relating this chain of events, Pitman inserted an important and startling bit of information that had gone unrevealed until now: "General Forrest is my uncle." Pitman eventually revealed who she really was to the general and said that she would leave the army if he desired. It was only then, according to this version, that he decided to employ her in his secret service.

Pitman's recounting of her capture, the time she spent at Fort Pillow, and her travels to St. Louis again brought out no new facts, but in regard to her decision to expose what she could about the Order of the American Knights, she admitted that Colonel Sanderson "and his Private Secretary William Thorpe," a person whose name had yet to surface in Pitman's record, "reasoned, argued, and persuaded with me for about a month, until I began to think I would be doing more good by telling what I knew than by keeping it a secret."

How much of the information Mary Ann Pitman related was true is debatable. There certainly is some truth in what she claimed. However, Provost Marshal General Sanderson had a habit of giving away information that he wanted confirmed in his examinations with Pitman, a habit that probably continued in conversations that were not recorded. Pitman, undoubtedly a clever woman, may have shaped many of her responses to his questions using what she knew from public knowledge, what she had learned from Sanderson and others, and what she thought Sanderson wanted to hear, because Sanderson remained committed to exposing a secret traitorous organization. Whatever the case, she convinced Sanderson of her trustworthiness. Her testimony played a central role in the case he built against the Order of American Knights. As he accumulated evidence, Sanderson consulted with William Rosecrans on a nightly basis, so the general must have had faith in Pitman's information, too. Upon being briefed by Sanderson on the investigation's findings during a visit to St. Louis, President Lincoln's secretary John Hay gave no indication in his diary that he doubted Pitman's honesty. Furthermore, in his final report on disloyal organizations, Judge Advocate General Joseph Holt called Pitman "a most intelligent" and "reliable" witness.[16]

On the other hand, Ohio Congressman and Southern sympathizer Clement Vallandigham disagreed, condemning Pitman for telling "preposterous and ridiculous" falsehoods. Others joined in on the attack. The Ohio-based pro-Democratic Party newspaper the *Cadiz Sentinel* reported:

> We are informed by one who knows that Mary Ann Pittman, the "Southern Lady" referred to in Judge Holt's infamous report, is a mulatto girl, and was take[n] from a plantation about ten miles from Fort Pillow.—She drinks, chews tobacco, smokes, dresses in men's clothing when necessary, and is addicted to all vices of a woman who is a regular camp-follower. She is shrewd, unscrupulous, and vicious to the last degree; will not hesitate at anything for pay. All

this must have been known to Mr. Stanton and Judge Holt, and yet they have the impudence and daring to issue such a report against a million loyal Northern m[e]n over the testimony of such an abandoned witness.[17]

This would not be the last time that Pitman fell victim to attacks on her womanhood, race, character, and morals.

Nevertheless, J. P. Sanderson continued to have faith in Pitman and so would Joseph Darr and James Baker, his successors as provost marshal general in Missouri, despite the fact that unanswered questions emanated from Memphis about her past activities. Shortly after Pitman arrived in St. Louis, J. A. Geary of the U.S. Police in Memphis contacted Sanderson suggesting that Mary Hays, also known as Mollie Turpin, "can throw some light on Steam Boat burning" that took place in or near that city. Evidently, Sanderson's men spirited Pitman off to St. Louis for his investigation before authorities in Memphis could question her and before Geary could get a receipt for her release to them. Apparently, Sanderson did not cooperate.[18]

Then, in September, a recent arrival to the city named Peter Tracy, who had been a hack driver in Memphis before moving to St. Louis, claimed that "Molly Hays, alias Mary Ann Pitman . . . [was] as late an occupant of the Iron Clad [,] the main Bawdy house & Brothel in the City of Memphis, Tenn." In a sworn affidavit he stated that he believed she had started working and living there about eighteen months prior and would stay there for six months at a time. He knew her because he stabled his horse in a location directly across from the Iron Clad, and on a number of occasions he had transported her from that place. He added that "she had the reputation for being a strumpet [prostitute]" and that she should not be believed. Pitman had been pointed out to Tracy, but why, where, and by whom remains unclear. Although Pitman was still in custody at the time, she later claimed that during the summer of 1864 she had been allowed to move about the city freely. Even then, Pitman's identity was not widely known. Whatever the case, the matter was handled by a captain in the St. Louis-district provost marshal's office and not Sanderson, and it was reported to Brigadier General Thomas Ewing, who had been appointed commander of the District of St. Louis in the Department of the Missouri under Rosecrans. Ewing and Rosecrans were friends, so it is doubtful that Ewing had any intention of discrediting his superior. Once again nothing came of the allegations, perhaps because Ewing soon was off chasing Sterling Price as he drove his invasion across the center of the state.[19]

Whatever questions there may have been about her past, Pitman began proving her value almost as soon as she arrived in St. Louis in May 1864. The evidence against John Beauvais and his father, St. Louis merchants accused of providing goods to the Confederates, includes a testimony from a person identified as Mary Simpson. Dated May 23—the day before Pitman gave her first formal statement to Provost Marshal General Sanderson—this statement asserted that Simpson "was captured by the Federal forces on or about the 1st of April 1864 in the rear of Ft. Pillow." It stated that two months prior to the capture, Simpson had been "ordered by Gen'l Forrest C.S.A. to proceed to St. Louis Mo and purchase percussion caps, pistols, powder etc. for the use of his command," and that these goods were obtained from John Beauvais. The Beauvaises were tried in August 1864 and among the witnesses listed against them appear the names "M. Simmons" crossed out and Mary Ann Pitman added.[20]

Soon Sanderson put Pitman to work in other ways. According to the story she told near the end of the war, while moving freely about St. Louis in July or August, she encountered a rebel colonel she knew named Ferris, who served under Sterling Price. With Sanderson's approval, she met with Ferris outside the city. He told her that he came there to learn what the Order of American Knights was doing and to assess the prospects of raising troops there for the impending invasion. He also wanted her to go with him to Price's headquarters. She declined, but told him that she would join Price when he returned to St. Louis. Pitman met with Ferris a second time in St. Louis; this time, she said, he had a letter from Nathan Bedford Forrest asking her to "return at all hazards." Over the next three days, she claimed, Ferris revealed to her the exact time and place of Price's raid. The two made plans for Pitman to travel south collecting information before meeting up with the invading force. Instead, all the information she gathered, she disclosed to Colonel Sanderson. She never followed through with the plan to meet with Price, perhaps through no fault of her own, since such action would have needed Sanderson's approval. No evidence suggests his willingness to support this. In fact, according to his successor Joseph Darr, while Sanderson at one time intended to use Pitman in "the Secret Service of the Department ... for some reason he did not do so," at least not outside of the prisons. Sanderson died on October 17. Four days later, in the thick of Price's raid, acting Provost Marshal General Darr recommended to General Rosecrans through the chain of command that he use Pitman as a spy, as she "would be a proper person to send to Price's Camp."[21] Rosecrans never responded.

The extent of the rest of Pitman's service to the United States government is hard to gauge because the records related to her activities are spread out over numerous files in the provost marshal general's records under her various aliases and variant spellings thereof, as well as in the records of others involved in or subject to her actions. Nevertheless, the details that can be found are fascinating. She was probably responsible for the arrest of the four Tennessee women who had obtained more goods to bring back home than was allowed by military law and took credit for giving information that led to the arrest of Emma Weaver of Arkansas, who was accused of spying. While Pitman exaggerated her responsibility for Weaver's capture, she definitely gave testimony against Weaver in her trial. Weaver, characterized by the *Missouri Democrat* as "a deceiver of the gayest kind," had been arrested under suspicion of spying for the Confederates in June 1864 in Carondelet, just south of St. Louis city. The night of her arrest, the matron of St. Charles Street Female Military Prison placed Weaver in a room occupied by Pitman, either by coincidence or design. Whatever the case, according to her statement, Pitman, using her Mollie Hayes alias, quickly won over Weaver's confidence by feigning disdain for the "wretched Yankees!" Weaver had been operating as a spy for the Confederate army for two years, Pitman attested, making seventy-five dollars a month. She had come to St. Louis with another spy named Leroy Tilly to gather information for General Jo Shelby on the number of troops and artillery in the city and its fortifications prior to Price's 1864 raid. Pitman next recounted that Weaver had smuggled a pistol into the prison and had given it to her for fear that if found in her possession it would ruin the chances of a quick release, which Weaver felt confident would happen. If she was not let out by authorities, she said she would "make her way out, if she had to shoot her way out," according to Pitman. Pitman saw to it that that never happened, handing the weapon over to Federal authorities and then telling Weaver it had been taken from her satchel.[22]

Because Pitman's testimony proved critical in finding Weaver guilty, Weaver's father, a Memphis merchant, began preparing "to destroy Miss Pitman's testimony" and to "render her infamous for all time to come." According to Peter Tallon of the U.S. Police, who investigated Abram Weaver's activities, Mr. Weaver claimed to have obtained a sworn statement from a river pilot also named Pitman who allegedly "kept [Mary Ann] Pitman & from whom she took her name." The elder Weaver maintained that he had forty people willing "to blast her reputation forever as a moral woman" through their testimony, and "effect his own purpose," getting his daughter released. One of the "strong" witnesses Mr. Weaver claimed was J. A. Geary, the officer who turned Pitman over to St. Louis authorities, but Tallon asserted reassuringly that he knew this to be untrue. "From what I see & hear in regard to this matter I am satisfied that there is a deep laid scheme in opperation [*sic*] for the purpose of extricating Miss Weaver from her present unenviable position & that there are some of our own officers in the plan or else Weaver could not be so bold in the matter." Thus, Tallon foiled Abram Weaver's attempts to discredit Pitman.[23]

Emma Weaver never shot her way out of the prison, nor did her father secure her release. Instead, before her sentencing, she escaped on September 26, two days after Tallon exposed to the provost marshal general the intrigues of her father, who, it was reported, had just left St. Louis because there was nothing more he could do for his daughter. About a month later, with Pitman again staying at the prison, two more woman escaped, sisters Clarinda Mayfield and Sarah Waitman. In the statement she gave about these escapes, Pitman told how she woke up early on the morning of Mayfield and Waitman's breakout and found the front door of the prison open. She immediately told William T. Dickson, who supervised the prison with his wife. Pitman revealed that the sisters had told her that they planned to escape before the expected closing of the prison because they did not want to be sent to Alton Prison; they also asked Pitman if she wanted to go with them. Pitman related that she had passed all this information along to Dickson, but he said that "he thought he had every thing secure."[24] Everything was not.

About this same time, another odd occurrence took place involving Pitman and Dickson. On October 29, Dickson gave a sworn statement about Pitman, referring to her as Mollie Hayes, concerning what he characterized as another escape from the prison by her. This alleged escape took place on October 21, the same day that Mayfield and Waitman fled. Dickson asserted that Hayes "was in no one's custody" and had permission to come and go as she pleased. When she left, he had no idea where she planned to go. Dickson then reported that just two days earlier he had heard that she was in Jefferson City and had been arrested for "being a woman in men's clothes." He said that Lieutenant Dodge, an officer assigned to the prison who had just returned from the state capital, told him this and that "she had Letters from this Dept. going on to General Rosecrans." The matter seems to have ended there, but more had been going on than Dickson realized. The day that Dickson claimed that Pitman had escaped, she actually swore her oath of allegiance to the United States government, probably in the presence of acting provost marshal general Joseph Darr. She then received a letter from Darr addressed to William Rosecrans's aide-de-camp Frank Bond, introducing her and recommending that the general use her as a spy in order to infiltrate Sterling Price's army. At the time, Rosecrans was in the field directing the pursuit of Price. Pitman probably would have passed through Jefferson City on her way to the general's headquarters, and she did have in her possession a letter from the provost marshal general of the department directed to Rosecrans's aide. It does not appear that Rosecrans put Pitman to work in any covert way, however.[25]

There is no evidence that Mary Ann Pitman, or anyone operating under any of her aliases, escaped from St. Charles Street Prison, Dickson's statement notwithstanding. In fact, it appears that Dickson had been questioned to see just what he knew about Pitman's whereabouts and activities. Furthermore, Joseph Darr went to great lengths to make it appear that Pitman was still in custody. On October 22 the *Missouri Democrat* reported that Darr had ordered "'Molly Hayes,' the notorious female spy of Forrest's command," sent from the St. Charles Street Prison to the Alton Prison. Furthermore, on October 25, right in the middle of the period when Dickson suggests she was on the lam, Darr wrote a letter to Brigadier General J. T. Copeland, who was commanding at Alton, concerning Pitman. Darr explained: "In case letters are received at the Military Prison for Mollie Hayes, Mary Ann Turpin, or Mary Ann Pitman, you will forward them to me; also that you will inform me of any inquiries that may be made for any of the person's named above before giving an answer to the same." The message continued: "The impression prevails, at present, that 'Mollie Hayes,' who is known by all of the above names, has been sent to Alton for confinement during the war, and it is very desirable that this impression should continue to exist."[26]

Whatever the case, by November 1, Pitman had arrived back at the Alton Prison, per the order of Joseph Darr. If not using her as a spy directly against the Confederate army, at least for now, Darr continued to use her in other matters. But first, authorities had to address some practical matters. Pitman owned very few clothes, and what clothes she had were falling apart. In early November, she wrote to Darr apprising him of her situation. Receiving no answer, she sent a letter directly to General Rosecrans. Calling him "friend," she claimed she "had no ladies clothes or dresses," and "no money to buy any." The clothing that Colonel Sanderson had bought her when she arrived in St. Louis had worn out, and for that reason she was wearing "gentleman costume," and that it was "very bad" for her to do so "when every one knows that i am a woman." That included Griffin Frost, who saw her the day she arrived. When she wrote this request, Pitman did not know that Darr had written to General Copeland the day before asking if she had "her female suit with her." Copeland replied that Pitman "has no outside apparel except an old dress unfit to wear." Furthermore, any new dress would have to be made for her at Alton so that it could be properly fitted. Copeland asked Darr for money for that purpose. He then included a list of things that Pitman needed: a black or dark dress; a cloak; a bonnet or hat; a pair of gloves; a half dozen hose; one corset; a veil; and a pair of shoes.[27]

Pitman's appeals eventually got the response she wanted, but it came at a slow pace. In fact, the delay in obtaining her new wardrobe interfered with her actual release from custody. On November 19, 1864, through Special Orders No. 407 of the War Department, President Abraham Lincoln issued a pardon for Pitman. Five days later, General Rosecrans issued Special Orders No. 326, directing that she be released from the Alton Prison. A day later, Darr wrote to General Copeland at Alton, informing him that "Mollie Hayes" had requested of Darr that she be allowed "to remain in prison until her clothes are made." Darr had no problems with this request, as long as it was "not inconsistent with the rules of the prison at Alton." Finally, on November 29, General Copeland ordered that Pitman be released from the prison and sent to Darr in St. Louis. In a separate move, he ordered that the clothes in her possession be inventoried and sent separately. It took another week for the trunk to arrive in St. Louis.[28]

Within days of her arrival in St. Louis, Pitman had a new task. On December 3, Pitman gave a long statement concerning things she had seen recently while in Alton Prison. First, she discussed inappropriate fraternizations committed by a Lieutenant Danforth with two of the female prisoners, Mollie Goggin and Florence Lundy. Goggin of Cooper County, Missouri, had been arrested for giving aid to the rebels in mid-1864 and sentenced to Alton for the remainder of the war. Lundy of Memphis, Tennessee, arrived at Alton having been found guilty of smuggling. One male prisoner described her as "a very fine looking young lady," but Goggin was Danforth's favorite of the two. Danforth granted the women special favors, including allowing them to leave the prison on their oath of parole. When they were in the prison, he spent long hours in their rooms behind closed doors. There were also two male prisoners who acted as servants for Danforth, receiving special treatment in return.[29]

Pitman next turned her attention to the commanding officer. While she admitted that he always treated her well and had made her letter inspector of the prison, going through all correspondence coming and going from the prison for inappropriate information, she implicated General Copeland as a member of the Order of American Knights. She also placed Copeland, a married man, in an inappropriate relationship with Florence Lundy. Finally, she revealed, Miss Lundy was using her special treatment to hatch a plan to send a large batch of uninspected letters from the prison. Later, Pitman would take credit for having Danforth and Copeland removed from their positions. The general, in fact, was removed from command in January 1865, after which he remained at the prison awaiting orders that never came.[30]

The year 1865 brought a new commander to the Department of the Missouri in Grenville M. Dodge and a new provost marshal general in Colonel James H. Baker. Baker quickly put Pitman to use, sending her beyond the confines of the department. In early January, he ordered her to Columbus, Kentucky, on the Mississippi River south of St. Louis, on business she would later describe as "secret." As she prepared to leave the town on a boat heading up river, an officer stopped her, asking if she had a pass. She showed the man the pass she received from Baker, issued by the order of General Dodge. It stated that she was on a "secret mission" in the service of the Department of the Missouri and was "entitled to the protection and assistance of our forces everywhere to enable her to carry out the purposes assigned to her." The officer found Baker's pass insufficient and arrested Pitman. He brought her to the colonel commanding the town, who also doubted her story. The colonel sent a telegraph to Baker asserting that "there is a Lady here named Mary M. Pitman purporting to be on a secret mission connected with your Dept. . . . Please inform me if she is actually employed by you, as her papers look suspicious." Pitman ended up spending two days in custody in Columbus before the matter was resolved. Upon her return to St. Louis, she sent a very indignant letter to Colonel Baker explaining in detail what had happened. She also mentioned that before her arrest she could not accomplish what she had gone to Columbus to do but gave no explanation.[31]

While Pitman carried out this secretive mission, she was involved in another mysterious matter. Just before Pitman left for Kentucky she wrote a letter to Abraham Lincoln, stating, "I am very desirous of visiting Washington and Seeing you in person both on business of importance for the government and some private affairs of my own none of which i [sic] would like to trust to paper and pray that you will grant my request." She added that the provost marshal general had told her that she could have the time away from her duties to go to Washington and return, but she felt that "he does not like to spare me that Long." She therefore asked the president if he could issue an order requiring her to travel to the capital so that she could carry out her business with him. What that business was remains unknown, and no evidence exists to suggest that the president responded one way or the other to the request.[32]

Soon Pitman had a new assignment in St. Louis. Using the name Ione Smith, she began investigating a smuggling operation involving George J. Jones, a book dealer who had been investigated two years earlier but let go for lack of evidence. Pitman and Jones had earlier dealings, and he knew her as a scout for Sterling Price, referring to her by her new alias. Pitman told him that she sought to do business with a man named "Dimmick," actually Horace E. Dimick, who also had been investigated once but released for want of evidence. She claimed that Dimick had been recommended especially by a Captain Bowles, perhaps Dick Bowles, who operated as a guerrilla in southern

Missouri in 1862. Evidently Bowles's sister had been arrested early in 1865 for aiding and feeding guerrillas and was in Gratiot Street Female Prison. Jones told Pitman that he could get a message to Miss Bowles in the prison through the Sisters of Charity. "We could send in by these ladies almost anything," he assured Pitman. "Some of them are good rebels."[33] In return, Pitman told Jones that Price planned another invasion in the spring.

Jones agreed to contact Dimick. He also brought Pitman to his house and introduced her to his wife as "Miss Smith, Gen. Price's female scout." Mrs. Jones was quite impressed. Two days later, Pitman filed another report with Colonel Baker. She told of spending more time with Mrs. Jones, a very devoted Confederate who hated Yankees. Mrs. Jones also offered to take Pitman to meet "a Madam" who is "a very good rebel." This woman turned out to be Angeline Augustine, a dressmaker originally from Canada. As for her clandestine business, Mr. Jones had explained to her that he had contacted Dimick and learned that Dimick could provide what she wanted. Jones's recounting of his meeting with Dimick suggests that the contraband dealer had his suspicions of the person who wanted these goods. He asked Jones who it was, to which Jones responded that it was none of his business. He then asked if it was a woman or a man. Again, Jones replied, it was not his business. Still, it appeared that the transaction would be made the next day, with Jones as the intermediate. The deal was consummated, but no arrests ensued. However, Pitman suggested that if Jones were arrested, his "servant girl," also should be taken into custody. "Just take the servant girl and put her in prison awhile, and She will tell all she knows."[34]

In this report Pitman also related an odd encounter she had at the Galt House hotel where she had a room. Upon returning to the hotel one evening, Pitman learned from the hotel's proprietor that a man in the hotel's parlor claimed to be her husband. When confronted, the man admitted that he had been mistaken, and that he and his wife "had had a little domestic trouble," and she left him. The man did not explain what drew him to the Galt House and Pitman, however. Pitman opined that she thought the man "a government detective or some one sent after [her] by Jones."[35]

Two months later Pitman sought out George Jones again to conduct more business with Horace Dimick. According to her report, she went to Jones's book business only to learn that he had sold it and moved to Mexico. The new proprietor of the store agreed to get her in touch with Dimick. Meeting for the first time face to face, Dimick agreed to sell Pitman pistols and cartridges through a third party again. That way he could remain "perfectly ignorant" of who bought them and for what purpose they were purchased. Before completing her business, Pitman learned that while Mr. Jones had fled the country, Mrs. Jones remained in town, staying at a St. Louis hotel. The two got together, joined by the rebel Madam Augustine who used her dressmaking business as a front for providing contraband goods to the Confederates. She, too, had been arrested before, twice in fact, along with her servant Louisa Rules, but had not been found guilty. Coincidently, Augustine told Pitman, or Ione Smith, of another woman named Smith who had been to her shop but two weeks earlier and had obtained cloth, buttons, and other goods through a clerk working there, Mr. Bolette, who was quite taken with the second Miss Smith. Madam Augustine also offered to facilitate a trade with John Beauvais if the dealings with Dimick did not work out. Pitman, knowing that Beauvais would recognize her as Mollie Hayes, insisted that Augustine did not need to do that.[36]

At the end of March, Provost Marshal General Baker moved to make arrests. A very dramatic account that somewhat resembled the events related in the three reports given by Pitman appeared in the *Missouri Democrat*. The paper stated that authorities had taken into custody Mrs. Jones, Madam Augustine, and Mr. Bolette (spelled Bolett in the newspaper). They paroled the two women but planned to banish them. Bolette, a British citizen, was ordered to Canada. The article made no mention of Horace Dimick. The big prize in this operation, however, was the arrest of Miss Ione Smith, who "had recently came [*sic*] from Price's army, and had credentials from Old Pap's headquarters." According to Mrs. Jones and Madam Augustine, the article continued, Smith's main purpose in coming to St. Louis had been to deliver to "a man from the East" a dispatch from Price and his superior, Lieutenant General Edmund Kirby Smith, and to receive a message from Richmond for Kirby Smith. Accordingly, Ione Smith, too, would be banished to the South. The information for this article, no doubt, came from the Office of the Provost Marshal General. Baker certainly had no intention of banishing Pitman. Such an article would serve to protect the cover of Pitman as Ione Smith so that in this persona she could be used again in the future.[37]

The article also included a rare description, actually two descriptions, of the woman calling herself Ione Smith. It described how she looked when she arrived at the hotel. She had "sparking blue eyes" that "contrasted with her dark complexion" and wore her hair in "long-jet-black ringlets." Her form "above the medium height and of exquisite proportions," Pitman "dressed in black" and "had the appearance of a well bred lady, of about 45 years of age." After her arrest, the article continued, further inspection at the provost marshal general's office disclosed that the spy they had in custody had been disguised. Her "jet black hair" turned out to be a wig, her actual hair being "a crop of short fair hair." Even her dark eyebrows were "painted." A "little soap and water" revealed a fair complexion" as well. Without the disguise, however, the subject looked "several years younger than formerly, and . . . more beautiful than ever." Considering that this "information" most likely came from the provost marshal general himself, one must question its accuracy. The description definitely did not match the image painted by Alton prisoner Griffin Frost of the "*female man*" he spied at the prison the previous November. "Arrayed in masculine attire," he noted, her "features are course, face round and full, a turned up nose, hands and feet small." It is doubtful that any of these portrayals do Pitman justice. She did have photographs of herself taken, but their location or even existence is unknown.[38]

The life Pitman chose to lead, especially in the last year of the war, must have been at times dangerous, tense, and frenetic, and all the time lonely. She could claim few if any friends outside of the provost marshal general's office and the Alton Prison staff. "Sometimes I wish I was back in Alton," she lamented. Even there she had alienated people through the investigation she conducted. She thought she may have found a connection with one of those officers, a lieutenant named F. A. Copeland (no relation to the general), but it did not play out. She wrote to him from St. Louis in early February 1865, regretting that he was unable to come there to visit her. "I always did like you exceedingly well perhaps better than I ought," for she had learned that he was married. "Why did you not tell me you had a wife and not have me braking my neck about another woman's husband." Nevertheless, she still wanted him to call on her if he did make his way to St. Louis and to reply to the letter. "I should be veary hapey [sic] indeed to hear from the noble lieut. As commander at Alton pris[on] tell me but if there is eny hoaps [sic] of you coming down hear [sic] . . . [I] must close hoping to hear from you ear [sic] long much love to my noble lieut." She signed the letter "Your devoted friend, Mollie M. Pitman." Copeland made a "true copy" of the letter and passed it along to be filed with the Office of the Provost Marshal General.[39]

During the winter and spring of 1865, Pitman carried out other activities as an operative for the Union army, especially in the area of Cape Girardeau, Missouri, about 115 miles south of St. Louis on the Mississippi River. April 21, 1865, found her reporting that she had heard that the notorious bushwhacker Sam Hildebrand was in the area of Cape Girardeau and she planned to go after him. If that proved untrue, she would turn her attention to "the Guerrilla [Nathan] Bolin," but for that she would "need a disguise." Both rebels managed to elude her.[40]

As the war neared its end, Pitman found her services no longer in demand. She also discovered that her efforts had left her with little or nothing in the way of compensation. She affirmed in a statement given in late March 1865 that when she first began working for the government Provost Marshal General Sanderson frequently gave her money in the amount of five or ten dollars out of his own pocket to get by on until she received regular pay. When Joseph Darr replaced Sanderson after the latter's death, Darr gave her two payments, one of forty dollars and the other of ten to pay her expenses. After her release from Alton Prison in late November or early December, Darr had Pitman sign a voucher for four or five hundred dollars. He then explained that a majority of the money would be sent to Sanderson's family as repayment for what the deceased colonel had advanced her; a large portion of the rest would go toward paying for her "disguise &c." The meager amount left, she said, was given to her five or ten dollars at a time. In the short time that he had been provost marshal general, James Baker proved to be a bit more generous, giving her one hundred dollars one month and another fifty the next. She also received another thirty-five dollars from the provost marshal of the District of St. Louis. With that money she had to pay not only her private expenses but also most of those related to her service. "I have had barely sufficient [funds] to live upon, and, though I still continue to work faithfully I am daily becoming more destitute." In response to her claim for proper compensation for the service she rendered to the government, in mid-May the judge advocate general recommended to the War Department that Pitman be paid the sum of five thousand dollars in compensation. According to a notation in the paperwork, the War Department approved the payment. After receiving her payment, Mary Ann Pitman vanished from the public record.[41]

CHAPTER 7

"Mere Friction and Abrasion . . . of the War"

During the Civil War, Mary Ann Pitman maneuvered between Confederate and Union, between Southern and Northern, between civilian and soldier, between male and female. While her efforts brought her into Federal custody, her ability to pass from one identity to the next enabled her to manipulate the circumstances she found herself in and to make the most of them. Pitman proved to be one of the more colorful individuals of the war. Unique circumstances and conditions characterized the cases of many other women arrested during the war. Some experienced arrest through no fault of their own. Others did not. In some instances, investigations, which could prove time consuming, revealed innocence or mitigating factors that influenced the accused's treatment. Other investigations provided the evidence that warranted stern punishment. Guilty or not, the arrested women's cases often reflected circumstances complicated by issues of gender, race, and other factors.

Mary Ann Pitman was not the only partisan woman among the St. Louis-area prisoners who transcended the boundaries of gender. Arrested in Macon County in north-central Tennessee, Sarah B. Keys was known to disguise herself in male attire as she associated with guerrillas operating in that region. In particular, she rode with William Callahan, "a notorious Guerrilla, Rober [sic] and Horse Thief," whom Keys had assisted in robbing the home of a discharged Union soldier across the border in Kentucky. First brought to Bowling Green, Kentucky, after her arrest in late May 1863, Keys next found herself sent to Gallatin, Tennessee, where her arresting officer believed that the provost marshal could find more evidence against her. By the second week of July, she was on her way to the Alton Prison, where she remained until late

September when she gained release. Evidently, authorities in neither Kentucky nor Tennessee could find sufficient evidence against her.[1]

Lack of evidence did not stop the provost marshal in Bowling Green from having strong opinions against Keys. "She is a rebel—a prostitute and a dangerous woman," he informed his counterpart in Gallatin. What proof he had that she prostituted herself is lacking in her file, and at that time prostitution in and of itself was not an offense in the eyes of civil or military law. Portraying one's enemies as sexual deviants, however, is a practice that goes back to Biblical times. Attacking Confederate women's sexual practices appears in the records, usually in witnesses' testimony. For example, a neighbor in Henry County, Missouri, described Mary Cull as "a woman of ill fame." Authorities arrested her in the summer of 1864, not for her sexual proclivities but for harboring and feeding bushwhackers. And in December 1864 a detective from the provost marshal general's office investigated a bawdy house operated by a woman named "Jinnie," described as a "notorious Rebel sympathizer." At issue was the rebel activity that allegedly went on in her establishment and not the business she conducted. Her accuser, by the way, was her recently divorced ex-husband.[2] Others faced accusations of being prostitutes or whores, as seen with Mary Ann Pitman, who encountered such characterizations on several occasions.

Union officials made no effort to regulate prostitution in St. Louis as they did elsewhere during the war. Nevertheless, a few prostitutes did face arrest for military-related infractions. For example, Clarinda Rasure, the Amesville, Kentucky, keeper of a house of ill repute, was taken into custody for passing counterfeit greenbacks. Mary Clark, already under arrest by St. Louis civil authorities for stealing $250 from a teamster at the brothel where she plied her trade, came under suspicion for being a Confederate spy after a search for the money found a rebel flag in her trunk. Accused of providing clothes and money to the Confederates and being a rebel mail operative, St. Louis prostitute Mary Byrne suffered banishment from the Department of the Missouri. A reopening of her case and new investigation found that she was the victim of vicious lies told by rivals who sought to get rid of her as their competition. Once exonerated, Byrne received transportation back to St. Louis, courtesy of the Union army. In one instance, however, five "lewd women whose presence endangered the health of the soldiers," presumably out of fear that they might spread venereal disease, were banished from Rolla and delivered under guard to St. Louis in June 1864. Nevertheless, Provost Marshal General Sanderson appears not to have done anything about them. The provost marshal general's office also routinely received complaints about brothels and saloons staffed by prostitutes, particularly when civil authorities failed to act. Such was the case of a saloon on Washington Avenue near the headquarters of the Department of the Missouri. According to the "Loyal Citizens" who signed a petition, "waiters of the female sex are in attendance" at the establishment. "These persons are of the vilest character, and in plain language it is a place of prostitution." The matter was delegated to the commander of the District of St. Louis, Colonel (and future provost marshal general) James H. Baker, who ordered the saloon to be shut down. He noted that "it is disreputable to have such a place so near [Department Headquarters], daily & nightly Enticing away the guard of the Maj. Gen. Comdg. himself." In this and other instances, the prevailing concern remained the impact these places had on the military and not necessarily the morality of the sex trade.[3]

Sarah Keys crossed not only gender lines in her disloyal activities, but also the lines of race. According to the account against her, she disguised herself as a "negro man" in carrying out the robbery of the former Union soldier. According to one source, the Alton Prison records listed Keys as a "white woman," which seems odd except for the fact that she arrived at the prison with another woman, a Mollie or Polly Jumper, identified as a "free Col'd woman." Authorities in Gallatin, Tennessee—the same authorities that took possession of Keys after her arrest—charged her with "belonging to a Guerrilla band." Jumper gained her release from custody at the same time that Keys did, with no further action brought against her. Jumper was not the only African American woman found in the custody of the Union army in St. Louis. In his diary, Alton prisoner Griffin Frost noted the arrival of "seventeen negro prisoners" sent from Vicksburg in mid-February 1865. "They were charged with mutiny," he continued, "tried by Commission, and sent here to serve out the sentence passed upon them." While the mutineers were most likely soldiers found guilty of disobedience, one prisoner was female. According to Frost, the other women in the prison, all white, put her to work as a "waiting maid." Frost tells no more about the female mutineer, and other records remain silent.[4]

More information is known about Sarah Guy and Harriet Martin, who both spent about three months together in the Gratiot Street Prison so that they could serve as witnesses in a case involving the steamer *White Cloud*. In mid-February 1863, inspectors discovered a large amount of mail along with other contraband on the boat when Federal authorities searched it while at Island No. 10 on the Mississippi River south of Cairo, Illinois. Along with the vessel's officers and crew, investigators arrested William J. Kribben of St. Louis, who was charged with helping to move the mail and for violating his oath of allegiance. They also took into custody Guy and Martin to serve as witnesses against Kribben. Exactly what information the two could provide that warranted arresting them and keeping them in prison is unclear from the records. Abundant evidence shows that African Americans, especially former slaves, quite willingly gave testimony against the disloyal when provided the chance. Nancy Kemp's former slave, for example, all too eagerly gave testimony concerning her ex-mistress's interactions with bushwhackers in Calloway County. Two others who knew Emma Weaver back in Arkansas gave testimony against her "Secesh" character and reputation. As for the testimony of Guy and Martin, the evidence against Kribben proved insufficient to find him guilty. Nevertheless, upon their release, Guy and Martin each received eighteen dollars for their appearances as witnesses.[5]

In another case, a "negro girl" known simply as Jennie was held as a witness against an accused thief. Known by several other aliases, Lizzie Hardin had been arrested along with a woman named Kate Slater for stealing money from a Union soldier in January 1864, only to be released three days later. A week and a half after that, military authorities again arrested Hardin and sent her to the Myrtle Street Prison. Evidently, this time the provost marshal had a witness against Hardin, Jennie, who was also taken into custody. In fact, the two shared the same room in the prison, no doubt creating a tense situation for both. A month after her second arrest, Hardin was ordered banished. What became of Jennie is unknown. In another case involving theft, a contraband woman named Mrs. Johnson testified that a Mollie Hobbs, a well-known customer in the local civil court, stole twenty dollars from her. In this instance, Hobbs gained release after returning the purloined money. These two incidents suggest that justice was not always meted out evenly, with the woman who stole from the soldier being punished much more severely than the one who took from the female former slave. Further, the Hardin case reveals the sometimes blurred lines between military and civilian justice during the war. The provost marshal's office handled Hardin's case of theft committed against a soldier, but that did not always happen. A year before Hardin's arrest, Anna Read and Mary Jasper got caught stealing a forty-dollar watch from a soldier. Civil authorities adjudicated their trial and punishment in the local criminal court, as was the case with Lizzie White, caught stealing from a soldier in July 1864. As the *Missouri Democrat* observed in early 1864, "It would seem that the boundaries between civil and military authority in criminal cases in this city are not very clearly defined, and a new code is much needed."[6]

Throughout the war that boundary between civil and military authority when it came to criminal activity remained ill defined. Early in the war, for example, when even the military remained unsure whether it could try the disloyal for treason in its courts, the April 1862 "Monthly Jail Report" from the St. Louis county jailor revealed inmates held on charges including larceny, robbery, selling liquor without a license, adultery, and six individuals committed to the jail on the charge of treason. The report gives no further record, and what became of the accused is unknown, but it is doubtful that they ever went to court on this charge. Nevertheless, the blurring of these lines apparently never became a major issue.[7]

In fact, in other cases, military authorities allowed some disloyal women to be dealt with by local authorities. For example, in an 1862 incident, Lieutenant Bishop of the St. Louis provost marshal's office decided to let his civil counterparts deal with a woman arrested on a Sunday evening for "rantingly abusing the Union soldiers, hurrahing for Jeff. Davis and creating a prodigious disturbance of the Sabbath tranquility." Also taken into custody were "two distracted cows" that the woman had with her when she committed this public disturbance. According to the *Missouri Democrat*, the "drunken she cessionist" had been brought to the Gratiot Street Prison after her arrest, but Bishop decided it best to turn her over to the "city calaboose." After all, she could be charged with being drunk and disorderly and disturbing the peace by the civil authorities, thus relieving the lieutenant from having to deal with the intoxicated troublemaker. What happened to the cows is unknown. Likewise, two years later military officials allowed the civil courts to prosecute Maggie Johnson, who in a drunken stupor had been loudly cheering Jefferson Davis.[8] Certainly, in many other cases where a Southern sympathizer publicly expressed support for the Confederacy, the accused suffered retaliation from the provost marshal's office, but not always.

If the influence of alcohol affected the military's response to certain disloyal females, sometimes so could their youth, as in the cases of sixteen-year-old Hannah Jane Martin and thirteen-year-old Katie O'Flaherty. Martha Longacre, the fourteen-year-old daughter of Nancy Longacre, gained her release from custody without a trial after her mother was acquitted by military commission of having fed bushwhackers. Age did not play a factor in dealing with fourteen-year-old Mattie Anderson. She and her nineteen-year-old sister Mollie had been banished from western Missouri through General Ewing's Order No. 11. Then, in December 1863, at least Mollie had been convicted of aiding guerrillas in Jackson County. She signed an oath and gave bond promising that she would not give further assistance to the rebels. A year later, military authorities arrested Mollie and Mattie in Howard County on unspecified charges. Sent to St. Louis, the two teens were ordered banished to the South. It did not help that they were the sisters of the notorious Missouri guerrilla "Bloody" Bill Anderson.[9]

Another teenage girl, Sarah Jane Smith, met with the full force of the Federal government. A native of Madison County, Arkansas, Smith devoted nearly two years to smuggling goods from Missouri to Confederate-occupied portions of her home state before escalating her activities to include sabotage. Caught in the act of cutting several miles of telegraph wire in southern Missouri, Smith first received a death sentence for the destruction. This sentence conformed with the dictates of General Orders No. 100, which states that "persons of the enemy's territory" caught cutting telegraph wires were not entitled to be treated as a prisoner of war with the protections that entails. "If captured," the code asserts, "they may suffer death." Found guilty by two thirds of the members of the commission that tried her, Smith was sentenced *"to be hung by the neck till dead, at such time and place as the General Commanding may direct."* General Rosecrans, commanding at the time, set the date for November 25, 1864. Until then, Smith would be confined to the Alton Prison.[10]

While Smith awaited her execution, the members of the military commission that found her guilty petitioned Rosecrans asking for "a mitigation of her sentence if consistent with public justice." Asking for mercy, they admitted that although she pled guilty to the charges, they thought Smith was "an ignorant country woman entirely unaware of the Enormity of the offence which she committed." Under the circumstances, the commission had no other course but to impose the penalty it did. Surprisingly, they did not mention her age as a factor. The *Missouri Democrat* described Smith as "green and untutored as a savage. In addition to her ignorance, she is subject to fits, and since her trial has had them every two or three days." Evidently swayed by the petitioners' argument, Rosecrans commuted Smith's sentence to imprisonment for the duration of the war. Nevertheless, he and others continued to press the teen to reveal the names of associates in her partisan activities. She refused.[11]

Griffin Frost gave a rather different image of Smith in his wartime journal. "The little telegraph girl" he described did not seem ignorant of what she had done. Rather, she appeared to be a defiant young woman proud of her actions. She boasted of being caught with the hatchet she used still in her hand and of refusing to reveal the names of her compatriots in sabotage. According to Frost, she told authorities that she would "rather be hung than tell." Smith had an "invincible determination not to be coaxed or scared into turning traitor against her friends," a trait that gained her the admiration and sympathy of Frost and the other female prisoners. Frost also never mentioned once that the young woman suffered from any kind of "fits." Smith remained in Alton until April 1865, when she gained release due to "extreme ill health," according to the *Missouri Democrat.*[12]

Teens were not the only minors found in the St. Louis-area prisons. Among the female prisoners could be found a number of their children. Many of the women banished south had their children with them as they spent time in one of the St. Louis female prisons before they departed together. In mid 1863, prisoner Edward Herndon Scott witnessed one child in the Alton Prison. A year later Griffin Frost noted that a Mrs. Mitchell had a daughter of five or six years old with her. He probably referred to Elvira Mitchel of Memphis, arrested for smuggling. Ten days before Caroline Billingsley of Carroll County, Arkansas, died from pneumonia on October 20, 1864, authorities at the Gratiot Street Prison turned her children Jesse and Blanche over to the care of the Sisters of Mercy religious order. Unknown is whether the Billingsley children were relocated due to their mother's illness or to the inappropriateness of the military prison as a place for the young. Also, Charles Grey, a boy of about ten orphaned when his mother Nancy Vaughn died in custody in March 1865, convinced authorities to send him to live with his uncle in Independence, Missouri. Another group of children ranging in age from fifteen to three, "having no friends or relations in this state," according to the *Missouri Democrat*, were sent to the House of Refuge, a reform school for juvenile offenders, on May 15, 1865, by order of the commanding officer of the Gratiot Street Prison. All initially had arrived in St. Louis with adults who had been ordered banished. With the war virtually over, however, the order was reversed. The children's mothers were released a week later, and the children presumably returned to them. Except for passing references in the military records, newspapers, and other accounts, very little is known about the children who spent time in the prisons with their mothers.[13]

At least one woman confined to the St. Louis-area military prisons was with child. Susan Kearney, the wife of a U.S. police officer working in the provost marshal general's office and five-months pregnant, arrived in the Myrtle Street Prison on late April 1864, having been accused of perjury and then conspiring "with the evil intent and wicked purpose of injuring, disgracing, and rendering infamous, the character and reputation of" the chief of the U.S. police, John Tallon. In a bizarre and convoluted case, Kearney claimed that earlier in April, while walking down the street she overheard Tallon talking with a woman she knew named Mary Douglas. She alleged that Tallon was trying to persuade Douglas to help him bring charges against a lieutenant named Henry H. Hines from a Colorado cavalry unit in order to get the soldier dismissed from military service. Accordingly, Douglas would go to Hines's apartment in St. Louis city early in the morning and offer to make shirts for him, but in the process somehow get Hines to insult her, enough so that upon her scream Tallon would enter the scene and arrest Hines. In exchange, Tallon would give Douglas one hundred dollars. Over the next several days, Kearney maintained, she met with Douglas and convinced her to swear a statement, or affidavit, exposing what Tallon plotted before Douglas left for New York state with her new husband, a Federal officer from that state. Kearney said that she went with Douglas to a lawyer and the affidavit was made. On Hines's behalf, Mrs. Kearney went to speak to Provost Marshal General Sanderson but found herself being interrogated by Sanderson and others about the crime of perjury. After five hours of questioning, Mrs. Kearney was allowed to leave but ordered to return the next day. When she returned, she was arrested. She spent several days in the Myrtle Street Prison before being transferred to the Gratiot Street Female Prison.[14]

Things went from bad to worse for Mrs. Kearney, as the provost marshal general moved to protect his chief of police. Furthermore, Olmstead Kellam, the lawyer who took the affidavit, and Alpheus Smith, the justice of the peace who notarized it, both swore that the woman who presented herself as Mary Douglas was, in fact, Susan Kearney. Authorities next arrested John Kearney for participating in what was now considered a conspiracy to destroy Peter Tallon's career. Once in custody, the Irish-born officer found other charges raised against him concerning his job performance. As for Henry Hines, who had been an assistant provost marshal general, he was already under investigation for aiding a slave trader in kidnapping African Americans in Missouri and spiriting them off to Kentucky for resale. Hines also warned the trader that the military police intended to arrest him. There were several other charges against Hines, and a court martial found him guilty on all counts in September 1864.[15]

As for Susan Kearney, she was pregnant with her fifth child. On May 12 the head of the Gratiot Street Prison hospital recommended to Sanderson that she be released, as she was "six months advanced . . . and in a delicate state of health." Sanderson declined. Husband John also sent numerous letter to Sanderson and to department commander William Rosecrans asking for Susan's release as well as a complete investigation of their cases, but to no avail.[16]

The Kearneys remained in custody into the summer of 1864, as Susan's due date fast approached. On August 9, Father F. J. Santois, a Jesuit priest affiliated with Saint Louis University, wrote to Colonel Sanderson on Susan's behalf. He stated that he had called on the Sisters of Charity at their hospital on Tenth and O'Fallon Streets and asked them if they could accommodate Mrs. Kearney. They told him that they had no objection and could provide a room for her, allowing no visitors except those on duty. Evidently, Kearney was moved and she had her baby, although the details remain elusive in the records. November 1 found Kearney still in the Sisters of Charity hospital, when orders were issued for her return to the Gratiot Street Prison. Two days later her trial began. The details of her trial are also unavailable, except that after a week the military commission hearing her case acquitted her of the charges and ordered her release.[17]

Oddly, one of the charges for which Lieutenant Hines was found guilty, "aiding and abetting the subordination of a witness, to the prejudice of military authority," related directly to the accusation against the Kearneys concerning the affidavit against Tallon allegedly filed by Susan. Her military commission found her not guilty of any wrongdoing in this matter. John Kearney, however, remained in custody. Three weeks after Susan's acquittal, he was released on oath and bond of $500 and ordered to report to the provost marshal general's office weekly in person or in writing. No record indicates that he ever faced a military commission of his own, leaving many details of this case left unanswered. It seems that the provost marshal general proved unwilling to pursue the matter any further.[18]

Considering how many women passed through the provost marshal general's custody in St. Louis during the war, it is likely that other pregnant women spent time in the female military prisons. Susan Kearney's pregnancy appears to be the only one that was recorded, and she did not give birth to the child in the prison. In a related note, however, Confederate prisoner Griffin Frost, at the time confined to the Gratiot Street Prison, noted "a scrap of gossip" circulating around the facility in April 1864, claiming that at the military prison at Rock Island, Illinois, "a portly young fellow in Confederate grey, was lately delivered of a fine boy—a new recruit for Uncle Jeff, of course." Eight months later the Sandusky, Ohio, *Commercial Register* reported from the Ohio military prison on Johnson's Island in Lake Erie that a Confederate officer gave birth to a "bouncing boy," or at least the author of the piece claimed to be "credibly informed" of such a birth. Considering the lack of corroborating evidence, one must wonder if the stories represent different versions of the same Civil War-era urban legend. Usually denied access to newspapers due to policy or circumstances, prisoners grasped for whatever information they could get.[19]

Occasionally in the prisons love was in the air, for better or for worse. Mollie Goggin, the Alton Prison inmate whom Mary Ann Pitman identified as having a romance with a lieutenant on the prison staff named Danforth gained her release from prison, according to Griffin Frost, "through the influence . . . of a gentlemanly Federal Lieutenant, to whom she is engaged to be married," probably Danforth. Goggin was not the only woman to obtain release through the intercession of an amorous soldier. On January 27, 1865, the *Missouri Democrat* reported the arrival in St. Louis of seven accused women from Chariton County. Originally eight women had been sent from that county, but the paper related that while delayed in Macon City, Missouri, one of them, Olivia Wall, fell in love with a Union soldier and agreed to marry him. Love, it seemed, had converted her from her disloyalty. Consequently, the provost marshal in Macon wrote to Provost Marshal General James Baker apprising him of the conversion of Miss Wall and pleading her case for a pardon. Baker agreed. The article continued, adding that another boy in blue smitten with one of the other women from this group directly petitioned Baker, requesting "the privilege of *Unionizing* one of the fair rebels in the same manner that his comrade had converted Miss Wall." In this case, Baker was not so accommodating. Four days after reporting of Olivia Wall's romance, the paper took pleasure in announcing that the lovelorn soldier, Corporal James H. Peyton, had been given permission by Baker to wed the "captivating captive," Miss Ada Boyce. He then ordered Boyce released "unconditionally," according to prison records, but unofficially on the condition that she become "Mrs. Corporal Payton."[20]

The *Missouri Democrat* further speculated that romance could be in the future for the remaining women, "five young girls and one middle aged female. . . . The girls are said to be good looking," and, the paper added snidely, "the old lady might do for a crippled soldier, or a Brigadier General without a command." A week later, the *Democrat* announced the impending marriage of a third woman from this group, Melissa Fox, who consented to wed Private William Coleman of the Missouri State Militia. Fox needed no pardon from Baker, as an investigation had deemed the evidence against her and her mother Isabella to be insufficient.[21]

Unknown is whether or not Mrs. Fox ever found herself a disabled veteran or unemployed brigadier general to espouse. Yet another woman from the group did find a husband. However, the marriage did not end well. While in custody, Miss Annie Payne caught the eye of a bugler from the Forty-Ninth Missouri Infantry named John C. Darnall. The *Missouri Democrat*, following the saga of the Chariton County women in serial form, reported that Darnall asked the new commanding general Grenville Dodge for permission to wed the "bushwhackeress" and he agreed. The provost marshal general sent for Miss Payne and when she arrived she confirmed her eagerness to marry the bugler. A justice of the peace was called for and the two were wed in the provost marshal general's office. The nuptials took place none too soon, as Darnall and his regiment were set to leave for Nashville that night. The separation served as a bad omen, as the Darnalls did not live happily ever after. Within two weeks it was discovered that Darnall already had a wife. Eighteen months earlier, according to several of the men of Darnall's regiment, the bugler had married another woman, who now resided with Darnall's cousin.[22]

Once in custody and back in St. Louis, Darnall told a melodramatic tale of love and betrayal. Two years prior, Darnall found true love with a young woman from Lincoln County, Missouri, near where his regiment was stationed.

The young woman's parents objected to the match, but Darnell persisted. Darnell finally forced the issue and thought that the resistant father had relented to the marriage. A ceremony took place, evidently with the bride heavily veiled, but when the ritual was done, Darnall claimed, he discovered that "another girl had been substituted for the one he loved!" He sought a divorce, but before it could be completed, his regiment was ordered to St. Louis. There he fell for Annie Payne, the new love of his life, and resolved to gain her freedom. Darnall and Payne wed, he left for Memphis, and she returned to Chariton County.

Darnall's fellow soldiers told a story that somewhat aligned with Darnall's, except for leaving out the part of a substitute bride and seeking a divorce. Whatever details clashed, one fact remained consistent: Darnall had a wife already. Upon Darnall's return to St. Louis, Provost Marshall General Baker decided to turn the whole matter over to civil authorities. The *Missouri Democrat* wrote sympathetically of Darnall, expressing hope that the circuit attorney in the case would "make some allowance . . . and not let the rude hand of the law scatter the tender blossoms of love." Darnall had "loved 'not wisely, but *two* well,' and many have thought that all was fair in love, as in war." Missing from the paper's account is any concern for the second Mrs. Darnall—Annie Payne.[23]

Not all Union soldier infatuations led to the release of a female prisoner. In July 1863, St. Louisan Mary Simpson was arrested for disloyalty and sent to the Female Military Prison. Soon after, Mrs. M. E. Hicks, the keeper of the prison, discovered the twenty-two-year-old prisoner attempting to escape with the aid of one of the guards, Jonathan Davis of the Eleventh Missouri Cavalry. Learning that the soldier had feelings for her, Simpson convinced him to help her escape, after which he should desert from the army so that the two could run off together to Kentucky. Instead, authorities arrested Davis, who maintained that he would eventually rescue Simpson from captivity. Simpson, on the other hand, admitted that she had no intention of going to Kentucky with Davis, nor did she harbor any love for him.[24]

While Davis ended up in prison for trying to help Mary Simpson escape, some women found themselves incarcerated for attempting to break men out. Anna Fickle's attempt to help a rebel guerrilla flee from custody went terribly wrong, and she suffered the consequences. In February 1864, Fickle participated in a plot to liberate Otho Hinton, a member of Andy Blunt's band of guerrilla fighters operating in central and western Missouri. Earlier in the war Blunt had served effectively under William Quantrill. Hinton had been captured in December 1863 and was being held in Lexington. On the night of February 22, two guards and their sergeant took the prisoner to the house of Mrs. Anna Reed for his evening meal. By all accounts a very attractive young woman, Fickle gladly agreed to help Hinton escape, as her bushwhacker brother had been killed by Federal soldiers a year earlier. Her role was to use her feminine wiles to ensure the cooperation of one of the guards, Private William Sabins. At seven o'clock, they plotted, the elderly Mrs. Reed, who was in on the scheme, would leave the dining room, then Sabins would disable the sergeant while Hinton made a break for the door with Blunt waiting outside. Sabins, however, chose not to cooperate. At the appointed time when Hinton made his move for the door the sergeant shot and killed him. Meanwhile, the other guard, who was in another room and had been bribed with money not to interfere, ran outside to find Blunt. Instead, he encountered other Federals and caught a lethal bullet from one of them. Blunt, too, was wounded, but managed to kill another Union soldier while making his escape, only to die two weeks later.[25]

Exposed by Private Sabins, Fickle and Reed were arrested, initially charged with "aiding and abetting the rescue of Hinton a Bushwhacker." They remained in custody in Warrensburg, Johnson County, through the rest of the winter and spring of 1864. On June 1, Reed gained release from "close confinement" due to "her age and infirmities" to await "further orders." It appears that she never experienced any kind of trial. Late that same month, Fickle also was released and sent to the residence of a local woman "in consequence of her serious Illness." Fickle would have her day in court, however. She was charged with a long list of infractions starting with "violations of the laws and customs of war." The specifics included "giving aid and comfort to the rebel enemies of the United States;" "murder" for the death of the soldier killed by Blunt; and "aiding and assisting the escape of military prisoners." Meeting in mid-August, the military commission found Fickle guilty on all charges, including second-degree murder, and sentenced her to ten years confinement in the Missouri State Penitentiary.[26]

Evidently, Anna Fickle had not learned her lesson about the dangers of trying to escape Federal custody. While in the Myrtle Street Prison awaiting her trial, Fickle caught the eye of a Nebraska soldier named Charles Warner, who was three quarters of the way through his one-year sentence for leaving his post and providing rebel prisoners with whiskey. The head cook for the prison guards, Warner evidently fell hard for Fickle and agreed to escape with her and run off together. Enlisting the aid of five other prisoners, Warner made a hole in the floor of the kitchen and then under the prison's floor they broke through two brick walls and almost through a third and to their freedom when guards discovered the six men and Fickle. The men, all Federal soldiers held for disobeying army regulations, could expect further punishment for their failed escape, except, of course, for the one already sentenced to death by firing squad. As for Anna Fickle, the prison staff was glad to see her off to the state penitentiary and to be done with her.[27]

Kate Beatty's apparent attempt to gain freedom for a Confederate prisoner, or at least to remove the death sentence from his head, did not go as planned, either. According to the *Missouri Democrat*, Beatty arrived in St. Louis on October 10, 1864, identifying herself as Mollie O. B. Wolf, the wife of Major Enoch O. Wolf, a Confederate officer in Federal custody in St. Louis. Wolf had the misfortune of being selected by then acting provost marshal general Joseph Darr to be executed in retaliation for the killing of a Union major and six other soldiers captured by Confederate guerrilla Tim Reeves. Beatty obtained a meeting with General Rosecrans at the Lindell Hotel and there she told him a tale of woe about how she had come to Missouri with her husband at the outset of Price's raid but stayed near Pilot Knob instead of joining the incursion. When she learned of her husband's capture and subsequent death sentence, she rushed to St. Louis to do what she could to get his life spared. After pleading for his life, the ersatz Mrs. Wolf offered to go back through the lines to convince Sterling Price to turn over the real culprit, Tim Reeves.[28]

After listening to Beatty and thinking her story questionable, the general sent for Darr and had her repeat it. She remained in the hotel under guard overnight and the next day again met with Darr who asked for further information. It took little time for her to stop cooperating. Under suspicion, Beatty found herself sent to the Gratiot Street Female Military Prison, while Darr had investigators look into details that she gave. The information they found did not match her story. Soon someone identified the imposter as Kate Beatty, who was already suspected of smuggling goods to the Confederates. Finally, when presented before Enoch Wolf, the major denied even recognizing Beatty.[29]

It is not clear exactly what Beatty wanted to accomplish. She simply may have sought to stop the execution, or perhaps she envisioned a broader plan to get Wolf released or to help him escape. Years later, an unexecuted Enoch Wolf claimed that guards told him Beatty intended to pass him money to use to bribe his way out of prison. Perhaps she just thought she could convince Rosecrans to let her back through the lines unmolested with contraband goods. She had offered to go to Price and ask him to turn over Reeves, which would have allowed her to return to the Confederacy. Instead, Beatty spent several weeks in close confinement, "alone . . . in irons [a ball and chain] . . . doubly guarded," per order of Rosecrans. Caught writing a letter to a fellow prisoner, a woman named Maria Ackerell with whom she was accused of smuggling, Beatty was also denied access to "books, papers, or writing materials."[30]

A military commission tried Beatty in early 1865 on charges of smuggling; "being a spy" on vague evidence that she had visited several Federal encampments on her way to St. Louis; and "fraudulent practices" for her impersonation of Mrs. Wolf. She pled guilty to the last charge, not surprisingly, as Major Wolf himself had testified against her. The commission, however, found her not guilty on the other charges and sentenced her to one month confinement, noting in the general order that reported the trial's result that "the Commission is thus lenient in this case, in view of the severity of the punishment inflicted upon the prisoner prior to her trial." Then the decision was made, most likely by new departmental commander Grenville Dodge, to remit the sentence, but to banish Beatty to the South "on account of the known disloyalty of the prisoner." As for Enoch Wolf, despite the protestations of outgoing commanding general William Rosecrans, President Lincoln ordered his execution suspended; in February, he gained release due to illness and returned to his home state of Arkansas to sit out the rest of the war. Inexplicably, the same day that Beatty departed for the South, the president telegraphed Dodge instructing that if Beatty "shall be sentenced to death," Dodge should notify Lincoln, and "postpone [the] execution till further order." By then, she was on her way down the Mississippi River.[31]

Kate Beatty's treatment while in custody represented the very rare exception and not the rule. Of the women held in custody in the St. Louis area, only Beatty appears to have been subjected to the ball and chain during the war. She probably received such harsh treatment because Rosecrans and Darr resented that she tried to pull the wool over their eyes so blatantly. Two other women imprisoned in the Gratiot Street facility at the same time as Beatty also were placed in close confinement and had pen and paper denied them. In this case the deprivation came in retaliation to the women managing to display a Confederate flag out of their window in the prison, a rather embarrassing situation for Federal authorities. In fact, in response the commander of the prison also recommended that the two be placed in irons as well, but it appears that their punishment did not go that far.[32]

Anna Fickle was not the only prisoner sent to the Missouri State Penitentiary. At least six others experienced the same fate, all found guilty of serious offenses. Five of the women had received sentences of specific durations, with Fickle facing by far the longest sentence at ten years, Martha Cassell receiving two years, and three others one year each. The two other women had been sentenced to confinement until the end of the war, but Pauline White's sentence also included hard labor, as did Martha Cassell's.[33]

It is unclear why President Lincoln believed that Kate Beatty had been sentenced to death, but such a sentence was not unheard of, such as in the case of

Mary Jane Smith. The sentence was never carried out, however. Accused spy Emma Weaver also received a death decree, but only after being sentenced in absentia because she had escaped from the St. Charles Street Female Prison. Weaver's sentence probably came in retaliation for her escape.[34]

While Smith and Weaver initially received death sentences, no Confederate women were executed during the course of the war. After the war, however, Federal authorities did put Mary Surratt to death for her involvement in the Lincoln assassination. Historian Elizabeth D. Leonard argues that while Victorian standards probably protected disloyal women from this extreme penalty, by the end of the war, especially after the president's death, the Northern public had grown weary of Southern women's treasonous activities. Thus, Mary Surratt became a surrogate for all rebel women who fought against the Federal government. On the other hand, a decade and a half after the war ended, Washington insider Horatio King claimed that President Andrew Johnson said on the eve of Surratt's execution that "there had not been 'women enough hanged in this war.'"[35]

Escapes from prison by women were rare, but not unknown. Isadore Morrison escaped in 1862, but from a hospital where she was being treated, not a prison. Susan Hardesty of Benton County, Missouri, arrested for spying in late October 1864, escaped from the Gratiot Street Female Prison a week later. And three women ordered banished in November 1863, Amanda Maddox, Mattie Maddox, and Mary Hall, failed to report to the steamer taking them south at the appointed time after having been released to settle their affairs.[36] Despite the dearth of escapes by women, in the fall of 1864, five female prisoners managed to escape from the St. Charles Street Female Prison—Emma Weaver, Clarinda Mayfield, Sarah Waitman, Elizabeth Newcome, and Missouri Wood—causing an investigation and the closing of that facility. With the exception of the fall 1864 escapes, the military did a good job at keeping its female prisoners behind bars. Nevertheless, the arrest of rebellious women by the Union army created many challenges that the military had to overcome or at least manage. Arguably, the biggest issue was related to providing proper housing for their rebels in crinoline. This ongoing situation would trouble officials, despite their best efforts to deal with it.

The early weeks of the war witnessed great tension and a few outbursts of violence in the streets of St. Louis. Original caption: "United States volunteers attacked by the mob, corner of Fifth and Walnut Streets, St. Louis, Missouri (sketched by M. Hastings, Esq.)." COURTESY OF THE LIBRARY OF CONGRESS, CIVIL WAR COLLECTION, LC-USZ62–132566.

Major General Henry Halleck commanded the Department of the Missouri before becoming general-in-chief of the army. COURTESY OF THE MISSOURI HISTORICAL SOCIETY, ST. LOUIS.

A former medical college, the Gratiot Street Military Prison held
Confederate prisoners of war as well as civilian prisoners, including many
women. COURTESY OF THE MISSOURI HISTORICAL SOCIETY, ST. LOUIS.

George E. Leighton served as provost
marshal in St Louis in 1861 and
1862. COURTESY OF THE MISSOURI
HISTORICAL SOCIETY, ST. LOUIS.

Confederate mail currier Absalom Grimes supervised a network
of operatives, including many women, who collected and passed
contraband mail between rebel soldiers and their loved ones behind
Union lines. COURTESY OF THE MISSOURI HISTORICAL SOCIETY, ST. LOUIS.

Right, Arrested for smuggling, passing contraband mail, and other offenses, Margaret A. E. McLure was banished beyond the lines in May 1863. After the war she became a major promoter of the Lost Cause myth. COURTESY OF THE MISSOURI HISTORICAL SOCIETY, ST. LOUIS. *Below*, New York native, Mexican War veteran, and Confederate general Daniel Frost commanded the pro-Confederate Missouri Militia that gathered at Camp Jackson in St. Louis during the early days of the war. COURTESY OF THE MISSOURI HISTORICAL SOCIETY, ST. LOUIS.

Left, Eliza Frost, the wife of Daniel Frost, was banished beyond the lines in 1863. Union authorities had intercepted illicit communications between her and her husband. COURTESY OF THE MISSOURI HISTORICAL SOCIETY, ST. LOUIS. *Below*, Before her arrest and banishment, Ada Haynes regularly exchanged letters with Confederate prisoners of war in the Gratiot Street Military Prison and other prisons in the North. COURTESY OF THE MISSOURI HISTORICAL SOCIETY, ST. LOUIS.

James O. Broadhead served as the provost marshal general of the Department of the Missouri in 1863. COURTESY OF THE MISSOURI HISTORICAL SOCIETY, ST. LOUIS.

Illinois's former state penitentiary, the Alton Military Prison (in the foreground), sat near the banks of the Mississippi River. It housed several dozen female prisoners who each spent many months in custody between 1863 and 1865. COURTESY OF THE MISSOURI HISTORICAL SOCIETY, ST. LOUIS.

The Commission was then cleared for
deliberation and having maturely
considered the evidence adduced
finds the accused as follows (viz)

Of the first specification Guilty. Two thirds of
the Commission concurring

Of the Second specification Guilty. Two thirds of
the Commission concurring

Of the Charge Guilty. Two thirds of
the Commission concurring

And the Commission does therefore
Sentence her the said Sarah J. Smith
to be hung by the neck till dead at
such time and place as the General
Commanding may direct. Two thirds
of the Commission concurring in
the Sentence

[signature]
2d Lieut 12th Mo Cavly
Judge Advocate

[signature]
Col 3 Mo Cavly
Prest.

A military commission in Arkansas found teenager Sarah Jane Smith guilty of cutting telegraph wires and sentenced her to death. The commission later reconsidered the sentence, which was commuted. She remained in custody in the Alton Prison until being released due to failing health. SARAH JANE SMITH TRIAL PROCEEDINGS—1864, SARAH JANE SMITH PAPERS, 1864–1865 [MC 736], SPECIAL COLLECTIONS, UNIVERSITY OF ARKANSAS LIBRARIES, FAYETTEVILLE.

Right, Union Major General William Rosecrans tangled with many disloyal women while leading forces in Tennessee in 1863 and then commanding the Department of the Missouri in 1864. COURTESY OF THE MISSOURI HISTORICAL SOCIETY, ST. LOUIS. *Below,* Horace E. Dimick operated a gun shop on North First Street in St. Louis. Acting as an undercover agent for Provost Marshal General Joseph Darr, Mary Ann Pitman attempted to engage Dimick in illegal sales of weapons. COURTESY OF THE MISSOURI HISTORICAL SOCIETY, ST. LOUIS.

Charged with smuggling,
Missouri Wood remained
confined to the St. Charles Street
Military Prison for Women
until her escape in October
1864. COURTESY OF THE MISSOURI
HISTORICAL SOCIETY, ST. LOUIS.

After the war, habitual troublemaker Drucilla Sappington apparently
remained well behaved. In the 1870s she moved with her husband
to Texas, where she died in 1906. COURTESY OF BETSY DEITERMAN,
CURATOR, POLK COUNTY MEMORIAL MUSEUM, LIVINGSTON, TEXAS.

The gravesite of Jane Foster in the Jefferson Barracks National Cemetery, St. Louis, Missouri. COURTESY OF THE AUTHOR.

The gravesite of Nancy Jane Vaughn in the Jefferson Barracks National Cemetery, St. Louis, Missouri.
COURTESY OF THE AUTHOR.

CHAPTER 8

"The Female Military Prison
. . . Is Continued"

When John Sanderson became incapacitated by the illness that took his life on October 14, 1864, Sanderson's first assistant Joseph Darr became acting provost marshal general. Previously, Darr had been the provost marshal in Wheeling, West Virginia, where he had his share of experience with rebellious women. According to a Southern sympathizer, Darr could be "amenable to reason." Perhaps that explains Darr's response when he learned of the whereabouts of St. Charles Street Prison escapee Missouri Wood. Just after Darr took over as provost marshal general, his officers intercepted a letter from Wood sent from Windsor, Canada, to her family in St. Louis. After about a month of considerable deliberation, Darr devised a plan of action. By then fears over the Order of the American Knights had dwindled, and any damage Missouri Wood could do from Canada as a spy was negligible. Rather than taking her family members into custody to force her return or sending agents to Canada to capture her, Darr simply wrote Wood a letter. Darr's letter, dated November 16, is not in Wood's file, but her response to it tells much. What Darr wanted to know about was how she escaped from the St. Charles Street Prison.[1]

The St. Charles Street Female Military Prison was one of several facilities used to house women during the war. In an environment in which the Union army was unprepared to deal with the influx of male military prisoners caused by the war, the addition of female prisoners made that task all the more troublesome. The issue of gender shaped and reshaped Federal authorities' approaches to the treatment of prisoners. By 1864, having female prisoners in custody in the St. Louis area had become commonplace but not without its problems. Many of these women found themselves held in the army's prisons for weeks or even months, either waiting for their cases to be adjudicated or serving sentences for their crimes. Little is known about life within the various facilities used as prisons for women, but the records do reveal some images. The extant evidence about the prisons that housed women exposes that as the war progressed, accommodating female prisoners remained a pressing problem. Furthermore, the picture we have of the female prisoners suggests that for many, arrest and imprisonment did little to weaken their rebelliousness and commitment to the Confederate cause.

In St. Louis, most of the women confined early in the war were held in the Gratiot Street Prison. A former medical college, the building had been confiscated from its owner Joseph McDowell after he fled St. Louis to join the Confederate army with his sons. The college, an imposing structure that resembled a fortress, sat on the northwest corner of Eighth and Gratiot Streets, extending northward along the former. At its center stood an octagonal-shaped domed building or tower, made of gray stone and taller than the two-story wings that reached out on either side to the north and south. Once the Federals possessed the building, they converted classrooms, laboratories, and other rooms to accommodate prisoners. In this transformation, the dissecting room became the prison's mess hall. The Gratiot Street Prison housed both Confederate prisoners of war as well as civilian prisoners arrested for disloyalty. Through mid-1862 and into 1863 that included the female prisoners kept for more than a day.[2]

An inspection that took place just before female inmates began populating the prison suggested that the facility was in fairly good shape at that time, although some improvements could be made. For example, a window in a room from which a neighboring building's roof could be accessed needed iron bars. Otherwise, the inspector concluded, "escape from the prison [was] impossible provided that the guard discharges its duty." The inspector's optimism about the security of the prison failed to match the determination and cleverness of the male prisoners in finding their way out. In fact, the inspector's recommendations to separate the military prisoners from civilian ones and to isolate prisoners sentenced to death contributed to the escape of Absalom Grimes, one of the most prominent civilian prisoners to come into the hands of Federal authorities. In the escape, female prisoners played a key role. In his memoir, Grimes recorded that in the prison he was isolated from the general population, placed in the structure identified as the "old McDowell dwelling," located behind the former school. The room on the first floor that held him shared a wall with a room confining two female prisoners, Drucilla Sappington and Elisabeth Sigler. Both women knew Grimes and had helped him in his work in the past. The wall between the two rooms, described by Grimes as parlors, contained a folding door, and although it was securely closed, Grimes and the women could speak with each other through it. Grimes also communicated with visitors that his neighbors were allowed. Grimes's room had only a rocking chair and a mattress on the floor; the decor of the women's room remains unknown. Considering that the women were permitted guests, their room was probably less spartan. Grimes also mentioned visiting an outhouse, which may or may not have been used by the women. As for his escape, Grimes slipped through a hole in the floor created by the removal of three planks and then cut his way through a wall to the outside with tools he obtained. This took more than one instance, and each time Grimes went into the hole, Sappington created the illusion that he was still in his room by rocking the squeaky rocking chair via a string attached to it that extending to her room through the secured door. Meanwhile, Sigler danced about the women's room singing loudly and otherwise making noise to cover up any sounds made by Grimes. Confinement did nothing to dampen these women's rebelliousness, especially Drucilla Sappington, who remained resolute in her convictions. Once out of prison she resumed her clandestine activities to aid the Confederacy and would have a second run in with Federal authorities.[3]

About six months later, Mary Louden and Lucie Nickolson spent time in the Gratiot Street Prison before they were banished beyond the lines in May 1863. Rather than occupying the old McDowell residence, the two stayed in the main prison. According to Nickolson's postwar account, authorities placed them in the former medical school's cadaver dissecting room, evidenced by the room's still blood-stained tables and floors. If true, the prison must have adopted a new mess hall. Nickolson also stated that their room was located below the prison hospital and underwent a deluge of dirty water coming through the ceiling every time prison personnel washed the hospital floor. Nickolson claimed that this shower usually came at meal times, befouling the women's food. The only thing that sustained them was food delivered by the Sisters of Charity, who came every day to visit the Catholic Mrs. Louden. Nickolson described a straw pallet on the floor upon which the two women slept. One evening, she recounted, Louden detected something moving in the straw; the source turned out to be two mice. Nickolson also reported that the commander of the prison verbally harassed the women on a regular basis during their stay in Gratiot Prison before Provost Marshal General Franklin Dick relocated the two women to Margaret McLure's Chestnut Street home. One might accuse the former rebel of exaggerating in her postwar reminiscence, but another prison inspection performed three months after Nickolson's stay confirmed the leakage problem during floor washings. Also, Colonel George W. Kincaid of the Thirty-Seventh Iowa Infantry, the regiment guarding the prison when it held Nickolson, had a strong antisecessionist reputation and often produced outbursts insulting Southern women in front of the male inmates.[4]

Margaret McLure's home on Chestnut Street, which quickly became known as the "female prison," surely must have been more comfortable than the prison on Gratiot Street, despite the fact that McLure's possessions and furnishings had been removed—they would be sold at auction by the government—and replaced with simple cots. There, McLure, Louden, Nickolson, and at least eight other confined women, including Drucilla Sappington, remained in the care of a matron, Mrs. M. E. Hicks, who would later be described as a "kind-hearted woman." According to one inmate's postwar account, the prisoners had little privacy in the mansion's now crowded space, and the food served remained inferior. Typical fare included hardtack, rotten bacon, and unpalatable coffee. After McLure and most of the first set of detainees left for the South, the house continued to hold female prisoners for another month before being closed, only to be reopened for that purpose later in the war. On June 11, 1863, the McLure house's remaining prisoners were transferred to a larger house, the former residence of Confederate sympathizers Edward Dobyns and his daughter Mary. The house, authorities believed with good reason, had been abandoned property. Located on Twelfth Street north of Howard Street, it was already empty, as the elder Dobyns had its contents packed up and put in storage before he left St. Louis. According to one source, the prisoners were "allowed the freedom of the house and yard, excepting the cellars and front parlor."[5]

Little more is known about the Dobyns house, except that the women were supervised by Mrs. Hicks, the same matron found at the Chestnut Street Prison. By now her kind heart had been tempered by the unruliness of her charges, as she noted that "the rebel women cut up awful shines." One prisoner Hicks encountered concerned her so much that she swore a statement to the provost marshal general. Marion Wall Vail, arrested as a member of the Confederate mail-carrying ring broken up in the spring of 1863, exhibited conduct that was "very riotous and abuseful to the Government," according to Hicks. Vail also used insulting language, "saying that she did not think it right for the Darned abolition Government to put such 'Darned' old union Hags over decent people." Too prim to write "damned," Hicks added, rather dejectedly, "I suppose, in fact I know that she meant me when she said 'old union Hags.'" In short, according to Hicks, Vail was "one of the most rebellious and insulting prisoners in my charge, in fact the worst—save Mrs. Sappington."[6]

Critical of all the female Confederate prisoners was a member of the Thirty-Seventh Iowa Infantry assigned to guard the St. Louis military prisons, who reported that "he would rather guard crocodiles and wild boars than secesh women. They sing the secession songs, and indulge in a variety of rebel demonstrations." A regiment primarily made up of men forty-five years of age and older, the "Greybeards," as they were known, had a reputation for kindness in the treatment of prisoners, their colonel notwithstanding. Evidently, the female prisoners had worn out this soldier's patience.[7] The Dobyns house continued as a prison until September 1863 when its last inmate, Hannah Ward, was banished. Ward, the sister of a former mayor of St. Louis, had been under the scrutiny of the provost marshal's office from September 1862, when neighbors presented a petition identifying Ward as "a scourge to the loyal people in her neighborhood and an avowed enemy of the Government of the United States" and calling for her banishment from the city. Authorities took no action at that time, but a year later after more accusations that she "frequently, causelessly, and wantonly exercised her lingual powers in impertinent abuse of her Union neighbors and the Union Government," arrest and banishment became her fate. Banishment did not hinder Ward's loyalty to the Confederacy. Instead of the South, Ward went to Canada, where evidently she became an operative of the Confederates. She was detained once in New York City only to be released due to lack of evidence, only to be arrested later in Detroit in August 1864.[8]

Authorities also used another building at 61 St. Charles Street as a prison for women. Located on the north side of the city, the St. Charles Street Female Prison may have been the residence situated between 5th and 6th Streets identified as a potential prison in February 1862. A major who inspected the site proposed that the structure might house up to seventy-five prisoners. Although it never entertained that many people, the facility opened for business by at least May 1864 and operated until October. Despite the use of this and other locations to hold them, the Gratiot Street Prison continued to receive women in 1864 and 1865. Authorities used different parts of the former medical college at different times to confine women. For instance, in an inspection report made in February 1864, U.S. surgeon and acting medical inspector of prisoners of war A. M. Clark described a room housing two female prisoners. This second-floor room, according to the report, was "about 12 by 5 by 8 feet in dimensions, with two windows, both of which were nailed down and the door locked. When the door was closed," the document continued, "the only possible supply of air was through a partly broken pane of glass." To make matters worse, according to Clark, the "air of the room was rendered still more foul by a close stool [portable toilet], which bore evidence of not having been cleansed for some time."[9]

The Myrtle Street Prison, the former slave pen, also continued to receive women. In August 1864, another investigator found ten women in a room larger than the one in Gratiot, but he estimated that this room, which contained no more than 2,400 cubic feet of air, was adequate for three prisoners at the most. In response, inspector of prisons Major Gustav Heinrichs recommended that the women in the Myrtle Street Prison be transferred to the Gratiot Street Prison and placed in "the so-called lower round room," the lower level of the building's central tower. He described it as "a large and airy room, and perfectly isolated from the other rooms." The room, sixty feet in diameter, at one time held 250 male prisoners. At the time that Heinrichs made his suggestion, the room was divided in half, holding one female prisoner on one side and a male—a counterfeiter ordered to be held in isolation—on the other.[10]

Just a few weeks later, a new female prison opened. The new facility, across the street from the existing Gratiot Street Prison—probably the three-story brick home that had housed prison guards earlier in the war—was deemed by Major Heinrichs "a very suitable place" for women. In fact, he had consulted an architect to verify the structure's safety, no doubt in response to the collapse of a building used to hold female prisoners in Kansas City a year earlier. Despite these moves, within a month Major Heinrichs and others discussed opening a new prison for women; in fact, he had already identified "a certain building situating on Tenth street between Clark avenue and Walnut street" as a possible new site.[11]

By this time, Heinrichs felt the new pressing need caused by the closing of the St. Charles Street Female Prison. On October 21, Joseph Darr ordered the location shut down after several successful and embarrassing escapes. Its remaining prisoners were sent to the new Gratiot Street Prison for women across the street from the original lock up. The *Missouri Democrat* called the St. Charles Street Female Prison "the receptacle of so many of the notorious female spies and mail carriers that have been caught in St. Louis." The building's first floor contained a kitchen and dining room as well as a sitting room. The second floor held the prisoners' bedrooms and a residence for the prison keepers William Dickson and his wife, Margaret, along with their teenage daughter and younger son. The prison staff also included an African American cook and a "colored girl" named Mary who carried out various errands for the staff and inmates. Guards could be found at the prison only over night; by breakfast time they were usually gone. The property had a backyard surrounded by an iron fence with a locked gate that led to an alley. Inside the building, according to Margaret Dickson, the women had "the run of the house."[12]

The prison's trouble keeping its inmates secured began in September 1864. Little is known about the first woman to escape, a Mrs. Newcome, who made her getaway shortly before Missouri Wood fled the prison. According to an affidavit sworn out by Wood, living safe from the long arm of the military law in Canada, one evening before sundown, Newcome went into the backyard, evidently negotiated the lock on the gate with ease, and made her way into the alley. From there she circled around to the front of the building on St. Charles Street. Watching for her from a second floor window facing the street, Wood threw a bonnet out to Newcome, as she would have drawn attention with her head uncovered in public. The bonnet landed in the street, according to Wood, right in front of a first floor window where William Dixon and an officer named Lieutenant Dodge were discussing a recent horse race. Newcome had to scoot to get it, and Wood found it surprising that neither Dixon nor Dodge saw her. With bonnet on head, Newcome then walked down St. Charles Street and got on a street car, never to be seen again.[13]

A few days later, on September 26, Wood made her escape along with Emma Weaver, who had sworn she would "make her way out" of the prison, even if she had to "shoot her way out." According to Margaret Dickson's witness statement, when the two did not come down for their breakfast and could not be found in their room upstairs, a search revealed that they had exited the property by way of the back gate using a filed key that they left behind. Asked if she knew how they got the key, Mrs. Dickson claimed she did not know but added that "there were 20 ways by which they could get it. It could have been thrown through the fence at the back of the prison; it might have been given them while they were talking to their friends, who had passes to see them. . . . They might have slipped the key from one to the other while [Mr.] Dickson had his back turned to open the door or something of that kind." She added that it might have been provided by Mr. Weaver, who recently brought his daughter crackers and doughnuts, implying that the key might have been hidden within the delivery. Whatever the case, Mrs. Dickson asserted that while the women may have found a key in the prison and altered it to open the lock, it was her "impression" that "it was got outside." Mr. Dickson thought that it was Weaver's father who provided the key, adding that he believed it was "Miss Weaver that get up the plans, & the other woman merely followed." Emma, the Dickson's teenage daughter, also insisted that the key must have come from outside the prison.[14]

Less than a month later, sisters Clarinda Mayfield and Sarah Waitman made their breakout. Mary Ann Pitman, who was in the prison at the time, reported that she had awoken at six thirty the morning of October 19 and noticed that the front door was ajar. She informed William Dixon, and when the two investigated, they found that the screws holding the clasp of the door's lock in place had been removed using the tip of a knife, which allowed the door to be opened. The clasp could not be found, but the screws were left lying by the door, along with a pair of women's hose, oddly enough. Asked if she had heard either prisoner suggest her plan, Pitman related that the two women told her that they learned that the St. Charles Street Prison was to be shut down and they would be sent to the Alton Prison, a fate they found unacceptable. Mayfield and Waitman asked Pitman if she wanted to abscond with them; she declined. Pitman stated that she had told Dickson of the prisoners' intent, but he did not act.[15]

Two days later, Provost Marshal General Darr closed the prison and transferred the remaining inmates to the new female prison on Gratiot Street. Nevertheless, the mystery of the exodus from the St. Charles Street Prison remained, that is, until Darr made contact with Missouri Wood in Canada. In response to Darr's request for information concerning her escape, Wood revealed that she would give evidence only if the military guaranteed protection for her mother, brother, sister, and children. Wood seemed anxious to help, but wanted assurances, adding that if she divulged what she knew, she feared that she would be "hunted down & persecuted" by friends of those her "testimony of the facts as they occurred will implicate." In his letter, Darr evidently suggested that he already suspected an officer who visited the prison regularly, Lieutenant Dodge, as an accomplice of the escapees. One reason suspicion fell on Dodge concerned information Mary Ann Pitman had related in her testimony against Emma Weaver. Dodge visited Weaver often, apparently having a romantic interest, and Weaver boasted that she could count on him to help her get out of the prison. "I can assure you now the person refered [sic] to in your letter," Wood stated, probably meaning Dodge, "is not the most guilty." That person had been "used as a tool in the hands of those higher in power."[16]

With assurances made that her family would be protected, Wood gave a sworn statement taken in Canada. "The whole management of my escape from the female prison in Saint Louis," she declared, "was made by [William] Dixon as far as I know." Wood explained that she had given Dickson $4,000 from money entrusted to her by her husband that she had smuggled into the prison hidden in her undergarments. Dickson said that he and Lieutenant Dodge would use the money to aid in securing from authorities in Washington her release. After a few weeks she pressed Dickson on the status of her case. He said that Dodge had made the application for her release, complete with her money, but to no avail. Dickson next proposed another course of action. For an additional $1,000 he could provide Wood with a key to the back gate, which she could use to escape. Wood agreed. Soon, Dickson provided the key, and Wood the money. The next day she made her escape. As she had while in custody, Wood continued to deny any guilt. "I made my escape from the prison—not because I have ever done anything to justify my imprisonment—but because I had learned so much, while I was in there, of the corruptness of the management of the prison that I almost despaired of ever getting out, by trial or otherwise," she explained. "During the time I was so imprisoned, I was badly treated by the said Dixon, and on several occasions heard him abuse, and ill treat others who were with me confined in said Prison." Dickson had told her that she would either remain in prison for the rest of the war or be shot. Thus, she became desperate to escape.[17]

Evidence arose prior to Wood's accusations suggesting that Dickson was up to something mischievous. Two weeks after Wood escaped, Michael Nolan, an officer who regularly escorted prisoners between the prisons and the provost marshal general's office, gave a statement relating that while escorting Wood, she had told him something he found suspicious. Wood told him that Dickson had informed Emma Weaver, who was awaiting sentencing, that the judge advocate general had already decided that she would be sent to the Alton Prison for the rest of the war. Nolan thought this information dubious, because he knew that the judge would not share this kind of information with the jail keeper. Soon after, he heard this same information from Weaver's father. Fear of being sent to Alton for the duration of the war in large part motivated both Wood and Weaver to escape. It also served as a catalyst for Clarinda Mayfield and Sarah Waitman's elopement. In each case, the information that these women would be sent to Alton—and Alton, in fact, may have been the destiny for some or all of them—originated with Dickson. At least one, Missouri Wood, paid him $4,000 to facilitate her escape. Upon receiving Wood's sworn statement, Joseph Darr ordered the arrest of William Dickson.[18]

Missouri Wood was not the only person to complain of corruption and bad treatment in the St. Charles Street Female Prison. Shortly after the authorities closed the prison, they launched an investigation of the Dicksons' management. The inquiry revealed demands for bribes, stealing from the prisoners, poor quality food, denial of use of the toilet facilities, and other wrongdoing. What came of these revelations is unclear, and considering that all charges against William Dickson were dropped in the end of January 1865, nothing probably resulted from the investigation. Years later, one woman who had been imprisoned on St. Charles Street during the location's last months of operation noted that when she and others were transferred to the new female prison on Gratiot Street, they "met men in Federal garb who were gentlemen. We were treated as human beings, every attention was shown us that was consistent with the rules and regulations of war."[19]

Identifying what women were assigned to any given prison in St. Louis at any given time is difficult, if not impossible, because of the incomplete, over-lapping, and at times inaccurate records that remain. The records do indicate that during 1864 at least two hundred women spent time in the female military prisons of the St. Louis region, including at least sixteen who were sent to the Alton Prison in Illinois. Alton began receiving female prisoners in 1863, sent primarily from Tennessee on charges related to spying and smuggling. In 1864 the prison also began to entertain rebel women from Missouri, found guilty of serious offenses and sent to Alton to complete their sentences. Sergeant Edward Herndon Scott of the Confederate Sixth Missouri Infantry left a vivid description of the prison as he found it in mid-1863, at a time when Alton held five women. Scott, who spent more than a month in Alton Prison between his capture in May 1863 and his transfer to Virginia for exchange in June, wrote the following:[20]

> Fifteen hundred of us were crowded into a place a hundred yards square at least two thirds of which space is occupied by buildings. You are aware that it has been condemned, as a place too loathsome and unhealthy for common felons, *so as the very place* it is made a Confederate prison. The hospital was full all the time we were there and loathsome contagion stalked abroad in the crowd. There were from a dozen to twenty cases of smallpox there all the time and I have seen men walking about the yard with it as pustules just breaking out on them, and men laid in the room where we slept till they got badly off with it before they were removed.
>
> We were constantly liable and some did take a still more loath-some and injurious contagion from the privies. Lice was as "thick as lice in Egypt." To keep clear of them was impossible. To walk across the yard after dark one would have to kick the rats out of the way and one was in positive danger of being bitten by them while he slept. . . . The water we had to use was a rotten limestone, that tasted sour and loathsome at first but I got used to it and the rats in it. It could only be drunk fresh from the well.[20]

The women Scott encountered at Alton, of course, were not housed among the general population of prisoners of war. Nevertheless, being within the prison compound, they certainly could not avoid being affected by the conditions Scott portrayed so vividly.

Scott provided no description of the accommodations made for the women, but a report that A. M. Clark, acting medical inspector of prisoners of war, filed with the commissary general of prisons, William Hoffman, on February 18, 1864, does shed some light. In his inspection of the prison, Clark found "three female prisoners now confined in a damp, half-underground room, only partitioned off from an open cellar." He added in disgust, the women's "present condition is an outrage on humanity." As a result, Clark requested that then prison commander Colonel William Weer—one of Alton's nine commanding officers—place the women "in quarters more appropriate to their sex" as soon as possible. To his satisfaction Clark found this request met before his next visit to the prison in late March 1864, although he failed to mention what Weer had done for the women.[21]

Providing adequate accommodations for female prisoners proved to be only one problem faced by prison officials at Alton, and no doubt elsewhere. There were others. For instance, on July 11, 1863, Weer's predecessor Major T. Hendrickson wrote to Hoffman questioning how clothing for destitute women prisoners was to be purchased. Arrangements already existed for providing male prisoners of war with replacement clothes when necessary. Hoffman resolved the issue by informing Hendrickson that such expenditures should come from the general prison fund. This practice continued, as revealed by the records of the prison account for April 1864. It reflected the purchase of "four complete Suits of Female Clothing," each costing $12.50. The record further specified that the clothes were "for use of Female Prisoners confined to the Alton Military Prison, discharged from the Small-pox Hospital."[22]

Hendrickson also contacted Hoffman concerning payment for washing Clara Judd's clothing. Evidently Judd was not expected to wash her own apparel as male prisoners were. Hendrickson's predecessor had used the general fund to cover the cost, but Hendrickson questioned whether this was proper. Finally, when Judd's health began to decline in May 1863, Andrew Wall, the surgeon in charge of the prison's hospital, informed Hendrickson that the "utter impossibility of having any of her own sex to attend her in sickness" made it hopeless to provide her with proper care. This fact contributed to the decision to release Judd.[23]

The Civil War disrupted the daily routines and rituals of women, especially in the South. With a high proportion of white southern men off to war, many new tasks and responsibilities fell on the shoulders of Confederate women, especially those of the slave-owning class. Moreover, Confederate women felt the personal loss of having their men gone, as wives sent to war their partners and mates, and single women lost their pool of suitors to the ranks of the military. The white population of many Southern communities during the war became overwhelmingly female, save the old men and young boys, and would remain so throughout the war. Soldiers, too, experienced this gender imbalance as they engaged in their new responsibilities in the army. Soldiers struggled to recreate what was familiar to them in their peacetime existences while enduring the hardships and rigors of military service. Particularly troublesome to the men was the masculine nature of army life. As Reid Mitchell observed in his study of Northern men going off to war, soldiering left the men in uniform desperate for the company of women, and not necessarily for sexual companionship. Northern soldiers sensed a sincere void in their lives because of the limited contact they had with women and the feminine influence that they felt missing in the military world.[24] Although the soldiers in gray had the advantage of spending most of the war on friendly turf, one can easily imagine Southern men making the same complaint of life in the Confederate camps.

This situation differed little, in fact, was even worse, for those imprisoned during the war. In the Alton Prison, however, a few Confederate officers and Southern women were able to re-establish some balance of the type of gender relationships they experienced before the war. The unique circumstances at Alton allowed at least some of the female inmates to maintain gender-related customs that stemmed from mid-nineteenth-century notions of domesticity. Within the walls of the prison, these women and their Confederate officer counterparts did their best to replicate the interactions with members of the opposite sex that they were accustomed to having during times of peace. Much of what we know about the developments in the Alton Prison comes from the postwar memoir of Missourian Griffin Frost, a captain who spent several months in Alton during the war's last year. Frost had been imprisoned at Alton for a short time in early 1864 before authorities sent him to the Gratiot Street Prison in St. Louis. Frost then returned to Alton on October 3, 1864; at this time he found conditions in the prison much improved since his first stay. He also characterized the officers in charge of the prison as being "very sociable," despite their strictness. This opinion of the camp's leadership changed little when the day-to-day oversight of the camp shifted from Lieutenant Robert St. G. Dyhrenforth to Major James M. Morgan a few weeks after Frost's arrival. While Brigadier General Joseph Copeland served as the prison commander during most of Frost's stay at Alton, it was Morgan with whom he and the other prisoners had most of their interactions.[25]

Frost took quick interest in the prison's female population. Three days after his arrival, he noticed that from the prison yard he could see the windows of the rooms of some of the women prisoners. It would be at these windows that the musical group organized by Frost and some of his fellow officers, "the band" as they called it, would serenade the women. The women found the attention quite enjoyable, and they rewarded the musicians with "very handsome bouquets" tossed from the window. Visiting the women and carrying on conversation with them at their window—what Frost called "window gossip"—became a common activity between the rebel officers and the female prisoners. Indeed, such contact proved to be the highlight of the day on several occasions. Interaction between the officers and the women did not end at the window, however. Shortly after Frost's arrival, prison authorities granted to the Confederate officers the privilege of visiting the quarters of the female prisoners for some innocent socializing. According to Frost, "an evening is never passed more pleasantly than in the enjoyment of [the female prisoners'] society."[26]

The interaction between the men and the women followed all the standards of proper Victorian decorum. That was seen to by Mrs. Eliza Haynie of Saline County, Missouri, imprisoned after admitting to harboring and aiding guerrillas back home as well as receiving stolen property. Now behind bars, Haynie entertained Confederate prisoners while playing the role of the matriarch of the "feminine household." According to Frost, Haynie was "possessed of a great deal of quiet womanly dignity" and a "perfect model in her way," as she "matronized the younger members of the company." In turn, the other female prisoners "looked up to and loved" Mrs. Haynie, showing her the deepest levels of respect. The younger female prisoners included Haynie's daughter Rachel, arrested on the same charges as her mother; Miss Florence Lundy of Memphis, arrested for smuggling; Miss Mollie Goggin, another Missourian who gave aid to the guerrillas; Miss Maggie Oliver, alias Maggie Kelly of Mobile, Alabama, arrested and found guilty in New Orleans with her aunt on unspecified charges and sentenced to one year's confinement; and young Sarah Jane Smith of Arkansas, arrested in southern Missouri while cutting several miles of telegraph wire.[27] They and several other older women shared a group of neighboring rooms in the Alton Prison with Eliza Haynie.

With the permission of Major Morgan, Mrs. Haynie and her circle of friends hosted a select group of Southern officers in their rooms usually once a week and on special occasions such as holidays or the eve of the departure of one of the female inmates. Visits could last anywhere from about three hours up to eight hours in at least two cases. According to Frost, the visits were so agreeable that "we all forgot we were in prison." Visiting the women generated fond memories of being home: "Seeing a lady sitting at the head of the table and receiving our coffee from her hands," Frost reminisced, "was a strong reminder of those 'days of auld lang syne.'" Just visiting the quarters of the female prisoners alone had a positive impact on Frost. He observed: "Their rooms [there were at least two shared by Haynie and her coterie] are good and comfortable, the floors nicely painted, and everything exhibited such perfect order that we were forcibly reminded of home. The fairy touch of woman's fingers," as Frost described the proverbial feminine touch, "had left its impress as far as her sphere extended." Such a quality, engendered by the women's sense of domesticity, could not be found by the men in their own quarters. The first visit took place on December 4, 1864; calling on the ladies at least once a week became a central part of the Confederate officers' routines. When they suffered a temporary loss of the privilege, the officers lamented. This deprivation proved to be a "deplorable misfortune" that made the day seem to drag on and on without end.[28]

Undoubtedly, Frost and his mates thought very highly of the women with whom they interacted at Alton Prison. Frost wrote: "I have never met in our most refined and select circles with greater delicacy and more eminent sense of feminine propriety, than is manifested within these strongly guarded prison walls." But evidence suggests that the women with whom the Confederate officers intermingled were themselves a select circle. Prison records and news-paper accounts show that other women, mostly from rural and less wealthy sections of Missouri, were sent to Alton prison during this time; evidently, they did not become part of Mrs. Haynie's circle of friends. Griffin Frost had little to say about these women, although he did briefly note once that a "poor ragged degraded woman" arrived at the prison. She was barefoot, "scantily clad," and suffering from the cold on that October morning. Beyond that, Frost had nothing to add. Frost also described the "*female man,*" whom he knew as Molly Hays, alias Mary Ann Pitman. Pitman was close enough to Frost's female friends to be able to expose the hanky-panky committed by General Copeland and his subordinate Lieutenant Danforth with certain female prisoners, but she was not among Mrs. Haynie's group or acquainted with Frost and the other Confederate officers. Pitman's masculine persona contradicted the image of domesticity valued in mid-nineteenth-century America. It certainly did not reflect the qualities of feminine etiquette that Frost admired. If proper etiquette was a factor in defining the group that socialized with the Confederate officers, race also had influence. In February 1865, a group of black prisoners was sent to Alton from Vicksburg, Missis-sippi, having been found guilty of the charge of mutiny. Among the group was one woman. Rather than welcoming her into their group or shunning her altogether, the lady prisoners of Mrs. Haynie's circle employed the black woman as a "waiting maid."[29]

When the officers visited the women's quarters, activities included the sharing of food received from friends and relatives outside the prison and the displaying of crafts (mostly jewelry) made by the male prisoners, but for the most part, the prisoners spent the time together in conversation. Frost noted in very complimentary fashion the pleasant discussions he had with many of the female prisoners during his stay at Alton. "There is a fountain of wit pent up in several of the feminine bodies," Frost observed. Some of the young women in particular had "conversational powers of the highest order." Even when the "conversation was general," Frost wrote, "some passages [were] decidedly rich."[30]

Unfortunately, the captain did not elaborate on any specific "passages" in this case, but often conversation centered on life before the war and any bit of news or gossip that may have found its way to the prisoners through letters, visitors, or "Madam Rumor." During the visits, the prisoners also discussed the Confederate cause and the conduct of the war, despite restrictions against such conversation. The prisoners were not allowed to converse on issues of a political nature, but they often did. Eventually, it came at a cost; caught in the act of "communicating political news" through their "window gossip," the women found their visitation privileges temporarily curtailed and their windows nailed and padlocked shut. The windows remained closed for two weeks; Major Morgan ordered them reopened only with the warning to the women to keep their window talking brief and to "a very limited scope," meaning no politics. That did not stop the prisoners from discussing political news. They just did it in more discrete ways. For instance, the prisoners spread news by using a form of sign language, spelling out words with their fingers in the palm of their hands.[31]

On several occasions the women prisoners also entertained guests from outside the prison—friends, virtually all female, who visited from nearby St. Louis—while they hosted the men. Such visits were usually a major source of outside news. One popular guest was Miss Sallie Linton, a frequent visitor to the women's quarters. Linton regularly brought with her tasty treats that she prepared for the prisoners, both female and male, and also donated raw materials such as silver, pearls, and gutta percha used by the men to make jewelry. She even purchased a set of tools for use by the men in making their "famous prison jewelry" and offered to sell the finished product in St. Louis to provide the men with some spending money. Much of the jewelry the men made became gifts to their lady acquaintances within the prison. In return, the women occasionally prepared treats to share with the men. For instance, Alabaman Maggie Oliver once presented the men of Frost's bunk with "a most delicious peach pudding," which the officers "received with abundance of thanks, [and] with continued applause." When the men visited the female quarters, it was not uncommon for the women to offer a meal or snacks and beverages to their company.[32]

Besides the regular weekly visits on Wednesdays, the women's quarters also hosted male visitors on special occasions. One such event included a festive Christmas dinner in 1864. The feast was prepared on December 27, and the men contributed items they received in packages from friends and family for the holidays. The women scheduled the festivities to begin at three in the afternoon. Upon the arrival of the men, "the usual form of introduction was gone through with," and then the hostesses led the men into one of the women's rooms which for the day served as a sitting parlor. For the next hour and a half the participants engaged in entertaining conversation, which "highly pleased" the hostesses. Then the company was called to the dining room where according to Frost, they "found a large table richly laden with everything the most epicurean taste could desire." The menu included a variety of roasted meats, including beef, turkey, goose, duck, and chicken. With the roasted items came such boiled favorites as bacon, cabbage, turnips, potatoes, and tomatoes. For side dishes the women prepared crackers, coleslaw, pickles, light bread and butter, and for dessert there was mince pie and cranberry tart. After dinner the women and their guests retreated to the room designated as the parlor. Some returned to conversing while others engaged in song, but the most popular activity was to promenade the hall, passing from one room to the next. Prison life offered rare occasion for such social walking, and the prisoners made the most of the moment. At eight p.m. the attendees were called back to the dining room for supper, which included fruit cake, jelly cake, pound cake, coffee, and tea. After supper they returned to their postdinner activities until eleven o'clock arrived and the officers "bade" their "lady friends an affectionate good bye."[33]

Not all the occasions that generated interaction between the female prisoners and the Confederate officers were so pleasurable. On several occasions, the men were permitted to visit the women's quarters to say their goodbyes to ladies being released. Such occasions were met with bittersweet feelings, as those left behind were pleased to see their acquaintances gain their freedom but at the same time they felt sadness for the departure of a friend from the social circle.[34]

Some departures could be even more somber. On March 19, 1865, one of the older female prisoners, Maggie Oliver's aunt Mrs. W. J. Reynolds of Mobile, Alabama, passed away. She had been seriously ill for several days before her demise. Four of the officers were asked to join with some of the women in keeping vigil over the corpse until the next day. The mourning continued for the next two days, during which the inmate officers who had known Mrs. Reynolds did what they could to comfort the womenfolk. Reynolds probably would have been buried in the Confederate graveyard, a potter's field, with the rest of the Confederate prisoners who died at Alton, had it not been for the fact that she was Roman Catholic. The local Catholic church allowed her to be interred in the Catholic burying ground, not far from the Confederate site. Being far from home and Reynolds's male kinfolk—her husband was in the Confederate army and had not been heard from in a long time—the corpse was in need of pallbearers. Once again the Confederate officers were called on to assist in this last intimate ritual of life, Mrs. Reynolds's funeral. With the prison commander's permission, five of the officer inmates attended the service at the nearby Catholic church and then accompanied Reynolds's body to the burying ground where a newly dug grave received her body.[35]

In many ways, Griffin Frost's memoir can be seen as a testament to the influence the ladies of Mrs. Haynie's corner of the Alton Prison had on the Confederate captain and his comrades. A good part of the explanation for this impact lies in the ways in which the ladies successfully carried on the practices expected of women in the mid-nineteenth century. Many of the actions of the women reflected the notions of domesticity that defined the expectations American society held for proper women. While maintaining the upkeep of the house and home, women were to be nurturing, moral, and devoted to their families; they were to foster for men a shelter in the home from the competitive world of business and politics. Visiting the women reminded the men of the positive qualities of home that they missed; it momentarily provided the men with a touch of womanhood that normally was lacking in military life.

On at least one occasion the women extended their nurturing skills beyond their usual officer guests. In November 1864, as some unidentified illness was besetting the prisoners, the women were allowed to visit the prison hospital, "and for a short time minister to the sufferings of the patients." It is not evident from Griffin Frost's recording of the incident exactly what the women did, but one can imagine that at least for a brief while the infirm prisoners enjoyed some level of comfort from their interaction with the visiting ladies.[36]

The women also may have had an impact on the spiritual needs of their male counterparts, as suggested by the experience of Griffin Frost. Frost exhibited a rather ambiguous interest in matters of faith, at least as reflected in his memoir, until his last weeks in custody as the war neared its end. On Sunday, March 12, 1865, Frost mentioned that two of the lady prisoners, Mary Russell and Maggie Oliver, had been permitted to attend church that day. One week later Mrs. Reynolds died, creating a set of circumstances that exposed Frost to the Catholic funeral ritual and other Catholic practices. Frost seemed to take a sincere interest in the preparations and their religious meanings, and he noted that he and the others were "impressed with the peculiar sadness and solemnity" of the funeral for their departed friend. Less than two weeks later, Frost received permission to attend a Catholic mass outside of the prison. He returned the following week and again the next. It is unknown whether Frost made a permanent habit of attending church services after this, but it appears that at least for a time and at least in part because of his interaction with the female prisoners, Frost felt the need to attend to his spiritual well-being.[37]

What may come as a surprise is that through all this interaction between the ladies and the Confederate officers at Alton, it appears that no romantic liaisons evolved, at least none recorded by Frost or in the prison records. Furthermore, despite Frost's keen eye for other matters, the romantic escapades reported by Mary Ann Pitman involving two female prisoners from Mrs. Haynie's group and the prison commander and another officer went unnoticed, or discreetly overlooked, except to acknowledge that an unnamed "gentlemanly Federal lieutenant" supposedly secured Mollie Goggin's release so that the two could wed.[38] Nevertheless, under the harsh circumstances of confinement, these Confederate men and women were able to foster relationships, the types that members of polite society were accustomed to having during peacetime. For a brief while, those Confederates were able to reestablish the gender relationships they enjoyed before the war.

By the spring of 1865, the prisons of the St. Louis region had witnessed more than four hundred women pass through their doors. By then, the war was nearing its end, and with it the need for the military prisons.

CHAPTER 9

"I Suppose She Could Be Released"

T he arrests of disloyal civilians in St. Louis and the rest of Missouri
continued into 1865, even as the war approached its end. While Federal authorities recognized that the death of the Confederacy appeared to be just a matter of time, they simultaneously continued to face the
reality that the state remained a very dangerous place. These circumstances
made dealing with rebellious women no less complicated.

Through late 1864 and early 1865, Union troops continued dealing with
the aftermath of Price's Raid while maintaining pressure on the women who
helped support Missouri's rebel guerrillas. For example, a group of six women
from western Missouri arrested in December arrived in St. Louis per the
order of Provost Marshal General Darr. There, Department of the Missouri
commander Grenville Dodge ordered them banished for "aiding and assisting Price during his late raid into this state," as well as "uniformly aiding
and giving comfort to the rebel enemies [*sic*] of the United States, feeding,
harboring and encouraging bushwhackers and guerrilla bands (to which
members of their families in and have been attached) and failing and refusing
to report said outlaws to the Federal authorities." The order of banishment
further threatened that the women were "expressly forbidden *under penalty
of death* from returning within the limits of this Department during the
war." Frustrated by banished women disobeying the dictate not to return,
Dodge determined it necessary to add this drastic stipulation.[1] A few weeks
later, however, Dodge approved the banishment of another group of eight
women on similar charges, except for the reference to aiding Price and the
penalty of death for returning without permission. Instead, they faced the
usual "penalty of such punishment as may be deemed just to be imposed
upon them."[2] Days later, nineteen women ordered banished from Chariton

County, most with children in tow, passed through St. Louis on their way south.[3] And the flow continued.

As late as the third week in April, Darr's successor James H. Baker was still searching for particular women suspected of aiding guerrillas in Missouri. The last such woman may have been Anna Reynolds of Lafayette County, who arrived in St. Louis on April 26, charged with disloyalty and harboring and feeding bushwhackers. Baker had ordered the twenty-one-year-old's arrest the previous month. Reynolds's case appears routine. In 1863 Reynolds's mother had been impacted by Thomas Ewing's General Order No. 11, which prompted her brother to leave the regular Confederate service and go into the bush in Missouri. Reynolds claimed that she had seen her brother only twice since then. The last time had been during Price's raid, when her brother was riding with Bill Anderson's gang. Nevertheless, while she acknowledged that she had seen other guerrillas on many occasions, Reynolds insisted that she never gave any aid or information to them. "I am southern in my feelings and friendly to the confederate cause," she admitted, "but am opposed to Bushwhacking." Apparently concerned that her youth and unmarried status might raise other suspicions about her interactions with guerrillas, Reynolds also insisted that she had "never lived or cohabitated with Bushwhackers or been intimate with them." Reynolds remained in custody in St. Louis until at least May 3, but her record remains silent on what happened after that. No doubt, she soon tasted freedom again.[4]

In the days after the surrender at Appomattox, department commander Grenville Dodge rescinded the orders banishing many of the women in custody and in the process of being sent beyond the lines, allowing them to swear an oath of allegiance and to go home. Such decisions did not come without protest. When the *Missouri Democrat* reported on May 5 that Dodge had ordered the release of several women awaiting banishment, Unionist Richard Bray quickly sent a letter to the general urging him to reconsider the case of four of the women—Mary and Louisa Archy and Rebecca and Martha Gilmore of Jasper County. "These people," he insisted, "have caused at least a dozen Union Soldiers to be Killed. They are vile rebels and so dissolute in character that the bushwhackers always hang around them." In addition, he added, because they were arrested and sent to St. Louis, another four soldiers and two "Union citizens" were killed in retaliation by bushwhackers. If allowed to return home, Bray concluded, these women would be arrested once again for new misdeeds within a month. Bray's protestation came to no avail.[5]

A few women did not escape banishment at this late date, however. Deemed by Judge Advocate O. B. Queen a "dangerous woman to the Federal cause" whom he was certain had been "aiding, giving information &c." to the rebel guerrillas, Ruth Brisco evaded conviction at her trial at Warrensburg, Missouri, in March 1865, due to a lack of witnesses. Nevertheless, Brigadier General John McNeil, who commanded the District of Central Missouri where Brisco was tried, decided to send her on to the provost marshal general in St. Louis with his recommendation that she be sent beyond the lines, despite the outcome of the trial. Likewise, Mary Vaughn and her daughter Susan faced banishment late in the war. The Vaughns were no strangers to the Federal military justice apparatus. In 1863 and again in 1864, various women in the Vaughn family circle spent time in custody in the Kansas border region, while several of the young men participated in the guerrilla war. In fact, in the fall of 1864 three of the Vaughn women were exchanged for two Union officers who had been captured by Mary's son Dan. Once again, in February 1865, Union authorities arrested several of the female Vaughns after an encounter between soldiers and guerrillas at Mary's house. This time the women were sent to St. Louis. Despite the cooperation they gave to the military, naming others who had helped rebels in the brush, and the loss of a third Vaughn, Mary's daughter-in-law Nancy, who died in Gratiot Prison a day after their arrival, the military showed no leniency. Neither did cooperation mitigate the treatment of Tabitha Rider, the teenage wife of guerrilla leader Jim Rider from Livingston County. According to the officer who arrested her, Tabitha had not believed her husband responsible for the depredations of which he had been accused, but in the summer of 1864, she joined him on several raids, and that convinced her that he was "a regular Bushwhacker and Robber." Soured on her marriage, in January 1865 she sought a divorce; before she could file the paperwork, a Federal detective arrested her. Her own admissions led to a guilty verdict, but she cooperated extensively, prompting authorities to put off her banishment. Sent to St. Louis, she continued to give information about disloyal Missourians. Nevertheless, on April 30 Tabitha found herself "sent South," along with Ruth Brisco and Mary and Susan Vaughn, no doubt per the orders of Grenville Dodge. The four were probably the last rebel women banished from St. Louis.[6]

While most other cases dealt with by the provost marshal general's office by this point in the war appear unremarkable, a few stand out. In January 1865 authorities arrested Sallie McPheeters, the wife of William McPheeters, head surgeon of Sterling Price's army. Prior to the war, Dr. McPheeters had been a prominent physician as well as a professor at the St. Louis Medical College. In 1862 his well-known Southern sympathies made him the target of taxes levied on pro-Confederates in the city by Provost Marshal General Bernard Farrar. McPheeters claimed that these taxes, combined with his fear of imprisonment for refusing to take an oath of allegiance, prompted him to flee St.

Louis and join the Confederate army, leaving Sallie and their children behind on their own. Mrs. McPheeters managed to stay out of harm's way until late in the war, when her attempt to send a letter through the lines to her husband ran afoul of Union general Joseph Reynolds, recently appointed Federal commander at Little Rock, Arkansas. McPheeters claimed that the previous commander, Frederick Steele, allowed Sallie's missives to pass through the lines, but Reynolds did not. According to Dr. McPheeters, upon receiving the letter with Sallie's request, Reynolds wrote to Major General Dodge in St. Louis with the instruction: "Send Mrs. Sally McPheeters down & I will put her through the lines at once." McPheeters was inaccurate only in the tone of Reynolds's response. Reynolds wrote: "Respectfully referred to Maj. Gen. Dodge . . . with the suggestion that the writer of this letter had better be sent to join her husband." Dodge concurred, ordering the doctor's wife to be arrested and sent south.[7]

Another Confederate officer's wife who faced arrest in St. Louis late in the war was Lisinka Ewell, the wife of Lieutenant General Richard S. Ewell of the Army of Northern Virginia. In March 1865, authorities learned that Mrs. Ewell was in town collecting money and other valuables, at least $100,000 in bank notes, paper money, and gold that she had deposited in various banks in the city after the death of her first husband but before her second marriage to the general. Upon Ewell's arrest, Provost Marshal General Baker ordered her valuables confiscated and her banished beyond Union lines. Ewell managed to make her way to Nashville, Tennessee, a city long since under Federal control but also a place where she owned a plantation she inherited. She convinced Union major general George Thomas, commanding at Nashville, that she had been allowed by Abraham Lincoln to take the amnesty oath and had done so in St. Louis before she left there. Somehow, Secretary of War Edwin Stanton learned of Mrs. Ewell's deception and ordered Thomas to have her arrested and sent back to St. Louis. Thomas telegraphed back with his understanding that she had been granted amnesty, but Stanton quickly dispelled that notion. Thomas carried out Stanton's order, sending the general's wife back to St. Louis, but once more the record falls silent on the final outcome.[8]

Two additional Missouri arrests merit attention. In mid-April 1865, Josephine Moore came into custody in St. Louis, accused of "using contemptuous language against the late president A. Lincoln, U.S." Moore's record does not state specifically what she said or relate the outcome of the case, but one might presume that Provost Marshal General Baker handled the situation the same way he did with Sarah Altridge, arrested in the town of Fulton, just north of Jefferson City about the same time. Upon learning from a soldier that Lincoln had been killed, Altridge stated that she was glad of it. Although she insisted that she thought the soldier was joking and that she responded in kind, the provost marshal in Fulton arrested her and referred her case to St. Louis. A week and a half later, he received the order from Baker to release Altridge upon giving her oath of allegiance. Considering how inconsequential whatever Moore said would have been at this point, it is likely that she too gained release with her oath.[9]

Through the winter and into the spring of 1865, women banished from the state earlier in the war began returning to Missouri with the permission of the provost marshal general. Those required to post bonds to ensure their good behavior received their money back, and women on parole who regularly had to check in with the provost marshal general were released from that obligation. In some cases, realizing this complete freedom from the military justice system took time. For example, records from mid-May identify four women still on parole and required to report either in person or by letter to the provost marshal general's office in St. Louis. Eleanor Ann King, who spent time in the St. Charles Street Prison for spying, and Fanny Houx, convicted of aiding bushwhackers, received release from their paroles a week into June. Obtaining freedom from the long arm of the law often took time. In August 1862, Fanny Barron of St. Louis was arrested for "inducing" a young man to "join a rebel band of bushwhackers." Barron spent only a few days in prison before being released; had this occurred later in the war, her treatment, no doubt, would have been more severe. She did, however, have to post a bond of $2,000 for her good behavior. Three years later, with the war over for more than three months, she requested that she be released from the obligations of her bond. A brief, rather indifferent endorsement on her letter reads "I suppose she could be released."[10]

Not all prisoners seemed eager to gain their freedom. Smuggler Florence Lundy completed part of the sentence she received—a six month prison stint—but refused to comply with paying a $3,000 fine, the rest of the sentence. Lundy even turned away offers to pay the levy from friends from Memphis concerned with her health, preferring, instead, in the words of fellow inmate Griffin Frost, to "let the Government vent the full force of its august and dignified anger on her own little person." Perhaps the real reason for her reluctance to depart the prison had to do with her relationship with General Copeland. Whatever the case, only when the friends paid the fine without her knowledge just days before the war's end did Lundy leave Alton Prison, more than a month after her prison term had expired. On a lighter note, the *Missouri Democrat* reported that during a tour of the female prison on Gratiot Street in January 1865, Provost Marshal General Baker observed a "lame rebel of the female sex playing a fiddle to while away the tedium of prison life."

Rather than being anxious to gain release, according to the news item, the prisoner "was contented as long as she could play the fiddle, and didn't care how long the war lasted." When she left the prison is unknown.[11]

Some female prisoners never tasted freedom again. At least four women died while in custody in St. Louis city. Coincidentally, three of them hailed from Arkansas and died within weeks of each other, although their deaths seem unrelated. On October 4, 1864, Caroline Billingsley and Nancy King were "committed for safe keeping in one of the buildings adjoining the Gratiot Street Military Prison," along with thirty-one other women and children who were probably refugees, but nonetheless treated as prisoners. Billingsley, a resident of Carroll County in the northeast corner of Arkansas just south of Springfield, Missouri, died from pneumonia ten days later; King, of Lebanon, Arkansas, not far from Arkansas's borders with Texas and the Oklahoma Territory, succumbed to the measles on October 31. Arrested in July 1864, Jane Foster of Randolph, County, Arkansas, stood accused of smuggling contraband letters through the lines. Her husband, Jacob, appealed to Provost Marshal General J. P. Sanderson for a speedy trial that he felt certain would prove her innocence, as she was illiterate and unaware that carrying such letters violated the rules of war, but to no avail. Jacob Foster, by the way, was at the time in the Gratiot Street Prison as a prisoner of war. He would never see his wife again. In September, he was transferred to the prison camp at Rock Island, Illinois, and then in March 1865 to Point Lookout, Maryland, for exchange. Jane, however, died of some unspecified illness on November 11, 1864.[12]

In March 1865, Nancy Jane Vaughn also died in custody in St. Louis. Arrested for feeding and harboring guerrillas in Jackson County on the western border, Vaughn arrived at the Gratiot Street Female Prison with Mary and Susan Vaughn.[13] At least three of the women who died in Federal custody in St. Louis were buried in the post cemetery at Jefferson Barracks south of the city. In 1866 the site became a national cemetery. Facing the Mississippi River, Billingsley's headstone identifies her as "C. Billingsly," barely discernable due to age and weather. She is buried in a section surrounded by Union soldiers, where she enjoys a "curved"-top stone standard for Federals instead of a "pointed"-top Confederate marker. At first, wooden markers identified the graves. In 1873 Congress funded the replacement of the markers with marble headstones, but only for Union soldiers. Not until 1906 did the Confederate dead receive marble stones. Foster's and Vaughn's remains lie among the Confederate dead, and both have had their headstones replaced since 1906. Foster's new stone with its pointed top bears a symbol associated with the Sons of Confederate Veterans. That organization probably replaced the original marker. Vaughn's stone, unlike that of Foster, has a rounded top, but according to one source, when first interred, her stone read "Henry Vaughn." Unknown is the final resting place of Nancy King.[14]

Death also visited the women in Alton Prison. Mrs. W. J. Reynolds of Mobile, Alabama, died just two months shy of the end of the war. A Catholic, she was buried in the local Catholic burying ground in a metal casket, should her family choose to retrieve her remains. Initially, prison officials opposed these arrangements, but upon learning that the nearby Catholic church planned to pay the costs of the burial, they agreed. Years later the bodies interred in the burying ground were relocated to the Greenwood Cemetery. It is unknown whether her family ever claimed her body. The cemetery, now known as St. Patrick's Cemetery, has no records of the remains moved from the old Catholic burying ground and thus no record of Mrs. Reynolds.[15]

Reynolds was not the first women to die in the custody of the Alton Prison. In September 1863, smallpox took the life of a prisoner whose story, as well as her name, is steeped in a bit of mystery. In July 1863, Federal authorities arrested Barbara Ann Donovan, or Dunovan, or Duvana, or Dunavant, or Dunevant in Memphis, Tennessee, with Elvira Mitchell and charged the two with smuggling. (One record has the woman as Barbary Ann and another as Anne B., but Barbara Ann is the most consistent.) Two months after arriving at Alton Prison, Barbara Ann died on Smallpox Island, also known as Tow Head Island, in the Mississippi River. In his 1895 memoir, wartime Memphis attorney John Hallum described meeting a young woman whose name he could not recall in Memphis's Irving Block Prison before she was sent to Alton. The woman had been caught trying to smuggle "ten yards of gray cloth, some buttons, thread, and gold lace trimming" to make a uniform for her fiancé. Barbara Ann may have been ill before she arrived in Alton. Hallum claimed that "this girl was in the incipient stages of consumption, aggravated by exposure in that cold, damp, fireless and bedless room," describing the accommodations usually used in the Irving Block Prison for women and inaccurately recalling the incident taking place in the winter of 1863–1864. Consumption and smallpox are diseases that a nineteenth-century observer probably would not confuse, but that does not mean that Barbara Ann was not already afflicted with some illness.[16]

Whatever her medical history, her name appears as Barbara Ann Dunevant, the only woman listed on a monument dedicated in 2002 to those who died on Smallpox Island while confined to Alton Prison. There the victims were buried, probably without caskets, rather than in the Confederate Cemetery. The specific location of the graves went poorly documented, and within a few years of the war, flooding had washed away any markers that had once existed showing their locations. In 1869 a report resulting from the inspection of national cemeteries recommended that if the bodies on the island could be found, they should be removed to the Jefferson Barracks National Cemetery. Nothing came of the recommendation. The remains, as well as the suffering that occurred on the island, went forgotten for decades. In 1874 witnesses reported that bodies had been exposed and washed away from the island due to a shift in the flow of the river channel caused by the building of a dike. Memories would have been fresh enough to recall the wartime use of the island and the prisoners who died there, but in 1935 when workmen uncovered skeletons while constructing a lock and damn system along the Alton riverfront, very few people cared about the connection between the remains and the war. Thus, the discovery did not stop the work. The unearthed bones, perhaps including those of Barbara Ann, apparently became part of the construction material.[17]

Aside from the confusion over her name, Barbara Ann is involved in another more interesting mystery. In the early twentieth century, Thomas Pinckney, a veteran of the Confederate Fourth South Carolina Cavalry, prepared a memoir that was never published. In it he revealed his shock at learning that a prisoner at the Alton Prison who had just died was, in fact, a woman. No one admitted knowing who she was, and her identity remained a mystery, according to Pinckney, but he added that a newspaper article that had recently appeared in the *New York Herald* of September 5, 1909 "may possibly afford the much desired information." The article, reproduced by Pinckney, identifies a "Confederate spy" imprisoned at Alton, "a frail little creature who gave the name B. A. Duravan." Duravan, the article continued, "had been there when the bullets were flying thick and fast, had been *in the long marches with Lee's army*," and "was strong in the belief of the Southern cause, eager to bring about the defeat of the Unionists." Although "comrades had a warm spot in their hearts for Duravan," it was not until she was found dead in her cell that anyone learned that "the pale little soldier was a woman."[18]

Of course, Barbara Ann had never disguised herself as a man and served in the army. Furthermore, she died on Smallpox Island, where she was buried. Interesting is the narrative the author of the article constructed about Barbara Ann as a brave soldier cherished by her comrades who had fought in many battles under the command of no less than Confederate icon Robert E. Lee. One cannot fault Thomas Pinckney for suggesting that Barbara Ann Duravan was his "fellow feminine-prisoner," although adding more intrigue to the story, Pinckney had been captured in Virginia in May 1864 and never actually spent time in Alton. According to his service record, he first had been sent to the prison camp at Point Lookout, Maryland, and then transferred to Fort Delaware on the Delaware River.[19]

Nevertheless, "Madam Rumor," as Griffin Frost called it, was a powerful thing, and the story Pinckney heard about a deceased female soldier at Alton, wherever he heard it, may have been based in truth. On August 2, 1904, the *Alton Evening Telegraph* reported the death of Michael Gleason, who during the Civil War had helped to bury bodies at the Confederate Cemetery near the Alton Prison. According to the article, Gleason, an Irish Catholic immigrant, was credited with being "probably the only one who knew the exact spot in the cemetery where lies the remains of the Confederate prisoner of war, who after death was discovered to be a woman." The paper reported that upon learning the true gender of this prisoner, Gleason pressed to have her interred at the Catholic burying ground because "she was of the sex of his mother" and therefore "should be buried in consecrated ground." Unsuccessful, Gleason personally maintained the upkeep of her grave, not only during the war, but for years afterward until he moved to St. Louis. The woman at the root of the story that Pinckney heard may have been the same woman that Michael Gleason buried. By the time of Gleason's death, the story of his connection with this unknown female prisoner was well known on both sides of the river. Several months before Gleason died, some residents of Alton began a movement to bring Gleason back to the town for one more visit so he could identify the exact spot where the woman could be found, but nothing came of it before his demise.[20]

Through late April and early May 1865, the population of the Gratiot Street Military Prison dwindled. The last women to pass through the facility were also the last three female captives released from the Alton Prison. Two of them still had time left on their sentences and were transferred to the Missouri State Penitentiary. Mary Russell and Maggie Oliver (alias Maggie Kelly) had been found guilty of smuggling and other charges in Vicksburg in the fall of 1864 and sent to Alton to complete the sentences they received, one year imprisonment each. Both would be pardoned and released before the completion of their terms, as had been the experience for the other women previously sent to the state penitentiary to serve their time. The third prisoner arriving from Alton, Mary Kirby, was also found guilty of smuggling in Baton Rouge, Louisiana, and sentenced to imprisonment for the rest of the war. From Gratiot Prison she obtained her release.[21]

The cessation of hostilities and the curtailment of martial law made the wartime prisons unnecessary. After the war, Joseph McDowell returned to St. Louis to reclaim his once prominent medical college. With a presidential pardon in one hand and control of the school in the other, McDowell went about the task of trying to reinvigorate the institution. He hired new faculty and began renovations of the building, but damages caused by the conversion of the school for military purposes combined with years of use as a prison and outright neglect had taken its toll. In the end the building could not be restored. After McDowell died on September 18, 1868, the new caretakers of the school renamed it the Missouri Medical College and moved it to a new location. The building remained dormant for a decade until the Saint Louis Fire Department ordered a portion of it demolished because it was unsafe. No stranger to the prison, Absalom Grimes visited what was left of it that same year and left the following description: "Bats and pigeons were aroused by our intrusion and flew about the deserted, silent rooms. Most of the flooring had been torn up and carried away; the outer walls . . . showed where they had been cut in thirty or more places by prisoners who had tried to escape. A great many had succeeded." Soon the rest of the building would fall by the wayside. The location presently is part of a parking lot on the property of the Nestlé Purina Company.[22]

The Myrtle Street Prison began to disappear even more quickly after the war, but part of it remained standing. On May 22, 1865, the *Missouri Democrat* reported that workmen could be seen tearing the building down, speculating that the space would soon be occupied by a "store or beer saloon." Rather than razing the entire structure, construction went up around it, and what was left of the former slave pen-turned-prison became part of the substructure of an edifice that for many years functioned as a drugstore. The location would soon be on the fringe of "Hop Alley," St. Louis's version of Chinatown that would develop in the postwar era. In the 1960s the buildings in the area made way for a new baseball stadium for the St. Louis Cardinals, Busch Stadium, and other urban renewal. According to a local urban legend, as workmen prepared to lay the foundation for the new stadium, they found a subterranean chamber, complete with chains and manacles attached to the wall, where Lynch's prewar business once stood.[23]

Likewise, the residences once owned by Margaret McLure and Edward Dobyns used as prisons for women during the war have long since disappeared, as has the structure on St. Charles Street. In fact, much of St. Charles Street in the modern downtown area of St. Louis has disappeared. On the east side of the Mississippi River, the Federal government and the state of Illinois had little use for the Alton Prison after the war and it came down. Many of the heavy stones used in the prison's construction gained new life in new buildings and residences erected after the war. Many years later, some of the remaining stones that had once been a part of the prison were relocated to a spot a few blocks away and on higher ground from the prison site, arranged as a monument to those who lived and died in the Alton Prison.[24] Besides those stones, nothing remains of the various locations that confined Confederate partisan women in the St. Louis region during the Civil War.

In the wake of Robert E. Lee's surrender to Ulysses S. Grant at Appomattox, the capture of Richmond, and the collapse of Confederate resistance elsewhere in the South in the spring of 1865, the Civil War came to an end. Confederate soldiers laid down their weapons, swore oaths that they would no longer take up arms, and began the long trek home. Confederate partisan women also abandoned their war against the Federal government and began putting the conflict behind them, although a few continued to cause problems for Union authorities. For example, Kate Beatty, who had been banished for her attempted impersonation of the wife of Confederate major Enoch Wolf, had been allowed to return to St. Louis in early April 1865. In September, Samuel Turner provided a statement to the provost marshal "in regard to one 'Mrs. Beattie.'" According to Turner, Beatty had come to live at the boarding house where he resided "about 4 weeks ago." There, Turner continued, Beatty "requested to have a room to herself as she was writing a history of the War." Turner became suspicious that Beatty was up to no good. She had several meetings with men she identified as "officers of the late Confederate army," including a colonel named Campbell and a captain named Miller, as well as a merchant that Turner could not identify. When she claimed that Captain Miller had great influence at West Point, Turner challenged that notion, and Beatty became extremely indignant and defensive, daring Turner to say that in front of Miller. Whether or not Beatty was writing a book or was up to some nefarious plot goes untold in the record. Certainly, her earlier activities made these suspicions worth investigating. Years later, Major Wolf encountered Beatty. He related that "she still bore on her wrists scars caused by sores made by the handcuffs that were fastened very tightly around her wrists because of her very small hands."[25]

Less than a year after her banishment, Ada B. Haynes was arrested in St. Louis again for having returned to the city without permission and was imprisoned in the St. Charles Street Prison. Haynes claimed that she intended to take the amnesty oath upon her return and behave as a "good citizen." Federal authorities found her claim dubious. "Her behavior since her return contradicts what she has heretofore sworn to, and shows that she is not to be trusted," asserted General Orders No. 125 of July 20, 1864. Authorities, however, decided to "give her an opportunity to make good her profession without temptation to herself or danger to the Government." Therefore, they ordered "that she be released on oath and bond not to reside west or south of the State of New York during the present rebellion." Haynes traveled to New York City, arriving in time to fall under suspicion of being involved in an attempt by Confederate operatives to start fires in Manhattan using Greek fire. Again in custody, she was kept under house arrest in her hotel per the order of the commander of the Department of the East, John Dix, until he determined that she had nothing to do with the arson plot. The fires caused limited destruction. Years later, in her defense and still defiant, Haynes claimed that had she been involved "she would have done a better job." In 1910 Haynes was still alive, eighty-one years old, and lucid enough to give a brief interview to H. W. Mizner about her wartime experience.[26]

Habitual troublemaker Drucilla Sappington, on the other hand, apparently remained on her best behavior once the guns fell silent. After her husband, William David, returned to Missouri, they resumed farming in St. Louis County. According to the 1870 census, the war had not impoverished the Sappingtons; the value of the family's real estate property was listed at $20,000, with an additional $1,000 worth of personal property. The family fell on hard times, though, and in about 1875 they moved to Sherman, Texas, near where Missouri Confederates had once quartered for the winter. In 1900 a seventy-six-year-old William David successfully applied for a Confederate pension from the state of Texas, claiming that due to old age and feebleness, he was unable to labor and that he owned no real or personal property. The former Confederate captain lived another seventeen years, but Drucilla died a decade earlier, on December 22, 1906.[27]

Another rebel woman who spent time in custody in St. Louis also made her way to Texas after the war. Virginia "Jennie" Knight, whom Drucilla Sappington, no doubt, encountered when the two were incarcerated in the home of Margaret McLure in the spring of 1863, had been arrested first at the age of seventeen for raising money to aid the Confederacy. Released on parole rather than being banished to the South, Knight was arrested again in January 1865 for giving aid and comfort to bushwhackers and for violating her oath. After the war, Knight married William H. Johnson, an attorney, and the two moved to Brownwood, Texas. After the death of her husband in 1890, she opened a home for wayward young women in Dallas, where she devoted much of the rest of her time until her death in 1934.[28]

Clara Judd, the first woman to be confined in the Alton Military Prison, returned to the South and her family after the war. The 1870 Census shows Clara and her three youngest children living with her son Harvey and his family in Murfreesboro, Tennessee. Harvey had been ordained a deacon and then a priest in the Episcopal Church, following in the footsteps of his father. In 1879, Harvey took a position at a church in South Carolina, but evidently

Clara did not make the move with his family. According to one source, she died in 1890. Early in the war Clara's three oldest sons, Harvey, Charles, and Amos, took work making percussion caps for the Confederate army, but according to Harvey's obituary in the *Confederate Veteran* in 1906, his brother "Charlie" at some point joined John Hunt Morgan's band of cavalry. Amos also confirmed that Charlie served under Morgan. In an extensive survey of Confederate veterans living in Tennessee conducted between 1915 and 1922, Amos reported that brother Charlie "was in Gen. Morgan's command and had been captured and sent North." It was Morgan that Clara had been accused of attempting to pass medicines and other contraband to when she was arrested in 1862. Neither Harvey's obituary nor Amos's survey mention their mother's arrest nor her prison ordeal at Alton.[29]

Ironically, Elvira Mitchell, who had been imprisoned with Clara Judd, sought to return to the town of Alton with her family near the end of the war. Now refugees from Tennessee, the Mitchells made their way to St. Louis, where Elvira petitioned the Refugee Bureau for aid in getting to Alton by river. According to the officer who endorsed the request, Elvira and her family "wish to go to their friends near Alton who will aid them & relieve the Govt. from any further expense." In another bit of a twist, in August 1864, Harriet Martin, one of the African American women who had been held at the Gratiot Street Prison as a witness in the *White Cloud* case, also requested transportation from Missouri to Illinois for her and her family from the Refugee Bureau. They would be sent to St. Louis, where Martin had been confined not as a prisoner, but until she gave her testimony in the case, before being ferried across the river.[30]

Melissa Fox of Chariton County, who with her mother Isabella gained release after authorities determined insufficient evidence existed against them, never married the soldier who claimed to have fallen in love with her. Instead, she went home and in 1868 married George Conrad. In 1887 both she and her mother succumbed to pneumonia nine days apart. Sarah and Dorotha Durritt returned to Johnson County from their banishment and also married. Sarah and her family moved to Kansas in the 1870s where she died in 1917. What became of Dorotha is unknown. Pardoned by Abraham Lincoln, Anna Fickle gained release from the Missouri State Penitentiary in late January 1865. The romantically inclined young woman returned to Lafayette County and married Confederate veteran George W. Parker. She remained there until her death in 1920. Emma Weaver, who had escaped from the St. Charles Street Prison, made her way back to Arkansas after the war. She, too, married, and like these other women apparently led a normal life until her death in 1917.[31]

After being banished from St. Louis in May 1863, Eliza Frost reunited with her husband, General Daniel Frost. Five months after her banishment, Eliza attempted to return to the North. She gained permission provided that she take the oath of allegiance, pay a bond of $10,000 for her good behavior, and live somewhere north of the Ohio and east of the Mississippi Rivers. Evidently, she found the terms unacceptable, but in February 1864 she again requested that she be allowed to return, this time to visit her aged parents. It is unclear when Eliza returned through the lines, but in September 1864 she, her husband and their family left the South for Matamoras, Mexico, where Daniel thought that the family would be safer. From there they travelled to Cuba and then to Canada where they remained until the war ended. Eliza and her family returned to St. Louis County where Daniel engaged in farming. Because Daniel never returned to the Confederate army, refusing efforts to get him back, he spent the next few decades defending himself against accusations of desertion. He died in 1900. Eliza, however, lived only until 1872.[32]

Margaret McLure, Eliza Frost's traveling companion in their banishment, also returned to St. Louis after the war. Confederate defeat did not hinder her commitment to the cause that was now lost. According to one source, she gave "her whole strength and thought . . . to her loved work, the care of Confederate soldiers." In the years after the war, McLure became a venerated icon among former Confederates for her contributions to the war effort, as well as for the ordeal she went through having her Chestnut Street house converted into a prison, with her as its first inmate, and being banished from the city. She contributed money for the erecting of statues dedicated to the Confederate dead and helped to raise funds for the creation of a home for aged and infirmed Confederate veterans. In 1891 "Mother McLure" was selected to be the first president of the Daughters of the Confederacy, a women's auxiliary for the Ex-Confederates Association that aided Missouri Confederate veterans in need. Soon, age and infirmity caught up with her, limiting the work she could perform for the organization. In 1902 she passed away.[33]

Even before the war ended, many women disappeared from the record completely. Sarah Jane Smith, who at one time had been sentenced to death, may have succumbed to the illness that led to her release from Alton Prison.[34] Isadore Morrison, who escaped from custody in 1862, remained at large and undetected. And after collecting her pay for the service she performed for the provost marshal general of the Department of the Missouri, Mary Ann Pitman was never heard from again. Certainly, she had burned many bridges in Tennessee and probably would not have received a warm welcome there. She also had made many enemies in St. Louis. Nevertheless, someone as resourceful and shrewd as Pitman probably successfully redefined herself in the postwar era.

As the nation recovered from the war and attempted to reconcile its differences, Southerners created a memory of the war that celebrated their defeated army, the brave men who went to war to protect home and family from a Yankee onslaught. This story of the Confederate Lost Cause had little room for inclusion of the partisan women who often found themselves under the scrutiny of Federal military authorities for their actions, a fact that would shape, or misshape, our understanding of Southern women's wartime experience into the twenty-first century.

CHAPTER 10

"The Heroines of This Most Disastrous Period Have Been Forgotten"

A s the Civil War generation faded away due to age, infirmity, and death, so, too, did the story of the arrest and imprisonment of the Confederate partisan women in St. Louis. In 1901 the very popular American author Winston Churchill published *The Crisis*, a romantic novel of the Civil War set in St. Louis. According to the introduction by Joseph Mersand included in a 1962 paperback edition released in time for the war's centennial, the first edition of *The Crisis* sold 320,000 copies in the first few months after it hit the shelves. The book has gone through many editions and has been translated into several languages. It spawned a short-lived 1902 Broadway play of the same name, written by Churchill, a movie version released in 1916, and even a Classics Illustrated comic book that appeared in 1958. In fact, *The Crisis* still can be found in print. Born in St. Louis six years after the war ended, Churchill did extensive research to provide an accurate depiction of the wartime river city, consulting both published works as well as residents of the city who lived through the war. When it came to the treatment of disloyal women, however, Churchill missed the mark. "No women were thrown into prison, it is true," his narrator relates, although one woman and her family faced house arrest for waving to Confederate prisoners of war being taken to prison, while another woman "was not permitted to shout for Jeff Davis on the street corner before the provost guard."[1] The instances Churchill describes certainly resemble a number of actual cases of rebel women running afoul of Union authorities, but his assertion that no women faced imprisonment is simply not true. By 1901, however, the number of people who actually remembered women being arrested and imprisoned was quickly dwindling.

Winston Churchill's fictional account *The Crisis* was not the only work of the turn of the century to reflect an amnesia about women in custody in Missouri. In his contribution to Clement A. Evans's twelve-volume collection *Confederate Military History*, John C. Moore wrote in 1899:

> The Southern women of Missouri were as loyal and true to their cause
> and as brave and heroic in the support they gave it and its defend-
> ers, as the women of any part of the South. At the hazard of their
> lives they made their homes hospitals to care for the sick and the
> wounded, and when they were not safe in their houses hid and fed
> them in the woods and in caves, until they recovered or died. . . .
> The spirit of heroism and disregard of consequences was not con-
> fined to the country. Nowhere were they more active and zealous
> and self-sacrificing than in St. Louis. No Southern soldier lacked
> for friends among the Southern women to feed him, to secrete him,
> to supply him with arms and money and whatever else he needed,
> to give him a horse and a guide, and to start him to the army—in
> a city crowded with Federal soldiers and alive with detectives and
> spies. Half the time Confederate commands in the West drew their
> medicines and lighter forms of ammunition from St. Louis through
> the aid of Southern women there.[2]

Moore acknowledged that the actively rebellious women of Missouri disre-
garded the consequences they might face while aiding the Confederate cause,
but he failed to discuss any of the women who suffered those consequences. In
fact, he mentions the arrival of Eliza Frost and her reunion with her husband
the general in Sterling Price's camp but asserts that she "had passed though
the lines [from St. Louis] with the consent of the Federals," stating nothing
of her banishment, nor anything of any other woman's arrest, imprisonment,
or banishment.[3]

Nevertheless, there were some efforts to keep the story of incarcerated
women alive, at least a version of it. The late nineteenth and early twentieth
centuries witnessed the production of myriad local, county, and regional
histories, often written by amateurs and designed, in large part, to highlight
a particular area's contribution to the Civil War. St. Louis was no different.
In 1882 J. Thomas Scharf, a prolific author who wrote many good quality
histories of this kind, published *History of Saint Louis City and County*. The
two-volume work includes more than one hundred and sixty pages of detailed
information and minutia about the war as it relates to St. Louis. Despite the
four pages Scharf devotes to the Gratiot Street Prison, he includes only two
brief mentions of its female prisoners. The first is embedded in a long quote

from the memoir of Absalom Grimes concerning his capture and imprisonment in the fall of 1862. Grimes mentions the "two well-known ladies
and two other ladies" confined to the "female prison," which happened to
be the room adjacent to the one Grimes occupied. Grimes does not reveal
why any of the women were in custody, and neither does Scharf. Although
not cited by name, the two well-known women were Drucilla Sappington
and Elisabeth Sigler, who, Grimes explains, aided him in escaping. The only
mention of women in Gratiot Street Prison in Scharf's own words comes in
a paragraph about Ada B. Haynes, who had been arrested and banished to
the South in May 1863 with Margaret McLure and Eliza Frost. According to
Scharf, Haynes had been "convicted of being engaged in the service of the
South as a kind of Confederate mail-carrier and agent." Scharf never admits
any guilt on Haynes's part, just that she was convicted. Haynes returned
to St. Louis without permission and was caught and placed in "the female
department of Gratiot Street prison" in 1864 until authorities released her
and allowed her to go to New York state until the end of the war. While not
mentioning any prison, Scharf also devotes two sentences to the arrest of
"Mrs. John Smith, a confederate spy," yet his brief description parallels the
well-publicized case of Ione Smith, who unbeknownst to Scharf was actually
the Union spy Mary Ann Pitman. Finally, Scharf notes in his treatment of
General Daniel Frost that "his wife," not mentioning Eliza by name, "was
'banished,' her only offense being that she had a husband in the Confederate
army."[4] Evident in what little Scharf includes in his discussion of Confederate
women in custody is his reticence to impart any guilt on them. With the
exception of "Mrs. John Smith," who never existed in the first place, Scharf,
himself a Confederate army veteran, attributes no actual military offenses to
these women that would warrant their arrests. With the women blameless,
they became victims of the Federal government, which Scharf implies bore
the onus of their arrests, incarcerations, and subsequent punishments.

An article in the *Missouri Republican* of May 19, 1903, written by Deborah
Isaacs and titled "Confederate Days in St. Louis—Female Prisoners of War"
continues these same themes. Appearing nearly forty years to the day of the
banishment of Margaret McLure, the article mentions her first, asserting
that this tireless visitor to the Confederate soldiers in the St. Louis prisons
and hospitals was charged with "aiding rebels [quotation marks in the orig-
inal]." Isaacs omits any reference to the role McLure played as a conduit for
Confederate mail and contraband or the aid she gave to escaped prisoners
and rebel men seeking to join the Confederate army, the specifics of the
charges against her. Isaacs also cites several other women banished to the
South from St. Louis, including Eliza Frost, a Mrs. Jeff Clark (perhaps Mrs.

Charles Clark), Lucy Welch, and Sallie McPheeters. Again, the author makes no mention of any actual charges these women faced. Ironically, Isaacs does reveal smuggling activities on the part of some of these women, but only after they had been found guilty and were preparing to head south, as they carried with them "comforts that had become luxuries to their relatives and friends in 'Dixie's Land.'"

Of the prisons housing women, Isaacs states, "There had been thought of fitting up a female prison in the college part of the McDowel prison, but later it was opened in the row on Eighth street, opposite the college, where at one time as many as seventeen female prisoners were under arrest." Isaacs then cites "Mrs. William McPheeters," who was "imprisoned for three weeks in the McDowel [*sic*] College female prison" before her banishment. The only other name of an imprisoned woman she gives is a "Mrs. Campbell of Memphis," arrested, claimed Isaac, only because she was from the South. "No women from the South could come to St. Louis at that time without incurring risk of arrest and imprisonment." Assumed to be a spy, Campbell gained release a week later after friends of her husband used their influence to allow her to be "banished beyond Federal lines," in other words, sent back home. Isaacs included one other unnamed woman, "a lady" who traveled to St. Louis to see "her sick and aged mother." Also assumed to be a spy, she was tried, found guilty, and "condemned . . . to the Alton prison until the close of the war." Like Scharf, Isaac portrays these women, whose only crime appeared to be tending to their family's needs and nurturing Confederate soldiers in the field, in prisons, and in hospitals, as victims of the Federal army. "No evidence was necessary for conviction," she claimed. "Sentences were stereotyped." While not ignoring the fact that women were confined in military prisons, she focuses on those banished rather than their incarceration. Furthermore, the examples she gives are names still recognized by many St. Louisans as late as 1903.[5]

Ten years after Isaacs's article appeared, the Missouri Division of the United Daughters of the Confederacy (UDC) published *Reminiscences of the Women of Missouri in the Sixties*. In her preface to the volume, Mrs. Blake L. Woodson laments that "for years the heroines of this most disastrous period have been forgotten." Therefore, the Missouri Division presented "this book to the world, that the youth of the future may read and learn of what material their forebears were made, and feel proud to say I am a descendant of the bravest, truest race that ever lived, whose women were as brave as lions when necessity arose, but always as pure and gentle as the dove." As Matthew Christopher Hulbert observes in his study of Civil War guerrilla memory, the women who contributed to this book "had no intention of letting their own services to the Confederate cause be neglected or forgotten in the postwar period." Nevertheless, their stories appear to have limits on what they revealed. Some of the accounts belong to women who spent time in the custody of the Missouri provost marshal in St. Louis. When asked by a member of the UDC to recount her experiences during the war for the volume, eighty-four-year-old Lucie Nickolson Lindsay only reluctantly consented. Once she began talking, she candidly revealed to her interviewer her involvement in aiding Confederate recruits making their way to Sterling Price's army and her activities smuggling goods to the rebel army, the things that led to her arrest and banishment in 1863. The short essay on Mary Cleveland, told thirdhand and somewhat convolutedly, also confirms Cleveland's guilt of the charges brought against her, helping with the distribution of contraband mail, that caused authorities to send her through the lines. In fact, it also substantiates that Cleveland was headstrong and a bit of a troublemaker. Author Virginia Yates McCanne notes that Cleveland's brother "could tell much of her banishment, as well as her adventurous life in the South, where she had a good time with the boys, and got into trouble more than once in trying to get letters through [the lines] to the parents and friends of the boys at home in Missouri."[6]

Not all items in the book are so forthcoming in disclosing service to the Confederate cause. Two entries relate to the wife of Confederate general Sydney Jackman, the first provided by the general's daughter Mary Jackman Mullins and the second by Mullins's daughter. In the first, Mullins tells of her mother's arrest and banishment without providing any explanation or context. She then describes how her mother and other kinswomen secreted and supplied Jackman and the men traveling with him during a recruiting trip he made back to Missouri. Mrs. Jackman also tended to the wounds her husband received during a skirmish with Federal soldiers. In this account, Mullins makes no connection between these activities and her mother's arrest and punishment, inferring that her mother's banishment stemmed simply from being married to a Confederate officer. In the second account, the author of which is identified only as "the daughter of Mrs. Mary Mullins," relates that the "crime" of which Mrs. Jackman and her relatives were accused "was that of allowing the husband, brother and son to visit his old home and seek shelter there for himself and men."[7] Both accounts imply that Mrs. Jackman's actions were simply those of a nurturing woman tending to the needs of her husband and others, and not military offenses that constituted aiding and abetting the enemy. They also stress Mrs. Jackman's frailty, having recently given birth and suffering from an unspecified illness, which evoked little sympathy from Federal officials.

Two items in the volume relating to Sue M. Bryant also insist on her innocence. The first is written by Bryant, now married and going by the name Carson. A nearly identical version appeared eight years earlier in the *Confederate Veteran*. Arrested in 1864 at the age of sixteen, the former Miss Bryant claims that her arrest stemmed from vendettas people had against her father, a judge who had "sentenced many criminals to state prison." The war, she posits, "gave them the opportunity to vent their ill-cherished feelings toward his family." The specific charges against her, she insists, were based on "false rumors and the display of southern colors" by her, specifically a red and white outfit she claimed she wore for a school presentation. She omits the accusation of sympathizing with rebel guerrillas, grounded in an intercepted letter she sent to a friend that stated, "If you see the bushwhackers, 'give them my never dying love,' and say to them, God bless them and all their wise undertakings."[8] While in custody, Bryant insisted on her innocence, but refused to take an oath of allegiance to the United States government, which prompted her captors to keep her locked up. Considering her age, authorities probably would not have responded as vigorously as they did had it not been for the fact that guerrilla activity recently had escalated in the state and Sterling Price's army was on the move. A half century later she never admitted to any wrongdoing and claimed that she eventually took the oath only because she thought her father was dying and wanted to return home.

Finally, no collection of essays about Missouri women would have been complete without an entry on Margaret McLure. Although "Mother McLure" had died in 1902, Mrs. P. G. Robert had conducted an interview with her in about 1898, and in 1906 used it to write a biography of McLure for the St. Louis chapter of the UDC, named in her honor. A version of it appears in *Reminiscences*. In it, McLure is portrayed as a women compelled to help the Confederacy out of concern for her own son who had joined the rebel army. Thus, she began visiting Confederate prisoners in St. Louis and those in the prison hospitals. Her reputation as a "friend of the Confederate soldier" escalated, and this drew her into other activities such as collecting rebel mail to be sent south, gathering contraband to be smuggled, hiding escaped prisoners, and aiding young men in making their way to the Confederate army in the South. McLure's activities are not denied; instead, they are framed as the actions of a devoted mother nurturing her son vicariously through her aid to the Confederate soldiers. The narrative then goes on to describe her arrest, the conversion of her home into a prison, her banishment with others, and their trip southward through the lines. In 1920 Matthew Page Andrews included a version of Robert's essay on McLure in his book *Women of the South in War*

Times. The only substantial change of note concerns Andrews's omission of any reference to the offenses that got McLure arrested and banished. Gone is any mention of McLure's involvement in collecting contraband mail for Absalom Grimes, her gathering of goods for smuggling, the escaped prisoners she hid, and the rebel recruits she helped send south. Accordingly, her only offense appears to be aiding "the unfortunate Confederates who were confined in the wretched military 'pens' of old St. Louis."[9]

This trend toward qualifying or even eliminating admission of involvement in the activities that aided the Confederate war cause, the very actions that led to the women's arrests, helped to shape the narrative of rebel women arrested and imprisoned in the St. Louis area. It is not the only trend evident, either. No matter how these stories were told, they usually conclude with the assumption that the real war was fought by the men, while the women played a secondary and, at times, passive role to their male defenders. Thus, while her "warm sympathy [was] with the South in its war for the maintenance of the liberties won in the long struggle of the revolution," others perceived Margaret McLure as "the soldier's friend," who "never refused aid or comfort to any Confederate soldier," and not an operative in the Confederate war machine. The only offense committed by Sydney Jackman's wife, besides being married to a Confederate officer, was providing nurture to her husband, and not aiding a "daring officer who was at all times an enemy to be feared by the northern soldiers." The former Sue Bryant asserted that her commitment to "the principles of the glorious South . . . caused her to suffer for the Confederacy and the 'Men who wore the Gray.'" As maintained in the second essay in *Reminiscences,* titled "The Origins of the United Daughters of the Confederacy," "the sting of injustice still rankles in the breast of those who fought for their homes and loved ones, for their pride, honor, manhood, their principles and rights, for all that men hold nearest and dearest in this life." Despite being a book by women about women during the war, *Reminiscences* identifies men as the fighters. The essay further assures its readers that "their fathers were never *rebels or traitors to their country,*" showing no need for exonerating their mothers for such wrongdoings. One contributor went so far as to suggest that only men can properly honor the now defunct Confederacy. In her essay about serving as a nurse during the Battle of the Seven Days, Mrs. P. G. Robert, who also penned the entry about Margaret McLure, ends her story with the revelation that since the end of the war "I have never seen a Confederate Uniform nor a Confederate flag that I have not wished for a moment that I was a man that I might have a hat to take off for it." Even in paying homage to the failed Confederate States, Robert gives deference to men as the appropriate actors.[10]

Historian Catherine Clinton has recently argued that women who trans-
gressed the roles of gender and aided the Confederate cause, especially as
"spies, scouts, and curriers," kept their stories to themselves after the war
because their actions would damage their reputations as ladies. "Females who
chose to defy the [gender] dictates of the era remain relatively unheralded
heroes; discretion was a necessary virtue," Clinton notes, "and after the war,
women might be excluded from tributes not just because of the secrecy sur-
rounding their missions but because women would be compromised if such
dealings were revealed. Ladies' reputations might be sullied permanently
if involvement [in these partisan activities] were acknowledged." There is
probably some truth to Clinton's observation, but it does not tell the whole
story. The source of the characterization of the rebellious women found in
Reminiscences and other sources, as well as the downplaying or ignoring of
their partisan activities and the repercussions some women faced, more likely
stem from the Lost Cause mythology that evolved after the war and its portrayal of the men who fought for the South. Through public commemorations,
newspapers, magazines, speeches, and other written accounts, especially
from the men who wore the Confederate gray, Southerners crafted an ideol-
ogy that served to rationalize the war and its outcome and to vindicate the
men who participated in it. The cause for which Southerners fought, usually
presented devoid of any connection to slavery, became one of protecting individual liberties, states' rights, and a traditional Southern—meaning white
Southern—way of life against an aggressive and dominating Northern society
and Republican Party. Thus, Southerners unified to resist the encroachment
of the Republican-dominated Federal government and the literal invasion
of the Yankee army. Accordingly, in the 1860s Southern men had taken up
arms not just for the political cause of the Confederacy, but more importantly
to protect their rights, their homes, and especially their families in a valiant
and noble effort. It ended in failure only because of the material superiority
that the North had over the South, and not because of any shortcomings
in the character and abilities of the men who served in the Southern army.
Although defeated, Southern men who served had nothing to be ashamed
of, having fought for what was right, honorable, and just.[11]

Women played a large role in creating the mythic Lost Cause as well as
in helping to rehabilitate their defeated menfolk. Southern women were in
the vanguard of the movement to erect monuments to honor the Southern
warriors and heroes, living and dead, and to commemorate Southern men
who died in Northern military prisons. Furthermore, they created the United
Daughters of the Confederacy to glorify the cause and to teach it to future
generations.[12] While women's endeavors did much to establish the Lost Cause

myth, the myth itself had little or no room for the wartime partisan endeavors of women. Innocent, helpless, and vulnerable, women were objects to be protected from the encroaching Federal army. The image of women participating in the fight in ways that could, and did, lead to their arrest and imprisonment, and theoretically could have brought on execution in some cases, placed the partisan women as actors in the struggle and suggested that these women were quite capable of protecting themselves. Thus, postwar narratives like those found in *Reminiscences* diminished women's military contributions to the war effort while deifying the efforts put forward by men.

One additional trend in the story of Missouri's Confederate partisan women becomes apparent by the second decade of the twentieth century. The story of these women became dominated by tales of banishment rather than of prison incarceration. Especially represented was the retelling of the departure of prominent St. Louis women. All but one of these women included in *Reminiscences* experienced banishment rather than a long incarceration. The one exception, Sue Bryant, spent about two months in custody—one of the articles about her suggests it was longer—only because she refused to take the oath of allegiance. Several later significant works about St. Louis and Missouri followed this pattern. In his epic 1981 history of St. Louis, *Lion of the Valley*, James Neal Primm offers one paragraph concerning banished women. He identifies the women as "wives of Confederate officers, some of whom were spies," mentioning Sallie McPheeters and Eliza Frost as wives but not implicating them as spies, and "women who too zealously promoted southern causes," noting Fanny Coons and her fundraising effort. A decade earlier, William E. Parrish includes only information on Coons in his contribution to the University of Missouri Press's "A History of Missouri" series, covering the Civil War and Reconstruction period. Louis Gerteis's history of wartime St. Louis gives most of the attention it pays to women prisoners to those banished with Margaret McLure and Eliza Frost in 1863, while William C. Winter's *The Civil War in St. Louis* discusses only those women. Finally, nearly half of the two and a half pages Katharine T. Corbett allots to Confederate women prisoners is devoted to McLure in *In Her Place: A Guide to St. Louis Women's History*.[13]

A 2009 essay about the 1863 banishment of McLure and company published by historian LeAnn Whites puts further emphasis on that incident as the primary story of Confederate women arrested in St. Louis. In it Whites asserts that prior to the spring of 1863, "The provost marshal had sporadically arrested a few women for disloyal behavior . . . , but they were generally held only for the day at Gratiot Prison, or at worst for a night, and even then with a notation like 'keep her for the night, teach her a lesson!'" Whites's portrayal grossly underestimates the numbers of women arrested during that time and the treatment they received. The research presented here identifies at least sixty women handled by Missouri's provost marshal office through May 1863, many of whom spent several days or weeks in custody with some heavily fined or banished from the state or the Department of the Missouri for their offenses. Whites further argues that the banishment of McLure and others "brought to a close an important chapter in a long and hard-fought battle between Southern sympathizing women in St. Louis—and in Missouri in general—and the Union soldiers who occupied a border area critical to the Northern war effort."[14] Again, the statement distorts the truth. The May 1863 banishment was the first of several mass banishments from St. Louis while the number of Confederate women spending time under lock and key continued to escalate through the war. If anything, that banishment, combined with the implementation of General Orders No. 100, opened a new chapter in the war between disloyal women and Federal soldiers in Missouri and its neighboring states.

The focus on banishment rather than imprisonment is tied to the memory of the war and the Lost Cause myth. Historian David Blight observes that "no other experience . . . caused deeper emotions, recriminations, and lasting invective than that of prisons. Civil War prisons were, by and large, hellholes of disease, misery, and death." As a result of these feelings, bitterness and condemnation concerning prisons and the treatment of prisoners continued to pervade postwar narratives of the Civil War, even as the war's participants began reaching a reconciliation with each other. Blight adds that "prison memory lacked heroes, personal resolutions, and life affirming elements of humane reconciliation, even among soldiers." Nevertheless, in the late nineteenth century many survivors of the prisons on both sides produced memoirs, just as veterans who never experienced the "hellholes" did. The prison survivors, as Benjamin Cloyd points out, sought to "redefine what wartime heroism meant." In addition to traditional military deeds such as "battlefield charges, last stands, brilliant tactics, or personal fighting prowess," this new definition also included the sacrifices, deprivations, brutality, and horrors experienced by those confined to prisons. Thus, the time the prisoners spent confined and away from the fighting was just as heroic as the experience of the soldiers on the battlefield. The fact that the Union army imprisoned a significant number of Southern women during the war is something that one would think would have made for powerful fodder in this war of words concerning prisons, yet the narratives from Confederates held as prisoners are virtually silent on female prisoners, instead stressing the terrible conditions and treatment that the men faced.[15] True, the conditions in the St. Louis-area prisons that housed Confederate women undoubtedly were nowhere near as bad as the prisons that held men in St. Louis and elsewhere in the North. Furthermore, nineteenth-century notions concerning gender tempered any harsh treatment the women may have experienced at the hands of the Union army. Nevertheless, while the fact that women remained in Union military prisons might have made for good propaganda, the notion of women in the prisons, some for weeks or months at a time, proved doubly vexing for veterans who spent time in a prisoner of war camp. First, it would have weakened the portrayal of Union prisons as intolerable places. Moreover, accounts of women enduring imprisonment would diminish the image of the heroic Confederate soldier surviving the horrendous experience of captivity. In other words, if frail and vulnerable women could tolerate imprisonment, then men experiencing prison was no valiant feat. Thus, tales of banishment of Confederate women proved to be more convenient for the Lost Cause mythology, less mitigating of soldiers' manhood, than stories of women's imprisonment during the war.

By the time that historians seriously began looking at the role of women in the Civil War, the story of disloyal women in custody had become mutated, submerged, lost, and forgotten. When historians did come across the residue of this story, they treated it as a novelty or curiosity, worthy of mention as an anecdote, if at all. As discussed in the introduction, historians have started to acknowledge and explore the depth of the political nature of Confederate women's activities during the war as well as the extent to which they were involved in partisan undertakings. But it took nearly a century and a half for historians to begin recognizing this. In her essay on the 1863 banishment of prominent St. Louis women, LeAnn Whites is exactly right in her assessment that "the story of the events that led to the banishment of these women . . . is . . . the story of how women's relational position became, in the course of the war, politicized and even treasonous from the perspective of the Union military."[16] Even then, the case of the banished women in question, while revealing, tells only part of the story.

In addition to scholars, some writers of fiction have also discovered Confederate partisan women, including a few covered in this book, as source material. For example, three works with neo-Confederate leanings introduce actual Missouri women known to the military justice system in St. Louis as characters. Jessica Jewett's 2006 novel *From the Darkness Risen* tells the story of Isabelle Cavanaugh, a Virginia slave mistress who in the spring of 1862 travels to St. Louis to find her husband, a captain from the Fifth Virginia Infantry captured in the Shenandoah Valley and sent to the Alton Prison. Once there, Isabelle enlists the aid of none other than Drucilla (spelled "Drusella" in the book) Sappington, who helps Isabelle concoct a farfetched scheme to break her husband out of prison. The plan goes terribly wrong, and Isabelle ends up herself a prisoner in Alton, where she reunites with her husband. Eventually, the two escape after a series of preposterous plot twists. Jewett acknowledges in "A Note to the Reader" at the book's outset that Sappington was a real person who lived during the war, but that her story had been "altered to fit this novel," meaning that it had been totally fabricated.[17] Key elements in the story, such as how a Virginia lieutenant and friend of the Cavanaughs would know to direct Isabelle to Sappington as someone who could help and exactly where to find her in St. Louis, or how Sappington, already under investigation for her disloyal activities, is allowed to organize and host an elaborate ball in St. Louis attended by many Federal officers and soldiers, go unexplained. Putting aside any literary defects in the novel, Jewett's melodramatic story shows a lack of awareness of the existence and function of the provost marshal system and other military practices and protocols.

A more realistic tale is woven by Fay Risner in *Ella Mayfield's Pawpaw Militia*, a fictionalized account of the wartime activities of the title character, who assisted and at times rode with rebel guerrillas in western Missouri during the war. While Ella never came into the custody of the Union army during the war, two of her sisters, secondary characters in the book, did. In July 1864, Clarinda (also known as Jane or Jennie) Mayfield and Sarah (also known as Sallie) Mayfield Waitman were arrested for aiding and abetting bushwhackers. Eventually sent to St. Louis, the two escaped from the St. Charles Street Prison. Broadly, the story remains true to actual events, its Southern sympathies notwithstanding, although Risner relied heavily on sources that one historian notes provides "an exaggerated and embellished account of" the Mayfield women's "wartime exploits."[18] Despite her sources, Risner's description of the sisters' escape from prison, while brief, parallels the actual historical narrative.

Taking greater liberties with the truth, although not to the extent that Jewett does, is James Ronald Kennedy's *Uncle Seth Fought the Yankees*. Known for the unreconstructed rebel polemic *The South Was Right!* authored with his brother, Walter Donald Kennedy, and several other right-wing publications, Kennedy here offers, according to the book's dust jacket, "his first foray into fiction, using a storytelling format." The book presents over one hundred vignettes of a few pages with titles such as "Why Do the Yankees Hate Us?," "Yankee Crimes against Women and Children," and "Yankee Materialism: The Root Cause of the War," told by the fictional elder veteran Uncle Seth to a young girl named Billie Jean, as well as numerous other short items of a paragraph or two and labeled *"Deo Vindice,"* or "God as Our Defender," the formal motto of the Confederate States of America. One of Kennedy's stories focuses on Georgia T. Read, who grew up in New Orleans but fled to Virginia after the Crescent City fell under Union army control in 1862. According to Uncle Seth, Read became a nurse with the Army of Northern Virginia. Not satisfied that she was doing all she could, Read cut her hair, disguised herself as a Union soldier, and strolled through Union army camps gathering what intelligence she could. She would then leave the camp the same way she came and pass through the lines, bringing to the Confederates what information she had. For some unspecified reason she relocated to the Western Theater, where she did the same thing and reported her observations to a General Price, perhaps Sterling, until her arrest and imprisonment in St. Louis.[19]

The provost marshal general's records do not specify the cause of Read's arrest, just that she was taken into custody in Weston, Missouri, on the western border in November 1864 and sent to St. Louis. From there she was banished on January 19. Kennedy uses no footnotes or documentation in this work. "Those who love the South do not need footnotes," he proclaims. "A man's word is his bound [*sic*]." Had he used footnotes, Kennedy no doubt would have cited the obituary of Read that appeared in the May 1910 edition of the *Confederate Veteran*, from which he draws and at times copies word for word. Kennedy echoes the obituary's claim that after the war Read settled in Fredericktown, Missouri, and began teaching, but when she refused to take an oath of allegiance to the United States, authorities ordered her banished from the state. The provost marshal general's records show no postwar banishment, only the January 1865 departure after her incarceration in St. Louis. Conversely, Kennedy and the obituary are silent on the documented banishment. Furthermore, Kennedy adds that as a "reward for maintaining her loyalty to her southern country, the Confederate States of America," Read "was to be known as the only female to ever be ordered out of the state of Missouri and the only female to suffer banishment because of her love of the South and disdain for the Yankee Empire."[20] Neither statement is true.

By far, a much better literary effort focusing on women in custody in St. Louis during the war is Paulette Jiles's *Enemy Women*. Published in 2002, *Enemy Women* follows the travails of eighteen-year-old Adair Colley, who with her family find it impossible to remain unaffected by the chaos that visits her native Ripley County in southeast Missouri. After the arrest of her father in late 1864, Adair is driven from her home and in short time she, too, is arrested under false charges of disloyalty. Sent to St. Louis, the innocent Adair enters the St. Charles Street Prison for Women where interrogators from the Office of the Provost Marshal pressure her to confess to helping the Confederates and to expose other rebel associates, even if she has to fabricate the facts. Helped by an officer with whom she falls in love, Adair escapes her captors, spending the rest of the novel working her way back to Ripley County, hoping that one day she will reunite with her love. Jiles claimed that she used "an unknown or 'lost' piece of the history of the Civil War in southeastern Missouri—the unjust incarceration of women" as a "dramatic background to a love story." Jiles's compelling story made its way to the *New York Times* bestseller list, met with critical acclaim, and even was featured on the cover of the *New York Times Book Review.*[21]

Jiles's novel is not without its critics, however. The selection of the book as the focus of a 2003 statewide community book club in Missouri generated criticism from some concerning the work's historical accuracy. In particular, the Ripley County Historical Society censured the work and its choice by the book club for its portrayal of an incident that took place in the county that Jiles characterizes as a massacre of civilians on Christmas Day 1863. The controversy generated an ongoing debate in the *St. Louis Post-Dispatch* from the time of the announcement of the book as the club's selection in October 2002 through the following March when the events related to the club took place.[22] This attention to the book generated no discussion of the truth of Jiles's depiction of the arrest and imprisonment of women.

Adair Colley is arrested after being falsely accused of "giving information to rebel spies, and other things." Arrests after untrue accusations certainly happened during the war, and Adair insists on her innocence. While in custody, however, she is encouraged, coaxed, and cajoled by officers of the provost marshal general's office to confess to the claims against her, which included cutting telegraph wires, harboring and feeding guerrillas, and holding money in a bank account for guerrillas. "Miss Collier," says one officer, "the provost marshal's department seems bent on extracting confessions from women. . . . You must plead guilty to one or the other [charge against her] and then write a confession." Failing at that effort, he later offers her the chance to plead guilty "to a vague charge of provisioning guerrillas," after which he said she would receive better treatment and perhaps even her release. "I want you to write a confession to assisting guerrillas, the one charge, and then I will do my best to see that it is taken lightly."[23] The historic record shows no such evidence of pressure being put on women to confess. Instead, there are convictions based on testimony of witnesses and other evidence, and plenty of women released when guilt could not be ascertained.

Also in conflict with the record is Jiles's portrayal of the women found in the St. Charles Street Prison. No one seems to be guilty of disloyalty. The women Adair meets in the prison derive from the lowest classes, in particular from the less than respectable segments of society, such as prostitutes and actresses. States one prisoner, "These here women might be whores and thieves and fortune-tellers and drunks but they are loyal." "Most of us are in here unjustly imprisoned," insists another, an "actress" with "bright red lips and cheeks . . . white skin and . . . sooty" eyelids. She had been charged with "theft." In reality, arrests cut across class lines from the richest to the poorest. Furthermore, many women willingly admitted to the charges against them, not to gain any favoritism or a release from custody but to express their defiance to the Federal government. Many, indeed, took great pride in the aid they gave to the Confederate cause. Finally, military authorities rarely involved themselves in civil crimes like theft, unless they involved the army or soldiers, or the crime interfered with military matters. One character did admit to soldiers "I stand for Dixie" when questioned, which led to her arrest. By 1864 such an admission alone would not have led to the three months of imprisonment that she had so far experienced, with no end in sight.[24]

In the century between the publication of Winston Churchill's *The Crisis* and Jiles's *Enemy Women*, much had changed concerning our understanding of the Civil War, particularly in regard to women's place in the conflict. While Churchill denied that the Union army arrested and imprisoned women, Jiles centered her narrative around imprisoned women, albeit in a flawed way. As critic John Vernon reminds us in his review of *Enemy Women*, "This is a novel, not a historical study."[25] The sad reality is that more people have read or will read *The Crisis* and *Enemy Women* than this book; still, we cannot expect novelists, or anyone else, to get the story right if historians do not.

Notes

Bibliography

Index

NOTES

Individual Civilians File · Record Group 109, War Department Collection of Confederate Records, Union Provost Marshals' File of Papers Relating to Individual Civilians [M 345], National Archives

MHS · Missouri Historical Society

O.R. · *War of the Rebellion: A Compilation of the Official Records of the Union and Confederate Armies.* 70 vols. in 128 books, Washington, D.C.: Government Printing Office, 1880–1901. O.R. is followed by the series number in Roman numeral (I-IV), the volume number, and the page number. The O.R. is also now available on CD-ROM and at various sites on the internet, allowing for specific and accurate searches that would be very difficult and time consuming using the hard copies.

Selected Records ... Alton Prison · Record Group 109, War Department Collection of Confederate Records, Selected Records of the War Department Related to Confederate Prisoners of War, 1861–1865, Alton, IL, Military Prison [M 598], National Archives

Selected Records ... Gratiot and Myrtle Street Prisons · Record Group 109, War Department Collection of Confederate Records, Selected Records of the War Department Related to Confederate Prisoners of War, 1861–1865, Gratiot and Myrtle Street Prisons, St. Louis, MO [M 598], National Archives

SLPL · Saint Louis Public Library

Two or More Civilians Files · Record Group 109, War Department Collection of Confederate Records, Union Provost Marshals' File of Papers Relating to Two or More Civilians [M 416], National Archives

*Quotes appear in the text as they appeared in the original,
with [sic] used sparingly for clarification.*

Introduction

1. Curran, "'On the Road to Dixie,'" 85.

2. Frost, *Camp and Prison Journal*, 40, 196.

3. A phrase used in Lincoln's "Appeal to Border-State Representatives for Compensated Emancipation, Washington D.C.," July 12, 1862, reprinted in *Abraham Lincoln: Speeches and Writings, 1859–1865*, 341.

4. Rable, *Damn Yankees*, 70, 168n6.

5. For examples of early works that cover women during the war see Brockett and Vaughan, *Women's Work in the Civil War*; Andrews, *The Women of the South in War Times*; Simkins and Patton, *The Women of the Confederacy*; Horan, *Desperate Women*; and Dannett, *Noble Women of the North*.

6. Massey, *Bonnet Brigades*.

7. *Civil War History* 61 (December 2015).

8. Such works include but are not limited to: Scott, *The Southern Lady*; Rable, *Civil Wars*; Ryan, *Women in Public*; Venet, *Neither Ballots nor Bullets*; Clinton and Silber, eds., *Divided Houses*; Leonard, *Yankee Women*; Burgess, *An Uncommon Soldier*; Whites, *The Civil War as a Crisis in Gender*; Joslyn, *Valor and Lace*; Faust, *Mothers of Invention*; Krug, "Women and War in the Confederacy"; Faust, "'Ours as Well as That of Men'"; Leonard, *All the Daring of the Soldier*; Giesberg, *Civil War Sisterhood*; Blanton and Cook, *They Fought Like Demons*; Cutter, *Domestic Devils, Battlefield Angels*; Silber, *Daughters of the Union*; Lowry, *Confederate Heroines*; Clinton and Silber, eds., *Battle Scars*; Silber, *Gender and the Sectional Conflict*; Ott, *Confederate Daughters*; Whites and Long, eds., *Occupied Women*; Giesberg, *Army at Home*; McCurry, *Confederate Reckoning*; and Clinton, *Stepdaughters of History*.

9. See especially Rable, *Civil Wars* and Faust, *Mothers of Invention*.

10. McCurry, *Confederate Reckoning*, esp. 85–217, quote on 163.

11. Baker, "The Domestication of Politics: Women and American Political Society, 1780–1920," 622.

12. McCurry, *Confederate Reckoning*, 163.

13. McCurry, *Confederate Reckoning*, 85–116.

14. See for instance Leonard, *All the Daring of the Soldier* and Blanton and Cook, *They Fought Like Demons*. Both works cover women from the Confederacy and the Union.

15. Bunch, "Confederate Women of Arkansas Face 'the Fiends in Human Shape,'" quote on 182.

16. McCurry, *Confederate Reckoning*, 96.

17. McCurry, *Confederate Reckoning*, 215.

18. See General Orders No. 100, also known as Lieber's Code, in *O.R.*, III, 3: 148–64.

19. See for instance Two or Move Civilians File, Roll 53, 15003.

20. I make this comment because on several occasions while giving presentations and in other discussions I have been challenged with the argument that these women were arrested primarily because they had been stepping out of their sphere and transgressing acceptable gender boundaries.

21. Individual Civilians File, Roll 176, Annie B. Martin; Individual Civilians File, Roll 85, Emma S. English; Individual Civilians File, Roll 252, Hattie Snodgrass; Individual Civilians File, Roll 144, Mrs. Edward Wm. Johnson [Johnston]; Individual Civilians File, Roll 246, Mary Simpson; Individual Civilians File, Roll 252, Harriet Snead.

22. For the Peace Democrats, or Copperheads, see Weber, *Copperheads*.

23. Individual Civilians File, Roll 197, Sarah Moss; Individual Civilians File, Roll 254, Eliza Spencer; Individual Civilians File, Roll 44, Elizabeth Campbell.

24. Neely, *The Fate of Liberty*, 130–33; Grimsley, *The Hard Hand of War*; Boman, *Lincoln and Citizens' Rights in Civil War Missouri*.

25. Lowry, *Confederate Heroines*. Lowry's research is also at times flawed by its incomplete nature. There are about three dozen women appearing in his book that are covered in this study.

26. Witt, *Lincoln's Code*, 269, 450; Blair, *With Malice toward Some*, 9, 11, 38, 120, 122, 129, 149, 154, 156–59; White, "'To Aid Their Rebel Friends,'" 11, 105–06, 252, 263–65, 272–76, 277–82. White also published an essay concerning a woman from Maryland arrested and convicted of aiding the Confederacy. See White, "All for a Sword."

27. Hesseltine, *Civil War Prisons*; Speer, *Portals to Hell*.

28. Herrera-Graf, "Stress, Suffering, and Sacrifice."

29. Belanger, "'A Perfect Nuisance.'"

30. Fellman, *Inside War*, 46, 71–72, 126, 127, 195–98, 206–07, 215, 221–22; Sutherland, *A Savage Conflict*, 31–32, 131, 201–02, 222, 234–35, 333n22; Gerteis, *Civil War St. Louis*, 174, 178–79, 180–81, 191, 192, 200–01, 232; Phillips, *The River Ran Backward*, 195–96, 263–68.

In addition, Harris in "Catalyst for Terror" focuses on the disaster that took the lives of four women of the ten held there because of their relations to guerrillas operating along the western Missouri border in the summer of 1863 and the incident's role as a catalyst for raid on Lawrence, Kansas. His treatment of the women is brief and he does not place the arrests in the broader context of Federal policy.

31. Beilein, *Bushwhackers*; Stith, *Extreme Civil War*, quote on 14.

32. Streater, "'She-Rebels' and the Supply Line," Long, "(Mis)Remembering General Order No. 28," and Whites, "'Corresponding with the Enemy,'" in *Occupied Women*, Whites and Long.

33. McCurry, "Enemy Women and the Laws of War in the American Civil War," quote on 668.

34. Hopkins, "'Tried by the Furnace of Affliction'"; Segura, "Dependent Independence."

35. See Lowry, *The Story the Soldiers Wouldn't Tell*; Lowry, *Sexual Misbehavior in the Civil War*, 114–82; and Barber and Ritter, "'Unlawful and against Her Consent.'"

36. Winthrop, *A Digest of Opinions of the Judge Advocate General of the Army, with Notes*, 327n1. Emphasis in the original.

37. Neely, *The Fate of Liberty*, 44; Blair, *With Malice toward Some*, 101. Blair identifies four different types of provosts: civilian, or "special" provosts, assigned to particular functions; army provosts, serving as military police for the soldiers; departmental provosts, operating under the head of specific geographic military departments; and state agents, serving as provosts with state militia. I would add to this district provosts, responsible for specific districts within departments and answerable to the departmental provost marshal general. This study makes reference primarily to departmental and district provosts.

38. McCandless, *A History of Missouri*, 2: 1–30, 270–76; Phillips, *Missouri's Confederate*, 23–52; Laughlin, "Missouri Politics during the Civil War," part 1: 400–402; Laughlin, "'Endangering the Peace of Society'"; Fehrenbacher, *The Dred Scott Case*; Potter, *The Impending Crisis, 1848–1861*, 199–224, 267–96; Fellman, *Inside War*, 3–22.

39. Laughlin, "Missouri Politics during the Civil War," part 1: 403; Van Ravenswaay, "Years of Turmoil, Years of Growth," 306–07, 317–18, quote on 303–04; Gerteis, *Civil War St. Louis*, 22; Primm, *Lion of the Valley*, 2nd edition, 173–82.

40. See Gerteis, *Civil War St. Louis*; and Arenson, *The Great Heart of the Republic*.

41. *O.R.*, I, 5: 373–75, II, 2: 125, 135–36, 153, 190, 236–38, 271–72, 277–79, 306, 309, 394–98, 577, 738–39; 781, 1027–40, 1315–21; II, 3: 719; II, 4: 461, 718–19; II, 5: 572–73, 743; II, 7: 450; II, 8: 34, 104; Robertson, "Old Capitol"; Christie, "The Prisoner."

42. *O.R.*, I, 33, 256, 686; I, 36, 3: 668, 684; I, 46, 2: 109–10, 123–24; II, 4: 482; II, 5: 121–22, 130–31, 155, 165–66, 340, 526–27, 547–48, 567–68, 705, 869; II, 6: 304–05; *Missouri Democrat*, July 7, 1862.

43. *O.R.*, II, 6: 1052, 1055; Christie, "The Prisoner," 123–24.

44. *O.R.*, II, 5: 920–22; *Newark Advocate* (Ohio), December 25, 1863; Buhk, *Memphis Vice, 1863*, 83–87.

45. *O.R.*, I, 9: 612–13; 1: 26, 1: 40–41; II, 4: 516, 880–85; II 5: 119–20; Arnold-Scriber and Scriber, *Ship Island*, 426, 427, 428, and 430.

46. *O.R.*, II, 4, 228–29, 247–48; II, 5: 247, 269, 447–48, 511, 514–15, 544, 943–44.

47. *O.R.*, II, 5: 436; II, 8: 261; Individual Citizen File, Roll 149, Clara Judd; Individual Citizen File, Roll 260, John A. Stuart; Harris, *Dr. Mary Walker*, 58–67.

48. *O.R.*, I, 19, 2: 563; I, 20, 2: 209; I, 22, 1: 702–04; II, 4: 918–19; II, 5: 178, 186–87, 189–90; 800–01, 816–17, 853; II, 6: 62–63, 69, 73–74; IV, 3: 267; [Brock], *Richmond during the War*; Davis, *Ghosts and Shadows of Andersonville*, 61–62, 145–52.

1. *"The Line Is Being Drawn Every Day"*

This chapter's title is from [Euphrasia Pettus?] to dear sister [Mrs. Charles Parsons?], May 20, 1861, Civil War Collection, MHS.

1. [Euphrasia Pettus?] to dear sister [Mrs. Charles Parsons?], May 20, 1861, Civil War Collection, MHS.

2. Phillips, *Missouri Confederate*, 222–40; Parrish, *A History of Missouri*, 3: 1–12; Anderson, *A Border City during the Civil War*, 40–62; Laughlin, "Missouri Politics during the Civil War," part 2: 588, 601; *O.R.*, I, 1: 675; I, 3: 4–5, 386–87.

3. Parrish, *A History of Missouri*, 3: 12–13; Rombauer, *The Union Cause in St. Louis in 1861*, 239; Anderson, *A Border City in the Civil War*, 160; Winter, "'Like Sheep in a Slaughter Pen,'" 61; *O.R.*, I, 3: 372.

4. The following account, except where noted, is drawn from Covington, "The Camp Jackson Affair: 1861," 197–212.

5. [F. A. Dick], "Memorandum of Matters in Missouri in 1861."

6. *O.R.*, I, 3: 5.

7. *O.R.*, I, 3: 5; Winter, *The Civil War in St. Louis*, 49–53, 164n60; Gerteis, *Civil War St. Louis*, 108–10.

8. Anderson, *A Border City during the Civil War*, 106–19; Rombauer, *The Union Cause in St. Louis in 1861*, 238–40; Krug, *Mrs. Hill's Journal—Civil War Reminiscences*, 13–22; *O.R.*, II, 1: 107. Quote from Louis Fusz Diary, 1862–1863, typescript copy, 1: 6 (May 10, 1862), MHS. Fusz penned his observations on the one-year anniversary of the incident.

9. Phillips, *Missouri's Confederate*, 257–60; Parrish, *A History of Missouri*, 3: 16–22; *O.R.*, I, 3: 381–82.

10. [Euphrasia Pettus?] to dear sister [Mrs. Charles Parsons?], May 20, 1861, Civil War Collection, MHS.

11. Parrish, *A History of Missouri*, 3: 23–28; McPherson, *Battle Cry of Freedom*, 350–51; Piston and Hatcher, *Wilson's Creek*.

12. Frémont, "In Command in Missouri," 279–83; Parrish, *A History of Missouri*, 3: 27–29. On June 6, 1861, Missouri was added to the military department that included Ohio, Indiana, Illinois, and parts of western Pennsylvania and Virginia, under the command of Major General George B. McClellan. The Western Department was created on July 3, 1861. *O.R.*, I, 3: 384, 390.

13. *Missouri Democrat*, August 15, 1861; *O.R.*, I, 3: 442, 466–67; Frémont, "In Command in Missouri," 278–79; Anderson, *A Border City during the Civil War*,

157–69; Laughlin, "Missouri Politics during the Civil War," part 2: 601; Parrish, *A History of Missouri*, 3: 23.

14. Knox, *Camp-Fire and Cotton-Field*, 54; *Missouri Democrat*, September 3, 1861.

15. Hesseltine, "Military Prisons of St. Louis, 1861–1865," 381–83; Anderson, *A Border City during the Civil War*, 184. See also Wright, *Discovering African American St. Louis*, 11.

16. Anderson, *A Border City during the Civil War*, 159–66; McCurry, "Enemy Women and the Laws of War in the American Civil War," 668–70.

17. *Missouri Democrat*, September 26, October 21, 1861; Gerteis, *Civil War St. Louis*, 147–48. McNeil replaced McKinstry as acting provost marshal in late September 1861.

18. Individual Civilians Files, Roll 40, Mrs. Burke; Individual Civilians Files, Roll 42, Ann Bush.

19. Massey, *Bonnet Brigades*, 30–31; Richardson, *The Secret Service*, 259; Individual Civilians Files, Roll 42, Ann Bush

20. Individual Civilians Files, Roll 42, Ann Bush. Burke evidently was released on the same day as her arrest.

21. Individual Civilians Files, Roll 40, Mrs. Burke.

22. *O.R.*, I, 3: 553, 559, 567; Parrish, *A History of Missouri*, 3: 37–42; Knox, *Camp-Fire and Cotton-Field*, 113; McElroy, *The Struggle for Missouri*, 258–59; Macartney, *Grant and His Generals*, 152–53.

23. Marszalek, *Commander of All Lincoln's Armies*, 1–104; Ambrose, *Halleck*, 3–10.

24. *O.R.*, II, 1: 234–36; Neely, *The Fate of Liberty*, 37; Boman, *Lincoln and Citizens' Rights in Missouri*, 80. Halleck reasserted martial law on December 26, 1861, through General Orders No. 34, but only in St. Louis City and "in and about all railroads in the State" (*O.R.*, II, 1: 155). In practice, however, martial law was applied throughout the entire state.

25. *O.R.*, II, 3: 454–55.

26. Mark Neely discusses the difficulty of trying captured Confederates for treason in Missouri in *The Fate of Liberty*, 42–43. See also White, *Abraham Lincoln and Treason in the Civil War*, 44–63.

27. *O.R.*, II, 1: 248.

28. See Faust's discussion of the order in *Mothers of Invention*, 207–12.

29. Campbell, "'The Unmeaning Twaddle about Order 28,'" 11–30; Grimsley, *The Hard Hand of War*, 53. Alecia P. Long challenges the order's effectiveness in "(Mis)Remembering General Order No. 28," 17–32.

30. *Missouri Democrat*, January 27, 1862.

31. *Missouri Democrat*, December 5, 6, 7, 11, 1861; Individual Civilians File, Roll 278, Nicholas Walton.

32. Individual Civilians File, Roll 55, Mary E. Cole; *Missouri Democrat*, December 28, 1861; Individual Civilians File, Roll 57, Bridget Connors; Two or More Civilians File, Roll 93.

33. *Missouri Democrat*, December 5, 6, 7, 11, 28, 1861; Individual Civilians File, Roll 278, Nicholas Walton; Individual Civilians File, Roll 55, Mary E. Cole; Individual Civilians File, Roll 57, Bridget Connors; Two or More Civilians File, Roll 93; *O.R.*, II, 2: 249–52. The generation of the list came in response to a request sent by Secretary of State William Seward on February 13, 1862, for such a list from all Union military prisons. *O.R.*, II, 2: 219. The copy Leighton received is now in Folder 2, George E. Leighton Collection, MHS.

34. *O.R.*, II, 1: 177.

35. See Marszalek, *Commander of All Lincoln's Armies*, 105–28.

36. *Missouri Democrat*, April 16, 17, 18, 29, May 3 and 15, June 16, 20, 21, July 11, August 14, 1862; Individual Civilians File, Roll 18, Mrs. Fanny Barron.

37. *Missouri Democrat*, July 14, 1862. Leighton was appointed acting provost marshal of "St. Louis and its vicinity," replacing John McNeil, on October 27, 1861. The appointment became permanent on December 4. See General Orders No. 27, Folder 1, George E. Leighton Collection, MHS; *O.R.*, II, 1: 233–34.

38. McCurry, "Enemy Women and the Laws of War in the American Civil War," 683; *Missouri Democrat*, July 7, 17, 1862; Knox, *Camp-Fire and Cotton-Field*, 113.

39. Mrs. Hannah Isabella Staggs, "Local Incidents of the Civil War," February 1899 (typescript manuscript), Civil War Collection, MHS; Peterson, McGhee, Lindberg, and Daleen, *Sterling Price's Lieutenants*, 110; *Missouri Democrat*, April 23, 1862; Compiled Service Records of the Confederate Soldiers Who Served in Organizations from the State of Missouri, Missouri State Guard, Hampton L. Boon (Roll 36).

40. Individual Civilians File, Roll 172, Daniel Lyons.

41. All information on Morrison, except where noted, is drawn from Individual Civilians File, Roll 196, Isadore Morrison.

42. Leonard, *All the Daring of the Soldiers*, 75–80.

43. *Missouri Democrat*, July 28, 1862.

44. The author thanks Anne Stirnemann of the Missouri Regional Poison Control Center in St. Louis for providing information on chloroform poisoning.

45. *Missouri Republican*, August 20, 1862; Individual Civilians File, Roll 196, Isadore Morrison. Halleck appointed Farrar provost marshal general on December 4, 1861 through General Orders No. 13.

46. Individual Civilians File, Roll 295, Mary Wolfe; Individual Civilians File, Roll 52, Lucinda Clark.

47. Individual Civilians File, Roll 89, Mrs. Catherine Farrell; *Missouri Democrat*, September 1, 1862.

48. Individual Civilians File, Roll 144, Mrs. Edward Wm. Johnson [Johnston], Roll 145, Margaret A. Johnston. See also Individual Civilians File, Roll 144, Edward Wm. Johnson.

49. Telephone interview, Ollie Sappington, July 18, 2000; *History of Southwest Missouri,* 913; 1860 U.S. Census, Missouri, St. Louis County, Central Twp., 851; 1860 U.S. Census, Missouri Slave Schedules, St. Louis County, Central Twp., 324. The author thanks Ollie Sappington for the biographical information he provided for both Drucilla and William David Sappington.

50. *Missouri Democrat,* September 4, 1862; Telephone interview, Ollie Sappington, July 18, 2000; Individual Civilians File, Roll 238, Mrs. W. D. Sappington; Individual Civilians File, Roll 185, George M. McKibben. The author thanks Mr. Sappington for the biographical information he provided for both Drucilla and William David Sappington.

51. *Missouri Democrat,* September 4, 1862; *O.R.,* II, 4: 486. The *Missouri Democrat,* September 8, 1862, identified the officer at Drucilla's house as Colonel John C. Boon, but Confederate mail carrier Absalom Grimes identified him as Hampton Boon. See Grimes, *Absalom Grimes,* 75. Information given by George McKibben also corroborates that it was Hampton Boon. See Individual Civilians File, Roll 185, George M. McKibben.

52. *Missouri Democrat,* September 17, 1862; Individual Civilian Files, Roll 245, Mrs. Sigler; Two or More Civilians File, Roll 93; Grimes, *Absalom Grimes,* 75, 85–93. See chapter 8 for a more thorough discussion of the escape.

53. *Missouri Democrat,* October 14, 1862, May 14, 1863; Individual Civilians File, Roll 290, Olly Williams; *O.R.,* I, 34, 2: 1077.

54. Prisoners: St. Louis, Mo. (Gratiot Street Prison) February–November 1865, and other Prisons (varying dates), Two or More Civilians File, Roll 93; *Missouri Democrat,* September 17, October 14, 1862; Individual Civilians File, Roll 269, Edward D. Trainor; Individual Civilians File, Roll 85, William Embree; Two or More Civilians File, Roll 8, 1986.

55. *O.R.,* II, 1: 140, 247–49; Individual Civilians File, Roll 152, Bridget Kelly; *Missouri Democrat,* June 20, 21, August 8, 13, 14, 1862.

56. *Missouri Democrat,* September 8, 1862.

57. Neely, *The Fate of Liberty,* 62.

58. *O.R.,* II, 2: 219, 236–38, 249–52.

59. *O.R.,* II, 2: 271–72; Leonard, *All the Daring of the Soldier,* 35–44. After being banished to the Confederacy Greenhow traveled to Europe where she tried to drum up support for the Confederacy and also published a memoir entitled *My Imprisonment, and the First Year of Abolition Rule at Washington* (1863). She attempted to return to the South in the fall of 1864 on a blockade runner, but when the ship was engaged in a pursuit by Union vessels off the coast of North

Carolina, Greenhow insisted upon being let off the ship in a row boat, and into threatening waters. She never made it to shore alive.

60. Leonard, *All the Daring of the Soldier*, 27; Boman, *Lincoln and Citizens' Rights in Civil War Missouri*, 63. From March 13 to September 19, 1862, Missouri became part of the Department of the Mississippi under Halleck's command. After his departure for Washington in mid-July 1862 the department was temporarily in the hands of John Schofield. The Department of the Missouri would be reestablished on September 19, 1862, with Samuel Curtis in command.

61. Grimsley, *The Hard Hand of War*, esp. 67–141.

2. *"On Account of the Difference of Sexes"*

This chapter's title is from General Orders No. 100, *O.R.*, III, 3: 158–59. A version of this chapter, titled "Lieber's Code, Henry Halleck, and the Concept of the War Traitor," was presented at the 13th Annual Mid-America Conference on History, Springfield, Missouri, September 26, 2008.

1. *O.R.*, III, 3: 148–64. For a brief summary of the far-reaching influence of Lieber's Code see Hogue, "Lieber's Military Code and Its Legacy," esp. 57–59. For other works on the code see Friedel, *Francis Lieber*; Baxter, "The First Modern Codification of the Laws of War.—Francis Lieber and General Orders No. 100"; Baxter, "The First Modern Codification of the Laws of War.—Francis Lieber and General Orders No. 100 (II)"; Childress, "Francis Lieber's Interpretation of the Laws of War"; Hartigan, *Lieber's Code and the Laws of War*; Mancini, "Francis Lieber, Slavery, and the 'Genesis' of the Laws of War"; Witt, *Lincoln's Code*; and Dilbeck, "'The Origin of This Tablet with My Name.'"

2. Hartigan, *Lieber's Code and the Laws of War*, 3, 13.

3. Hartigan, *Lieber's Code and the Laws of War*, 2, 3, 9–13, 18, 79–80; *O.R.*, III, 2: 301–09. The committee included Major Generals E. A. Hitchcock, G. Cadwalader, and George L. Hartsuff; and Brigadier General J. H. Martindale, along with Lieber. See *O.R.*, III, 2: 951.

4. *O.R.*, III, 3: 148–64. The following two paragraphs are drawn from the code and from Thomas F. Curran, "General Orders, No. 100."

5. For a discussion of Lieber's Code in practice, see Grimsley, *The Hard Hand of War*, 149–51. For recent analyses of the shortcomings of the code, see Stout, *Upon the Altar of the Nation*, 191–93; Nelson and Sheriff, *A People at War*, 153–56; Sutherland, *A Savage Conflict*, 128–29; and Carnahan, *Lincoln on Trial*, 30–31.

6. *O.R.*, III, 3: 158–59.

7. "A Code for the Government of Armies in the Field," 17, Francis Lieber Papers Ms. 71, Box 2, Folder 25, Special Collections, Milton S. Eisenhower Library, Johns Hopkins University; Lieber to Halleck, May 20, 1863, quoted in Hartigan, *Lieber's Code and the Laws of War*, 108–09; Lieber to Halleck, February 20, 1863;

February 25, 1863; March 2, 1863; March 16, 1863; March 17, 1863; [c. late March 1863]; April 17, 1863, Francis Lieber Collection, Huntington Library, San Marino, Cal.; Marszalek, *Commander of All Lincoln's Army*, 183. Carnahan incorrectly claims that "in the end, Lieber did all the writing," *Lincoln on Trial*, 30.

8. *O.R.*, III, 3: 158–59.

9. "A Code for the Government of Armies in the Field," 16.

10. "A Code for the Government of Armies in the Field," 16; *O.R.*, II, 1: 248. For more on the treason issue see Carso, "*Whom Can We Trust Now?*," esp. 197–201.

11. McCurry, "Enemy Women and the Laws of War in the American Civil War," 688–89; *O.R.*, I, 23, 2: 107–09; Jonathan White identifies Halleck's type of reframing the constitutional definition of treason as "constructive treason." See "'To Aid Their Rebel Friends,'" 40.

12. *O.R.*, I, 22, 2: 158–59. Sumner suffered a fatal heart attack and died on March 21, 1863, before he could arrive in St. Louis to begin his new assignment.

13. Lieber to Halleck, March 17, 1863, Francis Lieber Collection, Huntington Library, San Marino, CA.

14. Friedel, "General Orders 100 and Military Government," 552.

15. Lieber to Halleck, March 22, 1863, Francis Lieber Collection, Huntington Library, San Marino, CA. A few days later, Lieber admitted to Halleck that the letter to Rosecrans influenced several parts of the code. See Lieber to Halleck, [c. late March 1863], Francis Lieber Collection, Huntington Library, San Marino, CA.

16. Wheaton, *Elements of International Law*, 2nd annotated edition, Supplement, 41; Johnson, *An Argument to Establish the Illegality of Military Commissions in the United States*, 18.

17. Beale, *The Diary of Edward Bates, 1859–1866*, 490.

18. The essay has appeared in several publications. See for instance Alison, *Miscellaneous Essays*, 195–203. When the Civil War broke out, Alison supported the South's right to secede.

The source of the term "war traitor" remained a matter of controversy among military law scholars long after the war. See for instance Morgan, "War Treason"; and Garner, *International Law and the World War*, 95–97.

19. Baxter, "The Duty of Obedience to the Belligerent Occupant," 245; *O.R.*, II, 6: 46.

20. See comments on "A Code for the Government of Armies in the Field," Document LI 182A, Huntington Library, San Marino, CA.

A letter from political scientist Charles B. Robson to John C. French at Johns Hopkins University Library also asserts that the content of the comments of the draft at the Huntington Library originated with Halleck. The February 8, 1932, letter is filed with "A Code for the Government of Armies in the Field," Francis Lieber Papers Ms. 71, Box 2, Folder 25, Special Collections, Milton S. Eisenhower Library, Johns Hopkins University.

21. Baxter, "The Duty of Obedience to the Belligerent Occupant," 244–47, quote on 246. See also Baxter, "The First Modern Codification of the Laws of War.—Francis Lieber and General Orders No. 100 (II)," esp. 244–45.

22. The following section is drawn from Kerber, *No Constitutional Right to Be Ladies*, 3–33. For more on Revolutionary War-era state laws concerning treason see Carso, *"Whom Can We Trust Now?,"* 59–62.

23. Kerber, *No Constitutional Right to Be Ladies*, xxiii.

24. Stephanie McCurry explores this subject in "Enemy Women and the Laws of War in the American Civil War."

25. See Larson, *The Assassin's Accomplice.*

26. Individual Civilians File, Roll 53, Margaret Clifton; Individual Civilians File, Roll 12, Augusta Bagwell and Zaidie Bagwell; General Orders No. 37, May 22, 1863, U.S. Army, *General Orders, Department of the Missouri issued by General Curtis 1862 and 1863* (n.p., n.d.), SLPL.

27. Mark Neely argues that by the time it was released, the decision in *Ex parte Milligan* was in fact irrelevant. See *The Fate of Liberty*, 175–79.

28. Garner, "General Order 100 Revisited," 15; Marmon, Cooper, and Goodman, *Military Commissions*, 22, accessed at http://www.loc.gov/rr/frd/Military_Law/pdf/mil_commissions.pdf (accessed August 18, 2019).

The substance of the accusation of war treason can be found today in articles 103, 103a, and 103b of the Uniform Code of Military Justice (United States Code, title 10, subtitle A, part 2, chapter 47), accessed at https://www.law.cornell.edu/uscode/text/10/subtitle-A/part-II/chapter-47 (accessed August 18, 2019).

29. Halleck, "Retaliation in War," 116. According to an editorial notation, this essay was found in manuscript form among Halleck's belongings when he died in 1872. The content suggests that the essay was written in early 1865, and not in 1864 as the notation proposes.

30. See Grimsley, *The Hard Hand of War.*

3. *"To Know What to Do with Them"*

This chapter's title is from Provost Marshal General Franklin A. Dick to Union army Commissary-General of Prisoners William Hoffman, March 3, 1863, *O.R.*, II, 5, 320.

1. *Missouri Democrat*, November 11, 1862; M. Philip Lucas, "Curtis, Samuel Ryan"; *O.R.*, II, 5: 99–100.

2. 1860 U.S. Census, Missouri, City of St. Louis, Ward 4, 146; *O.R.*, I, 1: 680; I, 3: 5; II, 5: 99–100; Boman, *Lincoln's Resolute Unionist*, esp. 186–206. It is unknown whether Lincoln responded to Dick's proposal.

3. *O.R.*, II, 5: 319–21.

4. *O.R.*, I, 22, 1: 869; II, 2: 320–21.

5. *O.R.*, II, 1: 117; II, 5: 320.

6. *Missouri Democrat*, July 7, September 4, 1862; 1860 U.S. Census, Missouri, City of St. Louis, Ward 2, 640; 1860 U.S. Census, Missouri, St. Louis County, Central Township, 851.

7. *O.R.*, I, 22, 2: 278.

8. *O.R.*, II, 2: 252–53.

9. Grimsley, *The Hard Hand of War*, 113–14; *O.R.*, I, 17, 2: 88, 150.

10. *O.R.*, I, 13: 606, 616.

11. Leonard, *All the Daring of the Soldier*, 43, 77–78; *O.R.*, II, 2: 577; II, 3: 719–20.

12. *O.R.*, II, 5: 515, 537–38; III, 3: 164.

13. *O.R.*, II, 5: 447; Frost, *Camp and Prison Journal*, 39–40. The former cites Calhoun as Mrs. Colhoun.

14. Grimes, *Absalom Grimes*, 111.

15. Grimes, *Absalom Grimes*, 76–77; General Orders No. 39, May 23, 1863, in U.S. Army, *General Orders, Department of the Missouri Issued by General Curtis 1862 and 1863*, SLPL; Mrs. P. G. Robert, "History of Events Preceding and Following the Banishment of Mrs. Margaret A. E. McLure, as Given to the Author Herself," 78–79; Individual Civilians File, Roll 186, Margaret McLure.

16. Individual Civilians File, Roll 186, Margaret McLure.

17. *Missouri Democrat*, April 30, May 8, 9, 1863; Ann E. Lane to Sarah Lane Glasgow, April 19, 1863, William Carr Lane Papers, MHS.

18. *Missouri Democrat*, April 28, 1863; Grimes, *Absalom Grimes*, 105–07; Individual Civilians File, Roll 170, Mary Louden.

19. Floyd, "Reminiscences of Mrs. Lucy Nickolson Lindsay," 108; Individual Civilians File, Roll 203, Lucie Nickolson; *Missouri Democrat*, May 11, 1863. The letter is reproduced with some inaccuracies in *Missouri Democrat*, May 14, 1863.

20. Individual Civilians File, Roll 203, Lucie Nickolson; *Missouri Democrat*, May 11, 1863.

21. Individual Civilians File, Roll 98, Daniel M. Frost; Winter, *The Civil War in St. Louis*, 86; *O.R.*, I, 27, 1: 446; Individual Civilians File, Roll 252, Hattie Snodgrass; Compiled Service Records of the Confederate Soldiers Who Served in Organizations from the State of Missouri, 4th Missouri Cavalry, Joseph Chaytor (Roll 34).

22. Winter, *The Civil War in St. Louis*, 86.

23. Individual Civilians File, Roll 252, Hattie Snodgrass.

24. [Mattie Cassell] to Ada Haynes, February 7, [186?], Ada Byron Haynes Papers, MHS; William H. Duncan to Dr. T. Holmes, [ca. April 1862], Civil War Collection, MHS; *O.R.*, II, 5: 320.

25. J. Isaac Jones to Mrs. Hanes, September 20, 1862, Ada Byron Haynes Papers, MHS; *Missouri Democrat*, October 14, 1862, May 14, 1863; Individual Civilians File, Roll 290, Olly Williams; Two or More Civilians File, Roll 16, 4363; Two or More Civilians File, Roll 81, 22289; Individual Civilians File, Roll 238, Mrs.

Sapington [sic]. For the reference to "Mrs. Sapingtons Company" see A. H. Reed's January 1863 statement in Individual Civilians File, Roll 124, Samuel Hendel. Hendel, a St. Louis druggist, came under the scrutiny of Union authorities several times and eventually was ordered banished. Reed suspected him of being "One of the Secret members" who aided said band.

26. *Missouri Democrat*, May 14, 1863; Knox, *Camp-Fire and Cotton-Field*, 274.

27. Individual Civilians File, Roll 181, [Lewis] McLure.

28. *Missouri Democrat*, May 14, 29, 1863. For a thorough study of the Vicksburg campaign see Bearss, *The Campaign for Vicksburg*.

29. *Missouri Democrat*, May 14, 1863; Philip Gooch Ferguson Diary, May 31, 1863, MHS.

30. *Missouri Democrat*, April 10, May 26, 29, June 10, 1863; *O.R.*, I, 22, 2: 315.

31. *Daily Evening Bulletin* [San Francisco], September 30, 1863; *Missouri Democrat*, May 29, June 2, 10, October 29, 1863; *O.R.*, I, 22, 2: 318, 605; Winter, *Civil War St. Louis*, 127–28; Individual Civilians File, Roll 65, Mrs. Col. Cundiff.

32. *Missouri Democrat*, June 1, 1863; Grimes, *Absalom Grimes*, 49, 96–99, 138; Individual Civilians File, Roll 53, Mary S. F. Cleveland.

33. *Missouri Democrat*, June 6, July 10, 1863. What became of the two after this is unknown.

34. *Missouri Democrat*, June 12, 1863; 1860 U.S. Census, Missouri, City of St. Louis, Ward 10, 460.

35. Individual Civilians File, Roll 74, Edward Dobyns.

36. 1860 U.S. Census, Missouri, City of St. Louis, Ward 5, 163 (the Ruckers are also listed as residing in Ward 8, 341); Individual Civilians File, Roll 235, Elizabeth T. Rucker; *Missouri Democrat*, June 2, July 11, 1863; 1860 U.S. Census, Missouri, Buchanan County, St. Joseph, 3rd Ward, 509; 1860 U.S. Census, Pike County, Spencer Township, 512.

37. General Orders No. 50, June 15, 1863, in U.S. Army, *General Orders, Department of the Missouri Issued by General Curtis, 1862 and 1863*, SLPL; *Missouri Democrat*, September 23, 1863.

38. *Missouri Democrat*, June 17, 1863; General Orders No. 37, May 22, 1863, in *General Orders, Department of the Missouri Issued by General Curtis, 1862 and 1863*, SLPL. Augusta Bagwell's husband James was a wealthy Macon City merchant who could afford the bonds. 1860 U.S. Census, Missouri, Macon County, Macon City, 247.

39. *Missouri Democrat*, August 11, September 2, 1863, September 1, 1864; Individual Civilians File, Roll 279, Hannah Ward.

40. *Missouri Democrat*, November 23, 1863; Two or More Civilians File, Roll 25, 6947.

41. *Missouri Democrat*, May 14, 22, 29, December 1, 1863. See also June 2, July 11, September 22, October 29, and November 23, 1863.

42. *Missouri Democrat*, September 19, November 11, December 1, 3, 8, 1863, February 2, March 6, May 6, 10, 1864; Individual Civilians File, Roll 98, Lily Frost; Individual Civilians File, Roll 170, Mary Louden; Rule, "Sultana," 81–83. Rule argues that Robert Louden was responsible for sabotaging the riverboat *Sultana* carrying Union soldiers, including recently liberated prisoners from Andersonville, north on the Mississippi River, although the evidence is circumstantial. The late-April 1865 disaster claimed about seventeen hundred lives.

43. *Missouri Democrat*, September 16, November 23, 1863; inscription in volume 2 of Mrs. C. A. Howard, "Book of Copied Poems," 2 vols., ca. 1888, MHS; Oddly, Martin's April 1 statement is filed in the service record of Hampton L. Boon, the officer arrested in 1862 at the home of Drucilla Sappington. See Compiled Service Records of Confederate Soldiers Who Served in Organizations from the State of Missouri, State Guard, Hampton L. Boon (Roll 179). Emphasis in the original.

44. *Missouri Democrat*, July 22, October 4, November 14, 1864; General Orders No. 175, July 20, 1864 and General Orders No. 202, November 7, 1864, U.S. Army, *General Orders of Department of the Missouri, 1864 [In two parts, Part II]* (St. Louis: R. P. Studly and Co., Printers, 1864), SLPL.

45. *O.R.*, I, 22, 2: 461. For a fuller discussion of these two orders see Neely, *The Fate of Liberty*, 46–49.

46. Fellman, *Inside War*, 223–24.

47. Massey, *Refugee Life in the Confederacy*, 205.

48. Massey, *Refugee Life in the Confederacy*, 206; Grimsley, *The Hard Hand of War*, 118–19; Individual Civilians File, Roll 273, Marion Wall Vail; *O.R.*, I, 34, 2: 1077.

49. [Ann E. Lane] to Sarah Lane Glasgow, June 21, 1863, William Carr Lane Papers, Box 9–13, 1863–1869, MHS; Fellman, *Inside War*, 69; *Missouri Democrat*, May 29, June 10, 1863; Elder, "Virginia Johnson and the Dallas Rescue Home for 'Erring' Women, 1893–1941," 5; Individual Civilians File, Roll 158, Jennie Knight. Apparently Broadhead acted unwisely; after her release Knight continued to assist the Confederacy and early in 1865 she was again arrested for giving aid and comfort to bushwhackers.

50. "To an unidentified person in the East from an unidentified woman in St. Louis," Civil War Letter, 1863, WHMC. Stress in the original.

51. Individual Civilians File, Roll 23, Mrs. D. W. Bell.

52. Individual Civilians File, Roll 92, Mary Fitzgerald.

53. *Missouri Democrat*, July 16, 1863; Individual Civilians File, Roll 199, Joanna Murphy; Individual Civilians File, Roll 188, Maggie Melvin; Individual Civilians File, Roll 258, Louisa Stokes; Individual Civilians File, Roll 176, Emma Martin.

54. Individual Civilians File, Roll 44, Elizabeth Campbell (quote, emphasis in the original); *Missouri Democrat*, July 20, 1863.

55. *Missouri Democrat,* July 29, 30, 1863. What became of Devinney and William Carroll is unknown.

56. Individual Civilians File, Roll 246, Mary Simpson; *Missouri Democrat,* July 28, 29, 1863.

57. Individual Civilians File, Roll 85, Emma English.

58. Individual Civilians File, Roll 244, Amelia Shoemaker.

59. Fellman, *Inside War,* 46; Individual Civilians File, Roll 43, Margery J. Callahan.

60. Individual Civilians File, Roll 42, Mary Byrne.

61. Individual Civilians File, Roll 107, Mary Grandstaff; *Missouri Democrat,* December 11, 1863.

62. Individual Civilians File, Roll 208, Matilda Orme; Eakin, *Missouri Prisoners of War from Gratiot Street Prison and Myrtle Street Prison, St. Louis, Mo And Alton Prison, Alton, Illinois, Including Citizens, Confederates, Bushwhackers and Guerrillas; Missouri Democrat,* September 9, 1863.

63. Individual Civilians File, Roll 42, Mary Byrne; *Missouri Democrat,* January 28, 1864.

64. Individual Civilians File, Roll 187, Mrs. McRea; [Ann E. Lane] to Sarah Lane Glasgow, June 21, 1863, William Carr Lane Papers, Box 9–13, 1863–1869, MHS.

65. Toth, *Kate Chopin,* 63–70; Chopin, "As You Like It," *St. Louis Criterion* (March 20, 1897), reprinted in *The Complete Works of Kate Chopin,* 716.

66. Castel, "Order No. 11 and the Civil War on the Border," 257–68; Fellman, *Inside War,* 95–96.

4. *"They Have Five Ladies . . . at Alton"*

This chapter's title is from Curran, "'On the Road to Dixie,'" 85.

1. *O.R.,* II, 5: 227, 621.

2. Henry Halleck to J. B. McPherson, December 30, 1861, Henry W. Halleck Collection, MHS.

3. The following discussion of the history of the Alton State Penitentiary is drawn from Greene, "Early Development of the Illinois State Penitentiary System," 185–195.

4. *O.R.,* II, 3: 169; Winters, *The Civil War in St. Louis,* 153.

5. Winters, *The Civil War in St. Louis,* 153; *O.R.,* II, 2: 245–46, 257–58; Greene, "Early Development of the Illinois State Penitentiary System," 190.

6. The original statement is found in Individual Civilians File, Roll 149, Clara Judd. The statement is also reproduced in *O.R.,* II, 6: 621–24. Except where noted the following account is drawn from the statement.

7. Blakeslee, "'Examples Should Be Made,'" 3–5; 1860 U.S. Census, Tennessee, Franklin County, District No. 9, 159. The 1860 census lists Burritt Judd as

a carpenter, as well as the Judd's oldest son, and the next oldest as a carpenter's apprentice. The author thanks LaVonne Barac, a local historian in Minnesota, for details of the Judds' time in that state.

8. *Missouri Democrat*, May 21, 1863.

9. Data from the 1860 Census suggests that the boy may have been fourteen at the time.

10. The Federal government had yet to impose conscription.

11. Judd's account is a bit sketchy on this particular chain of events. A different, often clearer picture is given in Fitch, *Annals of the Army of the Cumberland*, 502.

12. *O.R.*, II, 5: 620.

13. Blakeslee, "'Examples Should be Made,'" 7; Fitch, *Annals of the Army of the Cumberland*, 503. Fitch continued to keep Forsythe's identity as a detective secret in his account. Judd may never have learned that he was with the Federal army.

14. This was the beginning of Morgan's 1862 Christmas raid into Kentucky. See Ramage, *Rebel Raider*, 134–37.

15. *O.R.*, II, 5: 620–21. Except where noted, the following is drawn from that source.

16. Fitch, *Annals of the Army of the Cumberland*, 502–07.

17. *O.R.*, II, 5: 621.

18. *O.R.*, II, 5: 277.

19. McCurry, "Enemy Women and the Laws of War in the American Civil War," 688–89; *O.R.*, I, 23, 2: 107–09.

20. Curran, "'On the Road to Dixie,'" 85.

21. Fitch, *Annals of the Army of the Cumberland*, 570; *O.R.*, II, 5: 684–85. Rosecrans ordered Hyde returned to Nashville in late July 1863. *O.R.*, II, 6: 153.

22. T. Hendrickson to William Hoffman, June 1, 1863, Letters Sent, February 1862—January 1864 (Roll 13), Selected Records . . . Alton Prison; Register of Confederate and Federal Soldiers and Civilians Sentenced, No. 5, January 1863—July 1864 (Roll 15), Selected records . . . Alton Prison; *O.R.*, II, 6: 153.

23. *O.R.*, II, 5: 768; General Register of Prisoners, November 1862–April 1864 (Roll 13), Selected Records . . . Alton Prison; Register of Confederate and Federal Soldiers and Civilians Sentenced, No. 5, January 1863—July 1864 (Roll 15), Selected Records . . . Alton Prison. See also Fitch, *Annals of the Army of the Cumberland*, 525–32.

24. Fitch, Annals of the Army of the Cumberland, 570, 573 (quote).

25. Register of Confederate and Federal Soldiers and Civilians Sentenced, No. 5, January 1863—July 1864 (Roll 15), Selected Records . . . Alton Prison, M 598; Individual Civilians File, Roll 258, Eliza Stillman.

26. Individual Civilians File, Roll 203, Ann Nichols; Missouri Democrat, January 18, 1864; Register of Civilian Prisoners, March 1863–June 1864 (Roll 15), Selected Records . . . Alton Prison.

27. Individual Civilians File, Roll 154, Sarah B. Keys; General Register of Prisoners, November 1862—April 1864 (Roll 15), Selected Records . . . Alton Prison; Letters Received and Orders Received, October 1862—November 1864 (Roll 13), Selected Records . . . Alton Prison; Individual Civilians File, Roll 149, Polly Jumper.

28. Individual Civilians File, Roll 149, Clara Judd; *Missouri Democrat*, August 18, 1863; *Valley Herald* (Chaska, Minnesota), August 29, 1863.

29. *Valley Herald*, August 29, 1863.

30. *Valley Herald*, September 19, 1863, reprints the *Argys* editorial (which may explain the typos) along with its response.

31. *Valley Herald*, December 5, 1863.

32. Individual Citizens File, Roll 149, Clara Judd; Individual Citizens File, Roll 260, John A. Stuart; Blakeslee, "'Examples Should Be Made,'" 10; *Valley Herald*, April 1, 1865.

33. This despite the fact that the prison fell under the jurisdiction of the provost marshal general of the Department of the Missouri. Scharf, *History of Saint Louis City and County*, vol. 1: 432.

5. *"Rebel Women . . . Are Engaged"*

This chapter's title is from the report of Colonel John P. Sanderson, provost marshal general of the Department of the Missouri, on the activities of the Order of American Knights, *O.R.*, II, 7: 236.

1. *O.R.*, I, 34, 3: 381; I, 34, 4: 527; Beilein, *Bushwhackers*; Boman, *Lincoln and Citizens' Rights in Civil War Missouri*, 233, 251; Whites, "Forty Shirts and a Wagonload of Wheat"; Streater, "'She-Rebels' on the Supply Line."

2. *O.R.*, I, 34, 2: 213.

3. See for instance the exchanges of correspondence between Grant and Rosecrans in *O.R.*, I, 34, 3: 381, 416–17. For the relationship between Grant and Rosecrans see Varney, *General Grant and the Rewriting of History*.

4. *O.R.*, I, 34, 4: 277; I, 41, 2: 716–17; Sinisi, *The Last Hurrah*, 51–52.

5. *Missouri Democrat*, June 8, 1864.

6. *O.R.*, II, 7: 228–29; "Rosecrans's Campaigns," 54, 112.

7. MSS 209, Box 1, Folder 5. J. P. Sanderson Papers, 1846–1865. Journal entry for March 7, 1864: Ohio History Connection.

8. Individual Civilians File, Roll 30, Sarah Bond; Two or More Civilians File, Roll 32, 8987.

9. *O.R.*, I, 34, 1: 994–95; Court-Martial Papers, Office of the Adjutant General, Record Group 133, Missouri State Archives, Jefferson City, Missouri; Register of Civilian Prisoners, March 1863–June 1864 (Roll 15), Alton Prison.

10. General Orders No. 154, August 22, 1864, and General Orders No. 190, October 6, 1864, in U.S. Army, *General Orders of Department of the Missouri*,

1864 [in two parts, part 2], SLPL; Two or More Civilians File, Roll 38, 10507; Individual Civilians File, Roll 76, Nannie L. Douthitt.

11. Individual Civilians File, Roll 133, N. E. Hough; *Missouri Democrat*, July, 8, 22, August 29, 1864; 1860 U.S. Census, Missouri, Jackson County, Kaw Township, 5.

During and after the war, stories circulated in the North that accused Southern women of possessing skulls, bones, scalps, and other body parts from the desecrated remains of Union soldiers for despicable purposes. See [Kirkland], *A Few Words on Behalf of the Loyal Women of the United States by One of Themselves*, 9, 10; Brockett and Vaughan, *Women's Work in the Civil War*, 781.

12. "Rosecrans's Campaigns," 113 (quote, emphasis in the original); Sinisi, *The Last Hurrah*, 51–56.

13. *Missouri Democrat*, October 18, 1864; Individual Civilians File, Roll 118, Mary Harlow; Individual Civilians File, Roll 80, Dorotha Durritt and Sarah J. Durritt.

14. Individual Civilians File, Roll 169, Martha Longacre and Nancy Longacre.

15. Kyle Sinisi provides the most thorough study of Price's Raid in *The Last Hurrah*. See also Hinton, *Rebel Invasion of Missouri and Kansas and the Campaign of the Army of the Border against General Sterling Price, in October and November, 1864*; Monaghan, *Civil War on the Western Border, 1854–1865*, 306–45; and Lause, *Price's Lost Campaign*.

16. Two or More Civilians File, Roll 46, 12720. Besides the Durritts and Harlow, the order included Eliza, Mary and Hattie Spencer; Julie Martin; Mary Cull; Jane Ward; and Elizabeth M. DeWitt. At least one, Jane Ward, returned to Missouri, was caught and banished to the South. See Prisoners: St. Louis, MO. (Gratiot Street Prison), October 1864–January 1865, Two or More Civilians File, Roll 92.

17. Two or More Civilians File, Roll 47, 13209; *Missouri Democrat*, December 7, 1864; Individual Civilians File, Roll 279, Mary Ward; Prisoners: St. Louis, MO. (Gratiot Street Prison) October 1864–January 1865, Two or More Civilians File, Roll 92.

18. Individual Civilians File, Roll 257, Emeline Stewart; *Missouri Democrat*, August 9, September 4, 27, October 29 and November 26, 1864; Two or More Civilians File, Roll 41, 11516 and Roll 416, 12102; Individual Civilian File, Roll 67, Delia Davidson. The Tennessee women included Harriet S. Brown, Julia Dennis, Martha Padgett, and Emma Whiston. They were also arrested with a James Clement.

19. Individual Civilians File, Roll 203, Ann Nichols; Individual Civilians File, Roll 192, Elvira Mitchel; Individual Civilians File, Roll 258, Elizabeth Stillman; Individual Civilians File, Roll 157, Mary E. Kirby; Individual Civilians File, Roll 57, Betty Conklin; Two or More Civilians File, Roll 43, 12027.

20. Individual Civilians File, Roll 252, Harriet Snead; Individual Civilians File, Roll 219, Anna E. Polk; *Missouri Democrat,* June 27, July 18, 22, 1864; General Orders No. 120, July 16, 1864, and General Orders No. 125, July 20, 1864, in U.S. Army, *General Orders of Department of the Missouri, 1864* [in two parts, part 2], SLPL.

21. Sterling Price, "Letter of recommendation from Sterling Price to General S. Cooper regarding Mr. John W. Polk for a position within his Quarter Master Department. Grenada, Mississippi, January 5, 1863," (1863), *The Broadus R. Littlejohn, Jr. Manuscript Collection,* Book 253, http://digitalcommons.wofford.edu /littlejohnmss/253 (accessed August 18, 2019); *O.R.,* I, 41, 2: 1062.

22. Individual Civilians File, Roll 30, Sarah Bond; Two or More Civilians File, Roll 32, 8987.

23. Individual Civilians File, Roll 96, Isabella Fox; *Missouri Democrat,* January 27 and February 8, 1865.

24. Individual Civilians File, Roll 135, Amelia Huckshorn; *Missouri Democrat,* January 27, February 4, 1865.

25. Individual Civilians File, Roll 19, Susan M. Bass; Two or More Civilians File, Roll 50, 14021.

26. See Klement, *Copperheads in the Middle West* and *Dark Lanterns.* Many historians have followed Klement's conclusion about the insignificance of these groups, but Stephen E. Towne has challenged that view with compelling research that merits further attention. See *Surveillance and Spies in the Civil War.*

27. Sinisi, *The Last Hurrah,* 50–51; *O.R.,* I, 34, 2: 304–05; II, 7: 228; *Missouri Democrat,* February 11, 1864; Boman, *Lincoln and Citizens' Rights in Civil War Missouri,* 234, 252.

28. Klement, *Dark Lanterns,* 64–90.

29. *O.R.,* II, 7: 231, 238. Sanderson's report is found in *O.R.,* II, 7: 228–366.

30. *O.R.,* II, 7: 236, 296–98.

31. General Orders No. 125, August 17, 1864, U.S. Army, *General Orders of Department of the Missouri, 1864* [in two parts, part 2], SLPL; Eakin, *Civil War Military Prisoners Sent to Missouri State Penitentiary,* 3; *Missouri Democrat,* August 30, 1864; Lowry, *Confederate Heroines,* 27 (Rodgers quote); Individual Civilians File, Roll 48, Martha Cassell.

32. *Missouri Democrat,* September 26, October 12, 1864; Individual Civilians File, Roll 296, Missouri Woods (see also Individual Civilians File, Roll 294, Missouri Wood); Individual Civilians File, Roll 48, Martha Cassell; Eakin, *Civil War Military Prisoners Sent to Missouri State Penitentiary,* 3.

33. *O.R.,* II, 7: 236; General Orders No. 125, August 17, 1864, U.S. Army, *General Orders of Department of the Missouri, 1864* [in two parts, part 2], SLPL; Individual Civilians File, Roll 286, Pauline White; Eakin, *Civil War Military Prisoners Sent to Missouri State Penitentiary,* 3.

34. *O.R.*, II, 7: 945, 951–52. Holt's entire report is found on pp. 930–53.

35. Neely, *The Fate of Liberty*, 135. Neely does not take into consideration those released from custody in order to be banished to the South.

6. *"Alias Mary Ann Pittman"*

This chapter's title is from Register of Civilian Prisoners, March 1863–June 1864 (Roll 15), Selected Records . . . Alton Prison.

1. Frost, *Camp and Prison Journal*, 193, 195 (emphasis in the original). Women prisoners both shocked and fascinated Frost. He made it a point to note all he could about those with whom he came into contact.

2. If you do not get the reference then you must rent and watch the film *The Usual Suspects*.

3. Register of Civilian Prisoners, March 1863–June 1864 (Roll 15), Selected Records . . . Alton Prison; *O.R.*, II, 7: 345, 347; For more on identity passing see Ginsberg, *Passing and the Fictions of Identity*, esp. her introduction, 1–18. See also Elizabeth Young, "Confederate Counterfeit," 181–217.

4. The following is based on "Examination of Mary Ann Pitman by Colonel J. P. Sanderson, Provost Marshal General, St. Louis, May 24, 1864," found in Individual Civilians File, Roll 218, Mary Ann Pitman.

5. Francis M. Stewart commanded the Fifteenth Tennessee Cavalry, C.S.A. in Brigadier General Robert V. Richardson's brigade. See Sifakis, *Compendium of the Confederate Armies: Tennessee*, 66.

6. Individual Civilians File, Roll 122, Ada Haynes; *Missouri Democrat*, July 20, 1864.

7. The following is based on "Examination of Mary Ann Pitman, by Colonel J. P. Sanderson, Provost Marshal General, St. Louis, May 31, 1864" found in Individual Civilians File, Roll 218, Mary Ann Pitman.

8. For the massacre see Ward, *River Run Red*; and Wills, *The River Was Dyed with Blood*.

9. In *River Run Red*, Andrew Ward briefly discusses Pitman's story, or a version of it, "none of which," he concludes, "could be proven or refuted after Forrest's attack on Fort Pillow." See 130–32, quote on 132. Ward bases his discussion primarily on a series of newspaper articles written by Earl Willoughby that appeared in the *Dyersburg* [TN] *State Gazette*, which this author has been unable to obtain.

10. The following is drawn from Individual Civilians File, Roll 218, Mary Ann Pitman. It is also reproduced in *O.R.*, II, 7: 345–55.

11. Sifakis, *Compendium of the Confederate Armies: Tennessee*, 125.

12. Records of the Provost Marshal General's Bureau (Civil War), entry 36, file for Pitman, Mary M., Record Group 110, National Archives.

13. Records of the Provost Marshal General's Bureau (Civil War), entry 95 (Secret Service accounts), 2nd quarter 1865, file for Pitman, Mary M., Record Group 110, National Archives.

14. 1860 U.S. Census, Tennessee, Dyer County, Dyersburg P.O., 390. For the issue of lying about one's age, see Curran, "A 'Rebel to [His] Govt. and to His Parents.'"

15. Ward, *River Run Red*, 131; Compiled Service Records of Confederate Soldiers Who Served from the State of Tennessee, 22nd Tennessee Infantry, Roll 52 [M 268], T. H. Phillips, Record Group 109, National Archives; Compiled Service Records of Confederate Soldiers Who Served from the State of Tennessee, 15th Cavalry and Fifteenth (Consolidated) Cavalry, Roll 49 [M 268], T. H. Phillips, Record Group 109, National Archives; Compiled Service Records of Confederate Soldiers Who Served from the State of Tennessee, 22nd Tennessee Infantry, Roll 52 [M 268], W. H. Craig, Record Group 109, National Archives.

16. "Rosecrans's Campaigns," 51; Towne, *Surveillance and Spies in the Civil War*, 180; Burlingame and Turner, eds., *Inside Lincoln's White House*, 206; O.R., II: 7: 932, 946 (Holt quotes).

17. Clement Vallandigham, "To the Editor of the New York News," October 22, 1864, reprinted in the *Boston Daily Advertiser*, October 27, 1864; *Cadiz* [Ohio] *Sentinel*, November 2, 1864. One hundred and twenty years later historian Frank L. Klement would also disregard her testimony. "None of her claims," he asserted, "would be borne out by either Confederate or Tennessee records." *Dark Lanterns*, 81n56.

18. Two or More Civilians File, Roll 37, 10171.

19. Two or More Civilians File, Roll 43, 11980; Records of the Provost Marshal General's Bureau (Civil War), entry 95 (Secret Service accounts), 2nd quarter 1865, file for Pitman, Mary M., Record Group 110, National Archives; David S. Heidler and Jeanne T. Heidler, "Ewing, Thomas, Jr."; Lamers, *The Edge of Glory*, 418–19.

20. Two or More Civilians File, Roll 47, 13159.

21. Records of the Provost Marshal General's Bureau (Civil War), entry 95 (Secret Service accounts), 2nd quarter 1865, file for Pitman, Mary M., Record Group 110, National Archives; Records of the Provost Marshal General's Bureau (Civil War), entry 36, file for Pitman, Mary M., Record Group 110, National Archives.

22. Records of the Provost Marshal General's Bureau (Civil War), entry 95 (Secret Service accounts), 2nd quarter 1865, file for Pitman, Mary M., Record Group 110, National Archives; *Missouri Democrat*, August 2, September 26, 1864; Two or More Civilians File; Roll 41, 11291; Individual Civilians File, Roll 218, Mary Ann Pittman; Individual Civilians File, Roll 282, Emily Weaver and Emma Weaver.

23. Individual Civilians File, Roll 282, Emily Weaver. Abram Weaver was arrested under suspicion of aiding his daughter in her escape. Joseph Darr ordered

his release on November 9 on his "parole of honor to report to this office the first Knowledge that he might obtain of the whereabouts of Emma Weaver." Prisoners: St. Louis, Mo. (Gratiot Street Prison) October 1864–January 1865, Two or More Civilians File, Roll 92.

24. *Missouri Democrat*, September 26, 1864; Two or More Civilians File, Roll 43, 12023 and 12024; Individual Civilians File, Roll 218, Mary Ann Pittman.

25. Individual Civilians File, Roll 122, Mollie Hayes; Individual Civilians File, Roll 218, Mary Ann Pittman; Records of the Provost Marshal General's Bureau (Civil War), entry 36, file for Pitman, Mary M., Record Group 110, National Archives; Lamers, *The Edge of Glory*, 429.

26. Individual Civilians File, Roll 122, Mollie Hayes.

27. Prisoners: St. Louis, MO. (Gratiot Street Prison) October 1864–January 1865, Two or More Civilians File, Roll 92; Individual Civilians File, Roll 218, Mary Pittman; Individual Civilians File, Roll 122, Mollie Hayes.

28. Individual Civilians File, Roll 218, Mary Ann Pittman; Individual Civilians File, Roll 122, Mollie Hayes.

29. Individual Civilians File, Roll 218, Mary M. Pitman; Individual Civilians File, Roll 106, Mollie Goggin; Frost, *Camp and Prison Journal*, 185.

30. Individual Civilians File, Roll 218, Mary M. Pitman and Mollie M. Pitman; Neil Hepburn, "West Bloomfield County Entrepreneur: Joseph Tarr Copeland," accessed at https://www.gwbhs.org/documents/2012/11/west-bloomfield-township-entrepreneur-joseph-tarr-copeland.pdf/ (accessed August 18, 2019); Carla Totten, "Alton Military Prison," 38.

31. Records of the Provost Marshal General's Bureau (Civil War), entry 36, file for Pitman, Mary M., Record Group 110, National Archives; Individual Civilians File, Roll 218, Mary M. Pitman.

32. Abraham Lincoln Papers, Series 1, General Correspondence, 1833–1916: Mary Ann Pitman to Abraham Lincoln, Wednesday, January 4, 1865 (Requests pass), Library of Congress, accessed at https://www.loc.gov/item/mal3981900/ (accessed August 18, 2019).

33. Individual Civilians File, Roll 147, Geo. J. Jones and George J. Jones; Individual Civilians File, Roll 73, H. E. Dimick; Nichols, *Guerrilla Warfare in Civil War Missouri, 1862*, 72; Nichols, *Guerrilla Warfare in Civil War Missouri*, vol. 4, *September, 1864–June 1865*, 393n25; Individual Civilians File, Roll 31, Mary Bowles.

34. Individual Civilians File, Roll 147, Geo. J. Jones; Two or More Civilians File, Roll 27, 7656 (This document appears to have been misfiled among those of January 1864.); Individual Civilians File, Roll 218, Mary M. Pitman; 1860 U.S. Census, Missouri, St. Louis City, 3rd Ward, 88.

35. Two or More Civilians File, Roll 27, 7656.

36. Individual Civilians File, Roll 218, Mary M. Pitman; Individual Civilians File, Roll 11, Mrs. Augustine; Two or More Civilians File, Roll 46, 12900; 1860 U.S. Census, Missouri, St. Louis City, 3rd Ward, 88.

37. *Missouri Democrat*, April 1, 1865.

38. *Missouri Democrat*, April 1, 1865; Frost, *Camp and Prison Journal*, 193, 195; Individual Civilians File, Roll 218, M. M. Pittman.

39. Individual Civilians File, Roll 218, Mollie M. Pitman.

40. Individual Civilians File, Roll 218, Mary A. Pittman and M. M. Pittman; Records of the Provost Marshal General's Bureau (Civil War), entry 36, file for Pitman, Mary M., Record Group 110, National Archives; Fellman, *Inside War*, 252–54; Nichols, *Guerrilla Warfare in Civil War Missouri, 1862*, 70–71; Nichols, *Guerrilla Warfare in Civil War Missouri*, vol. 3, *January–August 1864*, 18; Nichols, *Guerrilla Warfare in Civil War Missouri*, vol. 4, *September 1864–June 1865*, 212, 272, 281.

41. Records of the Provost Marshal General's Bureau (Civil War), entry 95 (Secret Service accounts), 2nd quarter 1865, file for Pitman, Mary M., Record Group 110, National Archives.

7. *"Mere Friction and Abrasion . . . of the War"*

This chapter's title is from Abraham Lincoln's "Appeal to Border-State Representatives for Compensated Emancipation, Washington D.C.," July 12, 1862, reprinted in *Abraham Lincoln: Speeches and Writings, 1859–1865*, 341.

1. Individual Civilians File, Roll 154, Sarah B. Keys; Alton Prison, Letters Received and Orders Received and Issued, October 1862–November 1864 (Roll 13), Selected Records . . . Confederate Prisoners of War.

2. Individual Civilians File, Roll 154, Sarah B. Keys; Knust, *Unprotected Texts*, 18; Individual Civilians File, Roll 64, Mary Cull; Individual Civilians File, Roll 143, Jennie. For more on prostitution and the war see Catherine Clinton, "'Public Women' and Sexual Politics during the American Civil War."

3. Lowry, *The Story the Soldiers Wouldn't Tell*, 61–92; Two or More Individual Civilians File, Roll 43, 12027; *Missouri Democrat*, June 15, 1863, February 25, January 28, June 20, 1864; Individual Civilians File, Roll 42, Mary Byrne; Two or More Civilians File, Roll 39, 10911.

4. Individual Civilians File, Roll 154, Sarah B. Keys; Eakin, *Missouri Prisoners of War*, vii; Alton Prison, Letters Received and Orders Received and Issued, October 1862–November 1864, 68 (Roll 13), Selected Records . . . Confederate Prisoners of War; General Register of Prisoners, November 1862–April 1864 (Roll 13), Alton Prison; Individual Civilians File, Roll 149, Polly Jumper; Frost, *Camp and Prison Journal*, 225. Eakin has the citation for Keys as a "white women," but the original source of the reference is unclear.

5. Two or More Civilians File, Roll 20, 5392; *Missouri Democrat*, February 18 and 21, 1863; Individual Civilians File, Roll 158, William J. Kribben; Two or More Civilians File, Roll 59, 16854.; Lowry, *Confederate Heroines*, 32–33; Individual Civilians File, Roll 282, Emily Weaver. For African Americans as witnesses see Fellman, *Inside War*, 66–67; Steers, "Dr. Mudd and the 'Colored' Witnesses"; and Romeo, "'The First Morning of Their Freedom.'"

6. Register of Prisoners Confined at Gratiot and Myrtle Street Prisons Compiled by the Office of the Commissary General of Prisoners, 1862–1864 [Book 2], 75, 88 (Roll 72), Selected Records . . . Gratiot and Myrtle Street Prisons; Two or More Civilians File, Roll 28, 7800, 7943, and 7948; *Missouri Democrat*, January 7, 1863, January 15, 20, February 1, 25, March 2, June 24, July 27, 1864; *O.R.*, II, 5: 983. The newspaper refers to Hobbs as Molly Hop.

7. *Missouri Democrat*, May 3, 1862.

8. *Missouri Democrat*, July 14, 1862, May 13, 1864.

9. Individual Civilians File, Roll 169, Martha Longacre and Nancy Longacre; General Orders No. 210, November 16, 1864, in U.S. Army, *General Orders of Department of the Missouri, 1864* [in two parts, part 2], SLPL; Individual Civilians File, Roll 7, Mattie Anderson and Mollie Anderson; Two or More Civilians File, Roll 25, 7173; *Missouri Democrat*, December 12, 1864.

10. Individual Civilians File, Roll 251, Sarah Jane Smith; Register of Civilian Prisoners, March 1863–June 1864 (Roll 15), Selected Records . . . Alton Prison; General Orders No. 210, November 16, 1864, in U.S. Army, *General Orders of Department of the Missouri, 1864* [in two parts, part 2], SLPL (italics in the original); Frost, *Camp and Prison Journal*, 207; *O.R.*, III: 3: 157.

11. The petition is filed in Individual Civilians File, Roll 250, Jane Smith; *Missouri Democrat*, November 22, 1864.

12. Frost, *Camp and Prison Journal*, 207, 217; *Missouri Democrat*, April 12, 1865.

13. Curran, "'On the Road to Dixie,'" 85; Frost, *Camp and Prison Journal*, 115; Individual Civilians File, Roll 192, Elvira Mitchel; Prisoners: St. Louis, MO (Gratiot Street Prison) October 1864–January 1865, Two or More Civilians File, Roll 92; Two or More Civilians File, Roll 59, 16837; Wood, *Bushwhacker Belles*, 58; *Missouri Democrat*, May 16, 1865; Hodes, *A Divided City*, 87; Prisoners: St. Louis, MO (Gratiot Street Prison) February–November 1865 (and other Prisons) (varying states), Two or More Civilians File, Roll 93; Two or More Civilians File, Roll 78, 21516; Two or More Civilians File, Roll 58, 16405; Two or More Civilians File, Roll 59, 16777, 16836, 16838. Children and the Civil War is a subject that is still underdeveloped. Recent research on the subject can be found in Marten, *Children and Youth during the Civil War Era*.

14. Individual Civilian File, Roll 150, Susan Kearney; General Orders No. 210, November 16, 1864, in U.S. Army, *General Orders of the Department of the Missouri, 1864* [in two parts, part 2], SLPL (quote).

15. Individual Civilians File, Roll 150, Susan Kearney and John Kearney; General Orders No. 180, September 27, 1864, in U.S. Army, *General Orders of the Department of the Missouri, 1864* [in two parts, part 2], SLPL. The commission sentenced Hines to two years confinement in the Alton Prison.

16. Individual Civilians File, Roll 150, Susan Kearney and John Kearney.

17. Individual Civilians File, Roll 150, Susan Kearney.

18. General Orders No. 180, September 27, 1864, in U.S. Army, *General Orders of the Department of the Missouri, 1864* [in two parts, part 2], SLPL; Individual Civilians File, Roll 150, John Kearney.

19. Frost, *Camp and Prison Journal*, 124; Sandusky *Commercial Register*, December 12, 1864; Kutzler, "Captive Audiences," 243–44. The author thanks Susan Youhn and DeAnne Blanton for information on these rumors.

20. Frost, *Camp and Prison Journal*, 218; *Missouri Democrat*, January 27, 31, 1865; Prisoners: St. Louis, MO (Gratiot Street Prison) October 1864–January 1865, Two or More Civilians File, Roll 92.

21. *Missouri Democrat*, January 31, February 8, 1865; Individual Civilians File, Roll 96, Isabella Fox.

22. *Missouri Democrat*, February 9, 28, March 3, 1865.

23. *Missouri Democrat*, March 3, 1865. The play on words derives from Shakespeare's *Othello.* The title character states that he has "loved not wisely, but too well" after killing his wife Desdemona in a jealous rage.

24. Individual Civilian File, Roll 246, Mary Simpson; *Missouri Democrat*, July 28, 1863.

25. Nichols, *Guerrilla Warfare in Civil War Missouri*, vol. 3, *January–August 1864*, 48–49, 54–55, 124–25; *Missouri Democrat*, March 25, 1864. Fickle may have been romantically involved with Blunt, as a photograph of her was found in his possession upon his death.

26. Two or More Civilians File, Roll 80, 21953; Individual Civilians File, Roll 227, Anna Reed; Individual Civilians File, Roll 91, Anna Fickle; General Orders No. 146, August 17, 1864, in U.S. Army, *General Orders of the Department of the Missouri, 1864* [in two parts, part 2], SLPL.

27. *Missouri Democrat*, August 15, 1864.

28. *Missouri Democrat*, January 20, April 3, 1865; Bruce Nichols, *Guerrilla Warfare in Civil War Missouri*, vol. 4, *September 1864–June 1865*, 72–74.

29. *Missouri Democrat*, January 20, 1865; Nichols, *Guerrilla Warfare in Civil War Missouri*, vol. 4, *September 1864–June 1865*, 74; Shiras, "Major Wolf and Abraham Lincoln," 356.

30. Shiras, "Major Wolf and Abraham Lincoln," 356; Prisoners: St. Louis, MO (Gratiot Street Prison) October 1864–January 1865, Two or More Civilians File, Roll 92; Individual Civilians File, Roll 21, Kate Beatty; Individual Civilians File, Roll 1, E. M. Ackerell; Two or More Civilians File; Roll 76, 20497.

31. General Orders No. 14, January 18, 1865, in U.S. Army, *General Orders of the Department of the Missouri, for 1865* (St. Louis: Missouri Democrat Print, 1866), SLPL; Shiras, "Major Wolf and Abraham Lincoln," 357; Lamers, *The Edge of Glory*, 435; Nichols, *Guerrilla Warfare in Civil War Missouri*, vol. 4, *September 1864–June 1865*, 74; Basler, *The Collected Works of Abraham Lincoln*, 8: 223.

32. Two or More Civilians File, Roll 76, 20497 and Roll 50, 14105. The two women were Amanda Cranwell and Georgia Reed.

33. Eakin, *Civil War Military Prisoners Sent to Missouri State Penitentiary*, 3, 4, 7, 11, 28; General Orders No 146, August 17, 1864, in U.S. Army, *General Orders of the Department of the Missouri, 1864* (in two parts, part 2), SLPL; *Missouri Democrat*, February 11, March 2, 1865. The other four women were Christiana D. Morse, Nancy P. Kemp (or Keogh), Maggie Kelly, and Mary (or Margaret) Russell.

34. *Missouri Democrat*, November 18, 1864.

35. Leonard, "Mary Surratt and the Plot to Assassinate Abraham Lincoln"; King, "Judge Holt and the Lincoln Conspirators," 956. King claimed he received his information from Johnson's private secretary, General R. D. Mussey.

36. *Missouri Democrat*, August 20, 1862, November 1, 8, 1864; Two or More Civilians File, Roll 25, 6947.

8. *"The Female Military Prison"*

This chapter's title is from the *New York Herald*, June 30, 1863.

1. *Missouri Democrat*, October 12, 15, 17, 1864; *Wheeling Intelligencer*, May 14, 1863; [Lawrence], *Border and Bastille*, 164; Individual Civilians File, Roll 294, Missouri Wood.

2. Scharf, *History of Saint Louis County*, 1: 417–18; Hesseltine, "Military Prisons of St. Louis, 1861–1865," 382–83. For a rather quirky biography of McDowell and a history of the building see Cosner and Shannon, *Missouri's Mad Doctor McDowell*.

3. O.R. II, 4: 57; Grimes, *Absalom Grimes*, 54–58, 88–93.

4. Floyd, "Reminiscences of Mrs. Lucy Nickolson Lindsay," 110–12; *Missouri Democrat*, May 11, 1863; O.R., II, 6: 150; Adams, "Greybeards in Blue," 33–34; Frost, *Camp and Prison Journal*, 31.

5. *Missouri Democrat*, May 9, 1863; Robert, "History of the Events Preceding and Following the Banishment of Mrs. Margaret A. E. McLure, As Given to the Author by Herself," 79, 80 (quote); *New York Herald*, June 30, 1863; Elder, "Virginia K. Johnson and the Dallas Rescue Home for 'Erring' Women, 1893–1941," 5; Individual Civilians File, Roll 74, Edward Dobyns; *Missouri Democrat*, June 12, 1863.

6. *New York Herald*, June 30, 1863; Individual Civilians File, Roll 273, Marion Vail.

7. *New York Herald*, June 30, 1863; McAdams, "Greybeards in Blue," 34.

8. *Daily Evening Bulletin* [San Francisco], September 30, 1863; Individual Civilians File, Roll 279, Hannah Ward; *Missouri Democrat,* August 11, September 2, 1863, September 1, 1864.

9. Two or More Individual Civilians File, Roll 4, 705; Missouri Democrat, May 14, 1864; *O.R.,* II, 5: 983.

10. *O.R.,* II, 7: 661; Hesseltine, "Military Prisons of St. Louis, 1861–1865," 387.

11. *O.R.,* II, 7: 772, 1019, 1142; Grimes, *Absalom Grimes,* 94; *Missouri Democrat,* October 22, 1864. For the collapse of the prison for women in Kansas City, see Harris, "Catalyst for Terror," 290–308.

12. *O.R.,* II, 7: 1019, 1142; *Missouri Democrat,* October 22, 1864; Individual Civilian File, Roll 73, Margaret E. Dickson.

13. Individual Civilians File, Roll 294, Missouri Wood.

14. Individual Civilians File, Roll 294, Missouri Wood; Individual Civilians File, Roll 282, Emma Weaver; Individual Civilians File, Roll 73, Margaret E. Dickson; Two or More Civilians File, Roll 43, 12023, 12024, 12025.

15. Individual Civilians File, Roll 218, Mary Ann Pittman.

16. Individual Civilians File, Roll 294, Missouri Wood; Individual Civilians File, Roll 282, Emma Weaver.

17. Individual Civilians File, Roll 294, Missouri Wood. Wood makes no mention of Weaver in her statement.

18. Two or More Civilians File, Roll 77, 20857; Individual Civilians File, Roll 73, William T. Dickson.

19. Fellman, *Inside War,* 221–22 (Fellman briefly discusses the investigation, but the source he cites in the provost marshal general's Two or More Civilians File cannot be verified); Individual Civilians File, Roll 73, William T. Dickson; Cason [*sic*], "Missouri Girl's Prison Experience," 506–8. Prior to her marriage, the author had been known as Sue Bryant. Eighteen years old at the time, the Cooper County native had been arrested for sympathizing with rebel guerrillas.

20. Curran, "'On the Road to Dixie,'" 83–84.

21. *O.R.,* II, 6: 967–69; II, 7: 82; Cox, *Alton Military Penitentiary in the Civil War,* 63.

22. *O.R.,* II, 4: 123; Cox, *Alton Military Penitentiary in the Civil War,* 99. On clothes for the male prisoners of war see *O.R.,* II, 3: 230, 237.

23. T. Hendrickson to W. Hoffman, April 21, 1863, Letters Sent, February 1862—January 1864, Alton, Ill. (Roll 13), Selected Records . . . Alton Prison; *O.R.,* II, 5: 619–20. No response from Hoffman to Hendrickson could be found.

24. Faust, *Mothers of Invention,* 31, 32, 51, 63–64, 115, 136–38, 140–46, 150–52; Mitchell, *The Vacant Chair,* 71–87.

25. Frost, *Camp and Prison Journal,* 184–86, 188, 191.

26. Frost, *Camp and Prison Journal,* 185–87, 206. The "band" consisted of two violins, a guitar, a banjo, and castanets.

27. Individual Civilians File, Roll 122, Eliza J. Haynie; Register of Civilian Prisoners, March 1863–June 1864 (Roll 15), Selected Records . . . Alton Prison; *O.R.*, I, 34, 1: 994–95; Frost, *Camp and Prison Journal*, 185, 187, 200, 217; Individual Civilians File, Roll 122, Eliza J. Haynie; Register of Confederate and Federal Soldiers and Civilians Sentenced, No. 6, February 1863–June 1865 (Roll 15), Selected Records . . . Alton Prison; Individual Civilians File, Roll 106, Mollie Goggin; *Missouri Democrat*, July 4, 29, 1865; Prisoners: St. Louis, Mo. (Gratiot Street Prison), February–November 1865 (and other prisons) (varying dates); Two or More Civilians File, Roll 93; Individual Civilians File, Roll 251, Sarah Jane Smith.

28. Frost, *Camp and Prison Journal*, 200, 223, 224.

29. Frost, *Camp and Prison Journal*, 193, 195, 225; Individual Civilians File, Roll 218, Mary M. Pitman.

30. Frost, *Camp and Prison Journal*, 200, 201–2, 205, 206–8, 216, 217, 219, 222.

31. Frost, *Camp and Prison Journal*, 187, 215, 216, 218, 219.

32. Frost, *Camp and Prison Journal*, 202, 204, 210, 222, 227.

33. Frost, *Camp and Prison Journal*, 207–8.

34. Frost, *Camp and Prison Journal*, 196, 228, 242.

35. Frost, *Camp and Prison Journal*, 234–37; Cox, Alton Military Penitentiary in the Civil War, 112.

36. Frost, *Camp and Prison Journal*, 199.

37. Frost, *Camp and Prison Journal*, 232, 234–37, 238, 240, 244. The few times Frost mentions attending church services on other occasions, his motivations appear to be to relieve his boredom. See 29, 63, 76, 82, 115–16.

38. Frost, *Camp and Prison Journal*, 218.

9. "I Suppose She Could Be Released"

This chapter's title is in regard to Fanny Barron's request that she be released from the obligations of her bond three months after the war ended. Individual Civilians File, Roll 18, Fanny Barron.

1. Two or More Civilians File, Roll 48, 13681; Roll 50, 14171 (quote, emphasis added).

2. Two or More Civilians File, Roll 53, 15003.

3. Two or More Civilians File, Roll 50, 14021.

4. Two or More Civilians File, Roll 59, 16779; Individual Civilians File, Roll 228, Anna Reynolds.

5. *Missouri Democrat*, May 5, 1865; Two or More Civilians File, Roll 53, 15003.

6. Individual Civilians File, Roll 35, Ruth Brisco; Wood, *Bushwhacker Belles*, 57–69; Fellman, *Inside War*, 197–98, 233–40; Two or More Civilians File, Roll 53, 15055; Roll 54, 15158; Roll 77, 20894, 20972; Individual Civilians File, Roll 230, Tabitha A. Rider; *Missouri Democrat*, April 29, 1865.

7. Individual Civilians File, Roll 187, Sallie McPheeters; William McPheeters, "Private. Reasons for Joining the Southern Army," July 24, 1865, and "Private. Banishment of My Wife," July 27, 1865, William McPheeters Papers, 1852–1903, MHS; *Missouri Democrat*, January 18, 19, and 20, 1865.

8. *Missouri Democrat*, March 16, 23, 1865; *O.R.* II, 8: 501, 506–07, 513; John C. Frederiksen, "Ewell, Richard Stoddert."

9. Individual Civilians File, Roll 194, Josephine Moore; Individual Civilians File, Roll 6, Sarah Altridge.

10. Report of Persons on Parole and Not under Bond Who Report to This Office [Department of the Missouri Provost Marshal General], Two or More Civilian File, Roll 93; Individual Civilians File, Roll 156, Eleanor Ann King; King, Eleanor Ann (1839–1884), Papers, 1856–1898, Western Historical Manuscript Collection, University of Missouri; Individual Civilians File, Roll 122, Fanny Houx; *Missouri Democrat*, August 14, 19, 1862, June 7, 1865; Individual Civilians File, Roll 18, Fanny Barron.

11. Register of Civilian Prisoners, March 1863–June 1864 (Roll 15), Selected Records . . . Confederate Prisoners of War; Alton Prison, Register of Confederate and Federal Soldiers and Civilians Sentenced, No. 5, January 1863–July 1864, 16 (Roll 15), Selected Records . . . Alton Prison; Frost, *Camp and Prison Journal*, 240; *Missouri Democrat*, January 28, 1865. From the article the "lame rebel" who played the fiddle could not be identified.

12. Prisoners: St. Louis, MO. (Gratiot Street Prison) October 1864–January 1865, Two or More Civilians File, Roll 92; Two or More Civilians File, Roll 38, 10507; Compiled Service Records of Confederate Soldiers Who Served in Organizations from the State of Missouri, Roll 62 [M 322] Fifteenth Cavalry, Jacob Foster, Record Group 109, National Archives. For some unknown reason Jacob Foster's letter to Sanderson is located in the file of Annie B. Martin. See Individual Civilians File, Roll 176, Annie B. Martin.

13. *Missouri Democrat*, March 18, 1865; Fellman, *Inner Civil War*, 197–98; Prisoners: St. Louis, Mo. (Gratiot Street Prison) February–November 1865 (and other prisons) (varying dates), Two or More Civilians File, Roll 93.

14. Winter, *The Civil War in St. Louis*, 144, 148–49; interview with Randy Watkins of the Jefferson Barracks National Cemetery, April 4, 2000; Hale, *Branded as Rebels*, 2: 332.

15. Frost, *Camp and Prison Journal*, 234–37; Cox, *Alton Military Penitentiary in the Civil War*, 112. The author thanks Dan Gedden of St. Patrick's Cemetery for his assistance.

16. *Missouri Democrat*, July 31, 1863; Cox, *Alton Military Penitentiary in the Civil War*, appendix A, vii; Lowry, *Confederate Heroines*, 98; Hallum, *The Diary of an Old Lawyer*, 334–35.

17. *St. Louis Post-Dispatch*, April 26, 2002; "Confederate POW Burials on Smallpox Island, West Alton, Il," http://www.usgwarchives.net/mo/civilwar /smallpox.htm (accessed August 18, 2019); Cox, *Alton Military Penitentiary in the Civil War*, 28–31, 113–15.

18. Pinckney's memoir, titled *My Reminiscences of the War and Reconstruction Times*, had been typeset and produced as page proofs but never published. The page including the *New York Herald* article is reproduced at "University of Virginia Online Exhibits/Hearts at Home: Southern Women in the Civil War," https://explore.lib.virginia.edu/exhibits/show/hearts/patriotism (accessed August 18, 2019).

19. "University of Virginia Online Exhibits/Hearts at Home: Southern Women in the Civil War," https://explore.lib.virginia.edu/exhibits/show/hearts/patriotism (accessed August 18, 2019); Compiled Service Records of Confederate Soldiers Who Served in Organizations from the State of South Carolina, Fourth Cavalry, Roll 29 [M 267], Thomas Pinckney, Record Group 109, National Archives.

20. *Alton Evening Telegraph*, August 2, 1904. The *St. Charles Chronicle* also published an obituary for Gleason with similar information. It can be found at http://www.genealogy.com/forum/surnames/topics/gleason/1600/ (accessed August 18, 2019). Six years later when Gleason's wife died, the *Alton Evening Telegraph* devoted half of her obituary to her husband and his role in burying Confederate dead, including the unknown woman. See "Alton Military Post and Prison," https://madison.illinoisgenweb.org/town_histories/alton/military _prison.html (accessed August 18, 2019).

21. Report of Persons Released from the Gratiot Str. Mil. Prison during the Month of April 1865 and Daily Morning Report, May 15, '65, Two or More Civilians File, Roll 93; Roll 62, 17418, 17699; *Missouri Democrat*, July 4, 29, 1865; Lowry, *Confederate Heroines*, 122, 128–29; Eakin, *Civil War Military Prisoners Sent to Missouri State Penitentiary*, 3, 4, 7, 11, 28.

22. Cosner and Shannon, *Missouri's Mad Doctor McDowell*, 102–03, 107, 116; Scharf, *History of Saint Louis City and County*, 1: 418, 421; Grimes, *Absalom Grimes*, 216.

23. *Missouri Democrat*, May 22, 1865; Wright, *Discovering African American St. Louis*, 11; Ling, *Chinese in St. Louis, 1857–2007*, 7–8, 24.

24. Winter, *The Civil War in St. Louis*, 154.

25. *Missouri Democrat*, April 3, 1865; Individual Civilian File, Roll 21, Mrs. Beattie; Shiras, "Major Wolf and Abraham Lincoln," 357.

26. General Orders No. 125, July 20, 1864, U.S. Army, *General Orders of the Department of the Missouri, 1864* [In two parts, part 2]; Johnson, "A Vast and Fiendish Plot"; Typescript history titled "Ada Byron Haynes," ca. 1910, Ada Byron Haynes Papers, 1861–1898, MHS.

27. 1870 U.S. Census, Missouri, St. Louis County, Central Township, 157; Interview with Ollie Sappington, July 18, 2000; W. D. Sappington, Alabama, Texas, and Virginia, Confederate pensions, 1884–1958, Texas, Pension File Nos. 06011–07516, Pension File Nos. 07186–07235, Application Years 1897 to 1929, W. D. Sappington, Ancestry.com; "Drucilla Williams Sappington," Find a Grave Memorial 92835871, West Hill Cemetery, Sherman, Grayson County, Texas, USA, https:// www.findagrave.com/memorial/92835871/drucilla-sappington#source (accessed August 18, 2019).

28. Individual Civilians File, Roll 158, Jennie Knight; Elder, "Virginia K. Johnson and the Dallas Rescue Home for 'Erring' Women, 1893–1941," 4–16.

29. 1870 U.S. Census, Tennessee, Rutherford County, Murfreesboro Ward 6, 47; "Theology," 296; Walter Edgar, *Chapters in Trinity's History*, chapter 13, "Reaching Out: 1879–1887," http://www.trinitysc.org/about/history/chapters-in-trinity -s-history (accessed August 18, 2019); 1880 U.S. Census, South Carolina, Richland Co., Columbia, 320; "Rev. H. O. Judd," 518; Dyer and Moore, comp., *The Tennessee Civil War Veterans Questionnaires*, 3: iii, xviii, 1268–69. The author thanks LaVonne Barac for supplemental information on Clara Judd.

Charlie did in fact serve under Morgan, at least until the general was killed in September 1864, but he did not join Morgan's command until well after his mother's arrest and imprisonment. Furthermore, according to his service record, Charlie voluntarily surrendered in mid-March 1865. Because he identified his home as Carver County, Minnesota, where his family had lived prior to the war before moving to Tennessee, he was released from custody provided he "remain North of the Ohio River during the war." Compiled Service Records of Confederate Soldiers Who Served in Organizations from the State of Kentucky, 2nd Battalion (Capt. Dortch's) Cavalry, Charles S. Judd (Roll 20); Compiled Service Records of Confederate Soldiers who Served in Organizations from the State of Georgia, 2nd Battalion Infantry (State Guards), Charles S. Judd (Roll 14).

30. Individual Civilians File, Roll 192, Elvira Mitchel; Roll 176, Harriet Martin.

31. Wood, *Bushwhacker Belles*, 78, 188–89, 227; Case Miner, "Emily Weaver (?– 1917)," *The Encyclopedia of Arkansas History and Culture*, http://www.encyclopedia ofarkansas.net/encyclopedia/entry-detail.aspx?entryID=5480 (accessed August 18, 2019).

32. Floyd, "Reminiscences of Mrs. Lucy Nickolson Lindsay," 113; Individual Civilian Files, Roll 98, Mrs. D. M. Frost and Eliza G. Frost; Hunter, "Missouri's Confederate Leaders after the War," 378; Winters, *The Civil War in St. Louis*, 140; Rolle, *The Lost Cause*, 221–22; Jenkins-Gamache, "Banished!" 65–66; "Elizabeth Frost," https://www.geni.com/people/Elizabeth-Frost/6000000028972750821 (accessed August 18, 2019).

33. Robert, "History of Events Preceding and Following the Banishment of Mrs. Margaret A. E. McLure, As Given to the Author by Herself," 82; Ankesheiln, *The Heart Is the Heritage*, 20–21, 66, 87–90, 120, 127; Hopkins, "'Tried in the Furnace of Affliction,'" 236–40.

34. Wood, *Bushwhacker Belles*, 213.

10. *"The Heroines . . . Have Been Forgotten"*

This chapter's title is from Woodson, preface, 3.

1. Churchill, *The Crisis*, quote on 358; Mersand, introduction, xiii; Schneider, *Novelist to a Generation*, 46–48; Titus, *Winston Churchill*, 25, 46, 49, 50, 154n31; "The Crisis" (play), Internet Broadway Date Base, https://www.ibdb.com/broadway -production/the-crisis-5656 (accessed August 18, 2019); Erish, *William N. Selig*, 142–46; Churchill, *The Crisis*, Classics Illustrated.

2. Moore, "Missouri," 183–84.

3. Moore, "Missouri," 179.

4. "Scharf, J. Thomas (John Thomas), 1943–1898," Social Networks and Archival Content, http://n2t.net/ark:/99166/w6nc6392 (accessed August 18, 2019); Scharf, *History of Saint Louis City and County*, 1: 420, 448, 504.

5. Deborah Isaac, "Confederate Days in St. Louis—Female Prisoners of War," *Missouri Republican*, May 10, 1903, clipping in William McPheeters Papers, 1852–1903, MHS.

6. Woodson, preface, 3–4; Hulbert, *The Ghost of Guerrilla Memory*, 74; Floyd, "Reminiscences of Mrs. Lucy Nickolson Lindsay," 105–14; McCanne, "Banishment of Miss Mary Cleveland," 241–42.

7. Mullins, "Sketch of Col. Sydney D. Jackman," 93–96; "Facts regarding Southern Women," 221–22.

8. [Carson], "Copy of the Oath of Allegiance," 189–90; "Reminiscences of the War between the States," 273–76. See also "Copy of the Oath of Allegiance," 508; *Missouri Democrat*, September 20, 1864.

9. Robert, "History of the Events Preceding and Following the Banishment of Mrs. Margaret A. E. McLure, As Given to the Author by Herself," 78–84; "The St. Louis Prison for Southern Women" in Andrews, *Women of the South in War Times*, 336.

10. Robert, "History of the Events Preceding and Following the Banishment of Mrs. Margaret A. E. McLure, As Given to the Author by Herself," 78, 82; "Facts regarding Southern Women," 222; [Mrs. John R. Carson], "Copy of the Oath of Allegiance," 190; "The Origins of the United Daughters of the Confederacy," 5; Robert, "Reminiscences of Richmond during the Seven Days' Fight, By a Chaplain's Wife," 90.

11. Clinton, *Stepdaughters of History*, 57–58. For more on the Lost Cause see Foster, *Ghost of the Confederacy*; and Blight, *Race and Reunion*.

12. Whites, "'Stand by Your Man'"; Cox, *Dixie's Daughters;* Mills and Simpson, eds., *Monuments to the Lost Cause;* Janney, *Burying the Dead but Not the Past;* Faust, *Mothers of Invention,* 248–54; Cloyd, *Haunted by Atrocity,* 56–110.

13. Daily Morning Report of Gratiot St. Mil. Prison, St. Louis MO, Oct. 10, 1864, Two or More Civilians File, Roll 92; [Carson], "Copy of the Oath of Allegiance," 189–90; Primm, *Lion of the Valley,* 262; Parrish, *A History of Missouri,* vol. 3, *1860–1875,* 73; Gerteis, *Civil War St. Louis,* 178–79, 180–81, 232; Winter, *The Civil War in St. Louis,* 85–86; Corbett, *In Her Place,* 95–97. See also Jenkins-Gamache, "Banished!"

14. Whites, "'Corresponding with the Enemy,'" quotes on 114 and 103 respectively.

15. Blight, *Race and Reunion,* 152, 184–85; Cloyd, *Haunted by Atrocity,* 56–82, quote on 60–61. One notable exception to the silence on female prisoners is Griffin Frost's narrative *Camp and Prison Journal,* published in 1866 just as the Lost Cause myth was germinating.

16. Whites, "'Corresponding with the Enemy,'" 106.

17. Jewett, *From the Darkness Risen,* quote on 1.

18. Risner, *Ella Mayfield's Pawpaw Militia;* Wood, *Bushwhacker Belles,* 41.

19. Kennedy, *Uncle Seth Fought the Yankees,* 128–29.

20. Daily Morning Report, Gratiot Mil. Prison, Saint Louis, Mo, Jan. 19, 1865, Two or More Civilians File, Roll 92, and Roll 51, 14396; Kennedy, *Uncle Seth Fought the Yankees,* 20, 129; "Death of a Woman Soldier," 214. As a "Deo Vindice" entry, Kennedy also retells the story of Sue Bryant that first appeared in the *Confederate Veteran* 13 (November 1905) and then in *Reminiscences of the Women of Missouri during the Sixties,* 189–90.

21. Jiles, *Enemy Women; New York Times Book Review,* February 24, 2002. Jiles's quotes come from "A Conversation with Paulette Jiles," 7, included as an appendix to the 2007 paperback version published by Harper Perennial.

22. Jane Henderson, "Fighting Words," *St. Louis Post-Dispatch,* October 13, 2002; Henderson, "Missourians Should Rally to 'Enemy Women,'" *St. Louis Post-Dispatch,* March 5, 2003; "Commentary: Readers Bring Different Perspectives to 'Enemy Women,'" *St. Louis Post-Dispatch,* March 19, 2003; and "'Enemy Women' Rekindles Civil War Discussion," *St. Louis Post-Dispatch,* March 26, 2003.

23. Jiles, *Enemy Women,* 51, 84, 86, 88.

24. Jiles, *Enemy Women,* 58, 59, 69.

25. Vernon, "P.O.W.," 9.

BIBLIOGRAPHY

Primary Sources

ARCHIVAL MATERIAL

The Huntington Library, San Marino, California
  Francis Lieber Collection
Library of Congress
  Abraham Lincoln Papers, Series 1, General Correspondence, 1833–1916, accessed at https://www.loc.gov/
  Franklin A. Dick Papers
Missouri Historical Society
  Civil War Collection
  Ferguson, Philip Gooch, Diary, 1847–1864
  Fusz, Louis, Diary, 1862–1863
  Halleck, Henry W., Collection
  Haynes, Ada Byron, Papers, 1861–1898
  Howard, Mrs. C. A., Book of Copied Poems, 2 vols.
  Lane, William Carr, Papers, 1813–1926
  Leighton George E., Collection
  McPheeters, William, Papers, 1852–1903
Missouri State Archives, Jefferson City, Missouri
  Record Group 133, Court-Martial Papers, Office of the Adjutant General
Milton S. Eisenhower Library, Special Collections, Johns Hopkins University
  Francis Lieber Papers
National Archives
  Record Group 109, War Department Collection of Confederate Records, Compiled Service Records of Confederate Soldiers Who Served in Organizations from the State of Georgia [M 266]

Record Group 109, War Department Collection of Confederate Records, Compiled Service Records of Confederate Soldiers Who Served in Organizations from the State of Kentucky [M 319]

Record Group 109, War Department Collection of Confederate Records, Compiled Service Records of Confederate Soldiers Who Served in Organizations from the State of Missouri [M 322]

Record Group 109, War Department Collection of Confederate Records, Compiled Service Records of Confederate Soldiers Who Served in Organizations from the State of South Carolina [M 267]

Record Group 109, War Department Collection of Confederate Records, Compiled Service Records of Confederate Soldiers Who Served in Organizations from the State of Tennessee [M 268]

Record Group 109, War Department Collection of Confederate Records, Selected Records of the War Department Related to Confederate Prisoners of War, 1861–1865 [M 598]

Record Group 109, War Department Collection of Confederate Records, Union Provost Marshals' File of Papers Relating to Individual Civilians [M 345]

Record Group 109, War Department Collection of Confederate Records, Union Provost Marshals' File of Papers Relating to Two or More Civilians [M 416]

Record Group 110, Records of the Provost Marshal General's Bureau (Civil War) [M 621]

Ohio History Connection, Columbus, Ohio
J. P. Sanderson Papers, 1846–1865

Saint Louis Public Library
U.S. Army, *General Orders, Department of the Missouri Issued by General Curtis 1862 and 1863* (n.p., n.d.)

U.S. Army, *General Orders of Department of the Missouri, 1864* [in two parts, part 2] (St. Louis: R. P. Studly and Co., Printers, 1864)

U.S. Army, *General Orders of the Department of the Missouri, for 1865* (St. Louis: Missouri Democrat Print, 1866)

Western Historical Manuscript Collection, University of Missouri
King, Eleanor Ann (1839–1884), Papers, 1856–1898

NEWSPAPERS

Alton Evening Telegraph [Illinois]
Boston Daily Advertiser
The Cadiz Sentinel [Ohio]
Commercial Register [Sandusky, Ohio]

Daily Evening Bulletin [San Francisco]
Missouri Democrat
Missouri Republican
Newark Advocate [Ohio]
New York Herald
St. Charles Chronicle [Missouri]
St. Louis Post-Dispatch
The Valley Herald [Chaska, Minnesota]
Wheeling Intelligencer

MISCELLANEOUS

1860 U.S. Census
1870 U.S. Census
1880 U.S. Census
Alabama, Texas, and Virginia, Confederate pensions, 1884–1958, accessed at
    Ancestry.com.
Price, Sterling. "Letter of recommendation from Sterling Price to General S. Coo-
    per regarding Mr. John W. Polk for a position within his Quarter Master
    Department. Grenada, Mississippi, January 5, 1863." (1863). *The Broadus
    R. Littlejohn Jr. Manuscript Collection*, Book 253. http://digitalcommons.
    wofford.edu/littlejohnmss/253.

Published Materials, Dissertations, and Unpublished Works

Adams, Benton. "Greybeards in Blue." *Civil War Times* (February 1998): 32–35,
    58–59.
Alison, Archibald. *Miscellaneous Essays*. New York: D. Appleton and Company,
    1860.
Ambrose, Stephen E. *Halleck: Lincoln's Chief of Staff*. Baton Rouge: Louisiana
    State University Press, 1990 [1962].
Anderson, Galusha. *A Border City during the Civil War*. Boston: Little, Brown,
    and Company, 1908.
Andrews, Matthew Page. *The Women of the South in War Times*. Baltimore: The
    Norman, Remington Co., 1920.
Ankesheiln, Wade F. *The Heart Is the Heritage: The Story of the Founding of the
    Confederate Home of Missouri*. Coral Springs, FL: Lumina Press, 2007.
Arenson, Adam. *The Great Heart of the Republic: St. Louis and the Cultural Civil
    War*. Cambridge, MA: Harvard University Press, 2011.
Arnold-Scriber, Theresa, and Terry G. Scriber. *Ship Island, Mississippi: Rosters
    and History of the Civil War Prison*. Jefferson, NC: McFarland and Com-
    pany, Inc., 2008.

Articles 103, 103a, and 103b of the Uniform Code of Military Justice (United States Code, title 10, subtitle A, part 2, chapter 47), accessed at https://www.law .cornell.edu/uscode/text/10/subtitle-A/part-II/chapter-47.

Baker, Paula. "The Domestication of Politics: Women and American Political Society, 1780–1920." *American Historical Review* 89 (June 1984): 620–47.

Barber, E. Susan, and Charles Ritter. "'Unlawful and against Her Consent': Sexual Violence and the Military during the American Civil War." In *Sexual Violence in Combat Zones: From the Ancient World to the Era of Human Rights,* edited by Elizabeth Heineman, 202–14. Philadelphia: University of Pennsylvania Press, 2011.

Basler, Roy P., ed. *The Collected Works of Abraham Lincoln.* 8 vols. New Brunswick, NJ: Rutgers University Press, 1953–1955.

Baxter, Richard R. "The Duty of Obedience to the Belligerent Occupant." *British Yearbook of International Law* 27 (1950): 235–66.

———."The First Modern Codification of the Laws of War: Francis Lieber and General Orders No. 100." *International Review of the Red Cross* 25 (April 1963): 171–89.

———. "The First Modern Codification of the Laws of War: Francis Lieber and General Orders No. 100 (2)." *International Review of the Red Cross* 26 (May 1963): 234–50.

Beale, Howard K., ed. *The Diary of Edward Bates, 1859–1866.* Washington, D.C.: United States Government Printing Office, 1933.

Bearss, Edwin C. *The Campaign for Vicksburg.* 3 vols. Dayton, OH: Morningside Press, 1985–1986.

Beilein, Joseph M., Jr. *Bushwhackers: Guerrilla Warfare, Manhood, and the Household in Civil War Missouri.* Kent, OH: Kent State University Press, 2016.

Belanger, Elizabeth. "'A Perfect Nuisance': Working-Class Women and Neighborhood Development in Civil War St. Louis." *Journal of the Civil War Era* 8 (March 2018): 32–63.

Blackman, Ann. *Wild Rose: The True Story of a Civil War Spy.* New York: Random House, 2005.

Blair, William A. *With Malice toward Some: Treason and Loyalty in the Civil War Era.* Chapel Hill: University of North Carolina Press, 2014.

Blakeslee, Merritt R. "'Examples Should Be Made': The Unhappy Story of Clara Judd." *Historical Tidings* 49 (April 2017): 2–11.

Blanton, DeAnne, and Lauren M. Cook. *They Fought Like Demons: Women Soldiers in the American Civil War.* Baton Rouge: Louisiana State University Press, 2002.

Blight, David. *Race and Reunion: The Civil War in American Memory.* Cambridge, MA: Harvard University Press, 2001.

Boman, Dennis K. *Lincoln and Citizens' Rights in Civil War Missouri: Balancing Freedom and Security.* Baton Rouge: Louisiana State University Press, 2011.

———. *Lincoln's Resolute Unionist: Hamilton Gamble, Dred Scott Dissenter and Missouri's Civil War Governor.* Baton Rouge: Louisiana State University Press, 2006.

[Brock, Sallie A.] *Richmond during the War: Four Years of Personal Observations.* New York: G. W. Carleton and Co., Publishers, 1867.

Brockett, L. P., and Mary C. Vaughan. *Women's Work in the Civil War: A Record of Heroism, Patriotism, and Patience.* Philadelphia: Zeigler, McCurdy and Co., 1867.

Buhk, Tobin T. *Memphis Vice, 1863: Sex for Sale and the Scandal That Rocked a Civil War City.* Lexington, KY: Tobin T. Buhk, 2016.

Bunch, Clea Lutz. "Confederate Women of Arkansas Face 'the Fiends in Human Shape.'" *Military History of the West* 27 (Fall 1997): 173–87.

Burgess, Lauren Cook, ed. *An Uncommon Soldier: The Civil War Letters of Sarah Rosetta Wakeman, alias Pvt. Lyons Wakeman, 153rd Regiment, New York State Volunteers, 1862–1864.* Pasadena, MD: The Minerva Center, 1994.

Burlingame, Michael, and John R. Turner, eds. *Inside Lincoln's White House: The Complete Diary of John Hay.* Carbondale: Southern Illinois University Press, 1997.

Bynum, Victoria. *Unruly Women: The Politics of Social and Sexual Control in the Old South.* Chapel Hill: University of North Carolina Press, 1992.

Campbell, Jacqueline G. "'The Unmeaning Twaddle about Order 28': Benjamin F. Butler and Confederate Women in Occupied New Orleans, 1862." *Journal of the Civil War Era* 2 (March 2012): 11–30.

Carnahan, Burrus M. *Lincoln on Trial: Southern Civilians and the Law of War.* Lexington: University Press of Kentucky, 2010.

Carso, Brian F., Jr. *"Whom Can We Trust Now?" The Meaning of Treason in the United States from the Revolution through the Civil War.* Lanham, MD: Lexington Books, 2006.

[Carson, Mrs. John R.] "Copy of the Oath of Allegiance." In *Reminiscences,* 189–90.

Castel, Albert. "Order No. 11 and the Civil War on the Border." *Missouri Historical Review* 57 (July 1963): 257–68.

Carter, Geri, ed. *Troubled State: Civil War Journals of Franklin Archibald Dick.* Kirksville, MO: Truman State University Press, 2007.

Cason [*sic*], Mrs. John R. "Missouri Girl's Prison Experience." *Confederate Veteran* 13 (November 1905): 506–08.

Childress, James. "Francis Lieber's Interpretation of the Laws of War: General Orders No. 100 in the Context of His Life and Thought." *American Journal of Jurisprudence* 21, no. 1 (1976): 34–70.

Chopin, Kate. "As You Like It." In *St. Louis Criterion* (March 20, 1897). Reprinted in *The Complete Works of Kate Chopin*. Edited by Per Seyersted. Baton Rouge: Louisiana State University Press, 1969.

Christie, Jeanne M. "The Prisoner: The Incarceration of Mrs. Mary M. Stockton Terry, 1864–1865." In *Valor and Lace: The Roles of Confederate Women, 1861–1865*, 15: 114–35. Journal of Confederate History Series. Murfreesboro, TN: Southern Heritage Press, 1996.

Churchill, Winston. *The Crisis*. New York: MacMillan Company, 1901.

———. *The Crisis*, Classics Illustrated 145. New York: Gilberton Company, 1958.

———. *The Crisis*. New York: Washington Square Press, Inc., 1962. Includes an introduction by Joseph Mersand.

Civil War History 61 (December 2015).

Clinton, Catherine. "'Public Women' and Sexual Politics during the American Civil War." In Clinton and Silber, *Battle Scars*, 61–77.

———. *Stepdaughters of History: Southern Women and the American Civil War*. Baton Rouge: Louisiana State University Press, 2016.

Clinton, Catherine, and Nina Silber, eds. *Battle Scars: Gender and Sexuality in the American Civil War*. New York: Oxford University Press, 2006.

———. *Divided Houses: Gender and the Civil War*. New York: Oxford University Press, 1992.

Cloyd, Benjamin G. *Haunted by Atrocity: Civil War Prisons in American Memory*. Baton Rouge: Louisiana State University Press, 2010.

Conard, Howard L., ed. *Encyclopedia of the History of Missouri*. New York: Southern History Company, 1901.

"A Conversation with Paulette Jiles." In Paulette Jiles, *Enemy Women*, appendix, 7–11. New York: Harper Perennial paperback edition, 2007.

"Copy of the Oath of Allegiance." *Confederate Veteran* 13 (November 1905): 508.

Corbett, Katharine T. *In Her Place: A Guide to St. Louis Women's History*. St. Louis: Missouri Historical Society Press, 1999.

Cosner, Victoria, and Lorelei Shannon. *Missouri's Mad Doctor McDowell: Confederates, Cadavers and Macabre Medicine*. Charleston, SC: The History Press, 2015.

Covington, James W. "The Camp Jackson Affair: 1861." *Missouri Historical Review* 55 (April 1961): 197–212.

Cox, Jann. *Alton Military Penitentiary in the Civil War: Small Pox and Burial on the Alton Harbor Islands*. St. Louis District Historic Properties Management Report 36. Alexandria, VA: Historic Properties Management, U.S. Army Corps of Engineers, 1988.

Cox, Karen L. *Dixie's Daughters: The United Daughters of the Confederacy and the Preservation of Confederate Culture*. Gainesville: University Press of Florida, 2003.

Curran, Thomas F. "A 'Rebel to [His] Govt. and to His Parents': The Emancipation of Tommy Cave." In Marten, *Children and Youth during the Civil War Era*, 65-76.

———. "General Orders, No. 100." In Heidler and Heidler, *Encyclopedia of the American Civil War*, 2: 819.

———, ed. "'On the Road to Dixie': A Missouri Confederate's Review of the Civil War at its Midpoint." *Missouri Historical Review* 96 (January 2002): 69-92.

Cutter, Barbara. *Domestic Devils, Battlefield Angels: The Radicalism of American Womanhood, 1830-1865*. DeKalb: Northern Illinois University Press, 2003.

Dannett, Sylvia G. L., ed. *Noble Women of the North*. New York: Thomas Yoseloff, Publisher, 1959.

Davis, Robert Scott. *Ghosts and Shadows of Andersonville: Essays on the Secret Social Histories of America's Deadliest Prison*. Macon, GA: Mercer University Press, 2006.

"Death of a Woman Soldier." *Confederate Veteran* 18 (May 1910), 214.

Dilbeck, D. H. "'The Origin of This Tablet with My Name': Francis Lieber and the Wartime Origins of General Orders No. 100." *Journal of the Civil War Era* 5 (June 2015): 231-53.

Driscoll, John K. *Rogue: A Biography of Civil War General Justus McKinstry*. Jefferson, NC: McFarland and Co., Inc., 2006.

Dyer, Gustavus W., and John Trotwood Moore, comps. *The Tennessee Civil War Veterans Questionnaires*. 5 vols. Easley, SC: Southern Historical Press, Inc., 1985.

Eakin, Joanne Chiles. *Civil War Military Prisoners Sent to Missouri State Penitentiary*. Independence, MO: Print America, 1995.

———. *Missouri Prisoners of War from Gratiot Street Prison and Myrtle Street Prison, St. Louis, Mo and Alton Prison, Alton, Illinois, including Citizens, Confederates, Bushwhackers and Guerrillas*. Independence, MO: Print America, 1995.

Elder, Jane Lenz. "Virginia Johnson and the Dallas Rescue Home for 'Erring' Women, 1893-1941." *Legacies: A History Journal for Dallas and North Central Texas* 26 (Spring 2014): 4-16.

Erish, Andrew A. *William N. Selig: The Man Who Invented Hollywood*. Austin: University of Texas Press, 2012.

Evans, Clement A., ed. *Confederate Military History*. 12 vols. Atlanta: Confederate Publishing Company, 1899.

"Facts regarding Southern Women." In *Reminiscences*, 221-22.

Farnham, Christie Anne, ed. *Women of the South: A Multicultural Reader*. New York and London: New York University Press, 1997.

Faust, Drew Gilpin. *Mothers of Invention: Women and the Slaveholding South in the American Civil War*. Chapel Hill: University of North Carolina Press, 1996.

———. "'Ours As Well As That of Men': Women and Gender in the Civil War." In *Writing the Civil War: The Quest to Understand,* edited by James M. McPherson and William J. Cooper Jr., 228–240. Columbia: University of South Carolina Press, 1998.

Fehrenbacher, Don E. *The Dred Scott Case: Its Significance in American Law and Politics.* New York: Oxford University Press, 1978.

Feimster, Crystal N. "General Benjamin Butler and the Threat of Sexual Violence during the American Civil War." *Daedalus* 138 (Spring 2009): 126–34.

Fellman, Michael. *Inside War: The Guerrilla Conflict in Missouri during the American Civil War.* New York: Oxford University Press, 1989.

Fitch, John. *Annals of the Army of the Cumberland.* Philadelphia: J. B. Lippincott and Co., 1863.

Floyd, Mrs. Tyler. "Reminiscences of Mrs. Lucy Nickolson Lindsay." In *Reminiscences,* 105–14.

Forster, Stig, and Jorg Nagler, eds. *On the Road to Total War: The American Civil War and the German Wars for Unification, 1861–1871.* New York and Washington D.C.: Cambridge University Press and the German Historical Institute, 1997.

Foster, Gaines M. *Ghost of the Confederacy: Defeat, the Lost Cause, and the Emergence of the New South, 1865–1913.* New York: Oxford University Press, 1987.

Frederiksen, John C. "Ewell, Richard Stoddert." In Heidler and Heidler, *Encyclopedia of the American Civil War,* 2: 665–66.

Fremont, John C. "In Command in Missouri." In *Battles and Leaders of the Civil War.* Vol. 1. New York: Thomas Yoseloff, Inc., 1956 edition [1887].

Friedel, Frank. *Francis Lieber: Nineteenth-Century Liberal.* Baton Rouge: Louisiana State University Press, 1947.

———. "General Orders 100 and Military Government." *Mississippi Valley Historical Review* 32 (March 1946): 541–56.

Frost, Griffin. *Camp and Prison Journal.* Iowa City, IA: Press of the Camp Pope Bookshop, 1994 reprint [1867].

Garner, James G. "General Order 100 Revisited." *Military Law Review* 27 (January 1965): 1–48.

Garner, James Wilford. *International Law and the World War.* London: Longmans, Green and Co., 1920.

Gerteis, Louis. *Civil War St. Louis.* Lawrence: University Press of Kansas, 2001.

Giesberg, Judith Ann. *Army at Home: Women and the Civil War on the Northern Homefront.* Chapel Hill: University of North Carolina Press, 2009.

———. *Civil War Sisterhood: The U.S. Sanitary Commission and Women's Politics in Transition.* Boston: Northeastern University Press, 2000.

Ginsberg, Elaine K. Introduction to *Passing and the Fictions of Identity*, 1–18.

———, ed. *Passing and the Fictions of Identity*. Durham, NC: Duke University Press, 1996.

Greene, William Robert. "Early Development of the Illinois State Penitentiary System." *Journal of the Illinois State Historical Society* 70 (August 1977): 185–95.

Grimes, Absalom. *Absalom Grimes, Confederate Mail Carrier*, edited by M. M. Quaife. New Haven: Yale University Press, 1926.

Grimsley, Mark. *The Hard Hand of War: Union Military Policy toward Southern Civilians, 1861–1865*. New York: Cambridge University Press, 1995.

Hale, Donald R. *Branded as Rebels*. Vol. 2. Independence, MO: Blue and Grey Bookshoppe, 2003.

Halleck, Henry Wager. "Retaliation in War." *American Journal of International Law* 6 (January 1912): 107–18.

Hallum, John. *The Diary of an Old Lawyer: Scenes behind the Curtain*. Nashville, TN: Southwestern Publishing House, 1895.

Harris, Charles F. "Catalyst for Terror: The Collapse of the Women's Prison in Kansas City." *Missouri Historical Review* 89 (April 1995): 290–308.

Harris, Sharon M. *Dr. Mary Walker: An American Radical*. New Brunswick, NJ: Rutgers University Press, 2009.

Hartigan, Richard Shelly. *Lieber's Code and the Laws of War*. Chicago: Precedent Publishing, Inc., 1983.

Heidler, David S., and Jeanne T. Heidler, eds. *Encyclopedia of the American Civil War: A Political, Social, and Military History*. 5 vols. Santa Barbara, CA: ABC-Clio, 2000.

———. "Ewing, Thomas, Jr.," in Heidler and Heidler, *Encyclopedia of the American Civil War*, 2: 667.

Herrera-Graf, Mercedes. "Stress, Suffering, and Sacrifice: Women POWs in the Civil War." *Minerva: Quarterly Report on Women and the Military* 16 (Fall/ Winter 1998): 1–24.

Hesseltine, W. B. "Military Prisons of St. Louis, 1861–1865." *Missouri Historical Review* 23 (April 1929): 380–99.

Hesseltine, William B. *Civil War Prisons: A Study in War Psychology*. Columbus: Ohio State University Press, 1930.

Hinton, Richard J. *Rebel Invasion of Missouri and Kansas and the Campaign of the Army of the Border against General Sterling Price, in October and November, 1864*. Chicago: Church and Goodman, 1865.

History of Southwest Missouri. Chicago: The Goodspeed Publishing Co., 1888.

Hodes, Frederick A. *A Divided City: A History of St. Louis, 1851–1876*. Stockton, CA: Bluebird Publishing Company, 2015.

Hogue, L. Lynn. "Lieber's Military Code and Its Legacy." In *Francis Lieber and the Culture of the Mind,* ed. Charles R. Mack and Henry H. Lesesne, 51–60. Columbia: University of South Carolina Press, 2005.

Hopkins, Rosemary. "'Tried by the Furnace of Affliction': Political and Social Activism among Civil War Era St. Louis Women." PhD dissertation, Saint Louis University, 2005.

Horan, James D. *Desperate Women.* New York: Bonanza Books, 1952.

Hulbert, Matthew Christopher. *The Ghost of Guerrilla Memory: How Civil War Bushwhackers Became Gunslingers in the American West.* Athens: University of Georgia Press, 2016.

Hunter, Lloyd A. "Missouri's Confederate Leaders after the War." *Missouri Historical Review* 67 (April 1973): 371–96.

Irwin, Ray W., ed. "Missouri in Crisis: The Journal of Captain Albert Tracy, 1861." Pt. 1. *Missouri Historical Review* 51 (October 1956): 8–21.

Janney, Caroline E. *Burying the Dead but Not the Past: Ladies' Memorial Associations and the Lost Cause.* Chapel Hill: University of North Carolina Press, 2008.

Jenkins-Gamache, Rachel K. "Banished! How Lily Frost, Lucy Nicholson, and Harriet Snodgrass Paid the Price for Disloyalty." *Gateway: The Magazine of the Missouri Historical Society* 31 (2011): 60–71.

Jewett, Jessica. *From the Darkness Risen: A Novel.* Middletown, DE: Jessica Jewett, 2006.

Jiles, Paulette. *Enemy Women.* New York: William Morrow, 2002.

Johnson, Clint. *"A Vast and Fiendish Plot": The Confederate Attack on New York City.* New York: Citadel Press, 2010.

Johnson, Reverdy. *An Argument to Establish the Illegality of Military Commissions in the United States.* Baltimore: John Murphy and Co., 1865.

Joslyn, Mauriel Phillips, ed. *Valor and Lace: The Roles of Confederate Women, 1861–1865.* Murfreesboro, TN: Southern Heritage Press, 1996.

Kennedy, James Ronald. *Uncle Seth Fought the Yankees.* Gretna, LA: Pelican Publishing Company, 2015.

Kerber, Linda K. *No Constitutional Right to Be Ladies: Women and the Obligation of Citizenship.* New York: Hill and Wang, 1998.

King, Horatio. "Judge Holt and the Lincoln Conspirators." *The Century: A Popular Quarterly* (April 1890): 955–57.

[Kirkland, Caroline M.]. *A Few Words on Behalf of the Loyal Women of the United States by One of Themselves.* New York: Loyal Publication Society, 1863.

Klement, Frank L. *Copperheads in the Middle West.* Chicago: University of Chicago Press, 1960.

———. *Dark Lanterns: Secret Political Societies, Conspiracies, and Treason Trials in the Civil War.* Baton Rouge: Louisiana State University Press, 1989.

Knox, Thomas W. *Camp-Fire and Cotton-Field: Southern Adventures in Time of War. Life with the Union Armies, and Residence on a Louisiana Plantation.* New York: Blelock and Company, 1865.

Knust, Jennifer Wright. *Unprotected Texts: The Bible's Surprising Contradictions about Sex and Desire.* New York: Harper Collins, 2011.

Krug, Donna Rebecca D. "Women and War in the Confederacy." In Forster and Nagler, *On the Road to Total War,* 413–448.

Krug, Mark M., ed. *Mrs. Hill's Journal—Civil War Reminiscences.* Chicago: The Lakeside Press, 1980.

Kutzler, Evan A. "Captive Audiences: Sound, Silence, and Listening in Civil War Prisons." *Journal of Social History* 48 (Winter 2014): 239–63.

Lamers, William M. *The Edge of Glory: A Biography of General William S. Rosecrans, U.S.A.* Baton Rouge: Louisiana State University Press, 1999 [1961].

Larson, Kate Clifford. *The Assassin's Accomplice: Mary Surratt and the Plot to Kill Abraham Lincoln.* New York: Basic Books, 2008.

Laughlin, Bonnie E. " 'Endangering the Peace of Society': Abolitionist Agitation and Mob Reaction in St. Louis and Alton, 1836–1838." *Missouri Historical Review* 95 (October 2000): 1–22.

Laughlin, Sceva Bright. "Missouri Politics during the Civil War." Part 1. *Missouri Historical Review* 23 (April 1929): 400–26.

———. "Missouri Politics during the Civil War." Part 2. *Missouri Historical Review* 23 (July 1929): 583–618.

Lause, Mark A. *Price's Lost Campaign: The 1864 Invasion of Missouri.* Columbia: University of Missouri Press, 2011.

[Lawrence, George Alfred]. *Border and Bastille. By the Author of "Guy Livingstone."* New York: W. I. Pooley and Co., [c. 1863].

Leonard, Elizabeth D. *All the Daring of the Soldier: Women of the Civil War Armies.* New York: W. W. Norton, 1999.

———. "Mary Surratt and the Plot to Assassinate Abraham Lincoln." In *The War Was You and Me: Civilians in the American Civil War,* edited by Joan Cashin, 286–309. Princeton, NJ: Princeton University Press, 2002.

———. *Yankee Women: Gender Battles in the Civil War.* New York: W. W. Norton, 1994.

Lincoln, Abraham. *Abraham Lincoln: Speeches and Writings, 1859–1865.* New York: Library of America, 1989.

Ling, Huping. *Chinese in St. Louis, 1857–2007.* Charleston, SC: Arcadia Publishing, 2007.

Long, Alecia P. "(Mis)Remembering General Order No. 28: Benjamin Butler, the Woman Order, and Historical Memory." In Whites and Long, *Occupied Women,* 17–32.

Lowry, Thomas P. *Confederate Heroines: 120 Southern Women Convicted by Union Military Justice.* Baton Rouge: Louisiana State University Press, 2006.

——. *Sexual Misbehavior in the Civil War: A Compendium.* Bloomington, IN: Xlibris, 2006.

——. *The Story the Soldiers Wouldn't Tell: Sex in the Civil War.* Mechanicsburg, PA: Stackpole Books, 1994.

Lucas, M. Philip. "Curtis, Samuel Ryan," in Heidler and Heidler, *Encyclopedia of the American Civil War,* 1: 533–34.

Macartney, Clarence Edward. *Grant and His Generals.* New York: The McBride Company, 1953.

Mancini, Matthew J. "Francis Lieber, Slavery, and the 'Genesis' of the Laws of War." *Journal of Southern History* 77 (May 2011): 325–48.

Marmon, Thomas C., Joseph E. Cooper, and William P. Goodman. *Military Commissions* (Charlottesville, VA: The Judge Advocate General's School, April 1953), accessed at http://www.loc.gov/rr/frd/Military_Law/pdf/mil_commissions.pdf.

Marszalek, John F. *Commander of All Lincoln's Armies: A Life of General Henry W. Halleck.* Cambridge, MA: Belknap Press of Harvard University Press, 2004.

Marten, James, ed. *Children and Youth during the Civil War Era.* New York: New York University Press, 2012.

Massey, Mary Elizabeth. *Bonnet Brigades.* New York: Alfred K. Knopf, 1966.

——. *Refugee Life in the Confederacy.* Baton Rouge: Louisiana State University Press, 2001 edition [1964].

McCandless, Perry. *A History of Missouri.* Vol. 2, *1820–1860.* Columbia: University of Missouri Press, 1972.

McCanne, Virginia Yates. "Banishment of Miss Mary Cleveland." In *Reminiscences,* 241–42.

McCurry, Stephanie. *Confederate Reckoning: Power and Politics in the Civil War South.* Cambridge, MA: Harvard University Press, 2010.

——. "Enemy Women and the Laws of War in the American Civil War." *Law and History Review* 35 (August 2017): 667–710.

McElroy, James. *The Struggle for Missouri.* Washington, D.C.: The National Tribune Co., 1909.

McPherson, James B. *Battle Cry of Freedom: The Civil War Era.* New York: Oxford University Press, 1988.

Mersand, Joseph. Introduction in Winston Churchill, *The Crisis,* xiii-xviii. 1962 paperback edition.

Mills, Cynthia, and Pamela H. Simpson, eds. *Monuments to the Lost Cause: Women, Art, and the Landscapes of Southern Memory.* Knoxville: University of Tennessee Press, 2003.

Mitchell, Reid. *The Vacant Chair: The Northern Soldier Leaves Home.* New York: Oxford University Press, 1993.

Monaghan, Jay. *Civil War on the Western Border, 1854–1865.* Boston: Little, Brown, 1955.

Moore, John C. "Missouri." In Evans, *Confederate Military History,* vol. 9.

Morgan, J. H. "War Treason." *Problems of the War* 2 (1916): 161–173.

Mullins, Mary Jackman. "Sketch of Col. Sydney D. Jackman." In *Reminiscences,* 93–96.

Murphy, Kim. *I Had Rather Die: Rape in the Civil War.* Batesville, VA: Coachlight Press, 2014.

Neely, Mark E., Jr. *The Fate of Liberty: Abraham Lincoln and Civil Liberties.* New York: Oxford University Press, 1991.

Nelson, Scott Reynolds, and Carol Sheriff. *A People at War: Civilians and Soldiers in America's Civil War.* New York: Oxford University Press, 2007.

Nichols, Bruce. *Guerrilla Warfare in Civil War Missouri, 1862.* Jefferson, NC: McFarland and Company, Inc., 2004.

———. *Guerrilla Warfare in Civil War Missouri.* Vol. 3, *January–August 1864.* Jefferson, NC: McFarland and Company, Inc., 2013.

———. *Guerrilla Warfare in Civil War Missouri.* Vol. 4, *September, 1864–June 1865.* Jefferson, NC: McFarland and Company, Inc., 2013.

"The Origins of the United Daughters of the Confederacy." In *Reminiscences,* 5–9.

Ott, Victoria. *Confederate Daughters: Coming of Age during the Civil War.* Carbondale: Southern Illinois University Press, 2008.

Parrish, William E. *A History of Missouri.* Vol. 3, *1860 to 1875.* Columbia: University of Missouri Press, 1973.

Peterson, Richard C., James E. McGhee, Kip A. Lindberg, and Keith I. Daleen. *Sterling Price's Lieutenants: A Guide to the Officers and Organizations of the Missouri State Guard, 1861–1865.* Shawnee Mission, KS: Two Trails Publishing, 1995.

Phillips, Christopher. *Damned Yankee: The Life of General Nathaniel Lyon.* Columbia: University of Missouri Press, 1990.

———. *Missouri's Confederate: Claiborne Jackson and the Creation of a Southern Identity in the Border West.* Columbia: University of Missouri Press, 2000.

———. *The River Ran Backward: The Civil War and the Remaking of the American Middle Border.* New York: Oxford University Press, 2016.

Pinckney, Thomas. *My Reminiscences of the War and Reconstruction Times.* Unpublished typeset manuscript accessed at "University of Virginia Online Exhibits/Hearts at Home: Southern Women in the Civil War," https://explore.lib.virginia.edu/exhibits/show/hearts/patriotism.

Piston, William Garrett, and Richard W. Hatcher. *Wilson's Creek: The Second Battle of the Civil War and the Men Who Fought It.* Chapel Hill: University of North Carolina Press, 2000.

Potter, David M. *The Impending Crisis, 1848–1861.* New York: Harper Torchbooks, 1976.

Primm, James Neil. *Lion of the Valley: St. Louis, Missouri.* 2nd edition. Boulder, CO: Pruett Publishing Company, 1990 [1981].

Rable, George C. *Civil Wars: Women and the Crisis of Southern Nationalism.* Urbana and Chicago: University of Illinois Press, 1989.

———. *Damn Yankees: Demonization and Defiance in the Confederate South.* Baton Rouge: Louisiana State University Press, 2015.

Ramage, John A. *Rebel Raider: The Life of General John Hunt Morgan.* Lexington: University Press of Kentucky, 1986.

"Reminiscences of the War between the States." In *Reminiscences*, 273–76.

Reminiscences of the Women of Missouri during the Sixties. n.p.: United Daughters of the Confederacy, Missouri Division, [1913].

"Rev. H. O. Judd." *Confederate Veteran* 14 (November 1906): 518.

Richardson, Albert D. *The Secret Service: The Field, the Dungeon and the Escape.* Hartford, CT: American Publishing Company, 1865.

Risner, Fay. *Ella Mayfield's Pawpaw Militia: A Civil War Saga in Vernon Co., Mo.* Lexington, KY: CreateSpace Independent Publishing Forum, 2008.

Robert, Mrs. P. G. "History of Events Preceding and Following the Banishment of Mrs. Margaret A. E. McLure, as Given to the Author Herself." In *Reminiscences*, 78–84.

———. "Reminiscences of Richmond during the Seven Days' Fight, by a Chaplain's Wife." In *Reminiscences*, 84–90.

Robertson, James I., Jr. "Old Capitol: Eminence to Infamy." *Maryland Historical Magazine* 65 (Winter 1970): 394–412.

Rolle, Andrew F. *The Lost Cause: The Confederate Exodus to Mexico.* Norman: University of Oklahoma Press, 1965.

Rombauer, Robert J. *The Union Cause in St. Louis in 1861.* St. Louis: St. Louis Municipal Centennial Year, 1909.

Romeo, Sharon. "'The First Morning of Their Freedom': African American Women, Black Testimony, and Military Justice in Civil War Missouri." *Missouri Historical Review* 110 (April 2016): 196–216.

"Rosecrans's Campaigns," in *Report of the Joint Committee on the Conduct of the War, at the Second Session Thirty-Eighth Congress.* Washington, D.C.: Government Printing Office, 1865.

Rule, D. H. "Sultana: A Case for Sabotage." *North and South* 5 (December 2001): 81–83.

Ryan, Mary P. *Women in Public: Between Banners and Bullets, 1825–1880.* Baltimore: Johns Hopkins University Press, 1990.

Scharf, J. Thomas. *History of Saint Louis City and County, From the Earliest Periods to the Present Day.* 2 vols. Philadelphia: Louis H. Everts and Co., 1883.

Schneider, Robert W. *Novelist to a Generation: The Life and Thought of Winston Churchill.* Bowling Green, OH: Bowling Green University Popular Press, 1976.

Scott, Anne Firor. *The Southern Lady: From Pedestal to Politics, 1830–1930.* Chicago: University of Chicago Press, 1970.

Segura, Allison. "Dependent Independence: Women in a Patriarchal Civil War–Era Society." Unpublished essay in the possession of the author.

Shiras, Frances. "Major Wolf and Abraham Lincoln: An Episode of the Civil War." *Arkansas Historical Quarterly* 2 (December 1943): 353–58.

Sifakis, Stewart. *Compendium of the Confederate Armies: Tennessee.* Bowie, MD: Willow Bend Books, 1992.

Silber, Nina. *Daughters of the Union: Northern Women Fight the Civil War.* Cambridge, MA: Harvard University Press, 2005.

———. *Gender and the Sectional Conflict.* Chapel Hill: University of North Carolina Press, 2008.

Simkins, Francis Butler, and James Welch Patton. *The Women of the Confederacy.* Richmond and New York: Garrett and Massie, Incorporated, 1936.

Sinisi, Kyle. *The Last Hurrah: Sterling Price's Missouri Expedition of 1864.* Lanham, MD: Rowman and Littlefield, 2015.

Speer, Lonnie R. *Portals to Hell: Military Prisons of the Civil War.* Mechanicsburg, PA: Stackpole Books, 1997.

Steers. Edward, Jr. "Dr. Mudd and the 'Colored' Witnesses." *Civil War History* 46 (December 2000): 324–36.

Stith, Matthew M. *Extreme Civil War: Guerrilla Warfare, Environment, and the Trans-Mississippi Frontier.* Baton Rouge: Louisiana State University Press, 2016.

Stout, Harry S. *Upon the Altar of the Nation: A Moral History of the Civil War.* New York: Viking Penguin, 2006.

Streater, Kristin L. "'She-Rebels' and the Supply Line: Gender Conventions in Civil War Kentucky." In Whites and Long, *Occupied Women,* 88–102.

Sutherland, Daniel E. *A Savage Conflict: The Decisive Role of Guerrillas in the American Civil War.* Chapel Hill: University of North Carolina Press, 2009.

"Theology." *Sewanee Alumni News* 23, no. 2 (August 15, 1957), 296.

Titus, Warren I. *Winston Churchill.* New York: Twayne Publishers, Inc., 1963.

Toth, Emily. *Kate Chopin.* New York: William Morrow and Company, Inc., 1990.

Totten, Carla. "Alton Military Prison." Master's Thesis, Southern Illinois University, Edwardsville, 1983.

Towne, Stephen E. *Surveillance and Spies in the Civil War: Exposing Confederate Conspiracies in America's Heartland.* Athens: Ohio University Press, 2015.

Van Ravenswaay, Charles. "Years of Turmoil, Years of Growth: St. Louis in the 1850's." *Bulletin.* Missouri Historical Society 23 (July 1967): 303–24.

Varney, Frank P. *General Grant and the Rewriting of History.* El Dorado Hills, CA: Savas Beatie, 2013.

Venet, Wendy Hamand. *Neither Ballots nor Bullets: Women Abolitionists and the Civil War.* Charlottesville: University of Virginia Press, 1991.

Vernon, John. "P.O.W." *New York Times Book Review,* February 24, 2002, 9.

War of the Rebellion: A Compilation of the Official Records of the Union and Confederate Armies. 70 vols. in 128 books. Washington, D.C.: Government Printing Office, 1880–1901.

Ward, Andrew. *River Run Red: The Fort Pillow Massacre in the American Civil War.* New York: Penguin Books, 2005.

Weber, Jennifer L. *Copperheads: The Rise and Fall of Lincoln's Opponents in the North.* New York: Oxford University Press, 2006.

Wheaton, Henry. *Elements of International Law,* edited by William Beach Lawrence. 2nd annotated edition. Boston: Little, Brown, and Company, 1863. Supplement.

White, Jonathan W. *Abraham Lincoln and Treason in the Civil War: The Trials of John Merryman.* Baton Rouge: Louisiana State University Press, 2011.

———. "All for a Sword: The Military Treason Trial of Sarah Hutchins." *Maryland Historical Magazine* 107 (Summer 2012): 155–74.

———. "'To Aid Their Rebel Friends': Politics of Treason in the Civil War North." PhD dissertation, University of Maryland, 2008.

Whites, LeeAnn. *The Civil War as a Crisis in Gender: Augusta, Georgia, 1860–1890.* Athens: University of Georgia Press, 2000.

———. "'Corresponding with the Enemy': Mobilizing the Retaliation Field of Battle in St. Louis." In Whites and Long, *Occupied Women,* 103–116.

———. "Forty Shirts and a Wagon Load of Wheat: Women, the Domestic Supply Line, and the Civil War in the Western Border." *Journal of the Civil War Era* 1 (March 2011): 56–78.

———. "'Stand by Your Man': The Ladies Memorial Association and the Reconstruction of Southern White Manhood." In *Women of the South: A Multicultural Reader,* edited by Christie Ann Farnham, 133–149. New York and London: New York University Press, 1997.

Whites, LeeAnn, and Alecia P. Long, eds. *Occupied Women: Gender, Military Occupation, and the American Civil War.* Baton Rouge: Louisiana State University Press, 2009.

Wills, Brian Steel. *The River Was Dyed with Blood: Nathan Bedford Forrest and Fort Pillow*. Norman: University of Oklahoma Press, 2014.

Winter, William C. *The Civil War in St. Louis: A Guided Tour*. St. Louis: Missouri Historical Society Press, 1994.

——, ed. "'Like Sheep in a Slaughter Pen': A St. Louisan Remembers the Camp Jackson Massacre, May 10, 1861." *Gateway Heritage* 15 (Spring 1995): 56–74.

Winthrop, Bvt. Colonel W. *A Digest of Opinions of the Judge Advocate General of the Army, with Notes*. Washington, D.C.: Government Printing Office, 1880.

Witt, John Fabian. *Lincoln's Code: The Law of War in American History*. New York: Free Press, 2012.

Wood, Larry. *Bushwhacker Belles: The Sisters, Wives, and Girlfriends of the Missouri Guerrillas*. Gretna, LA: Pelican Publishing Company, 2016.

Woodson, Mrs. Blake L. Preface in *Reminiscences*, 3–4.

Wright, John A. *Discovering African American St. Louis: A Guide to Historic Sites*. 2nd edition. St. Louis: Missouri Historical Society, 2002.

Young, Elizabeth. "Confederate Counterfeit: The Case of the Cross-Dressing Civil War Soldier." In Ginsberg, *Passing and the Fictions of Identity*, 181–217.

Websites

"Alton Military Post and Prison," https://madison.illinoisgenweb.org/town _histories/alton/military_prison.html.

"Confederate POW Burials on Smallpox Island, West Alton, IL," http://www. usgwarchives.net/mo/civilwar/smallpox.htm.

"*The Crisis* (play)," Internet Broadway Date Base, https://www.ibdb.com /broadway-production/the-crisis-5656.

Edgar, Walter. *Chapters in Trinity's History*, chapter 13, "Reaching Out: 1879–1887," http://www.trinitysc.org/about/history/chapters-in-trinity -s-history.

"Elizabeth Frost," https://www.geni.com/people/Elizabeth-Frost /6000000028972750821.

Find a Grave, database and images (https://findagrave.com: accessed 18 August 2019, memorial page for Drucilla Williams Sappington (17 Jul 1826–22 Jan 1906), Find A grave memorial no. 92835871, citing West Hill Cemetery, Sherman, Grayson County, Texas, USA; Maintained by Don Rubarts (contributor 46951019), https://www.findagrave.com /memorial/92835871/drucilla-sappington#source.

Hepburn, Neil. "West Bloomfield County Entrepreneur: Joseph Tarr Copeland," https://www.gwbhs.org/documents/2012/11/west-bloomfield -township-entrepreneur-joseph-tarr-copeland.pdf/.

"Michael Gleason, Alton, Ill. D. 1904," http://www.genealogy.com/forum
/surnames/topics/gleason/1600/.

Miner, Case. "Emily Weaver (?-1917)," *The Encyclopedia of Arkansas History
and Culture,* http://www.encyclopediaofarkansas.net/encyclopedia
/entry-detail.aspx?entryID=5480.

"Scharf, J. Thomas (John Thomas), 1943–1898." Social Networks and Archival
Content, https://n2t.net/ark:/99166/w6nc6392.

"University of Virginia Online Exhibits/Hearts at Home: Southern Women
in the Civil War," https://explore.lib.virginia.edu/exhibits/show/hearts
/patriotism.

INDEX

THOMAS F. CURRAN is the author of *Soldiers of Peace: Civil War Pacifism and the Postwar Radical Peace Movement*. He earned his doctorate from the University of Notre Dame and currently teaches American history at Cor Jesu Academy in St. Louis, Missouri.